Texas

Little Trips

Great Getaways Near You

Sharry Buckner

Copyright © 2009 by Sharry Buckner

No part of this book may be reproduced or utilized in any form or by any means: electronic, mechanical or otherwise, including photocopying, recording or by any informational storage and retrieval system without permission in writing from the author.

Although the author has researched all sources to ensure the accuracy and completeness of the information contained within this book, no responsibility is assumed for errors, inaccuracies, omissions, or inconsistency herein. Any slights of people, places or organizations are completely and totally unintentional.

ISBN
1-933177-19-5 (10 digit)
978-1-933177-19-9 (13 digit)

Library of Congress Control Number: 2009943449

First Edition

Printed in the United States of America
Published by Atriad Press, LLC
13820 Methuen Green
Dallas, TX 75240
(972) 671-0002

Table of Contents

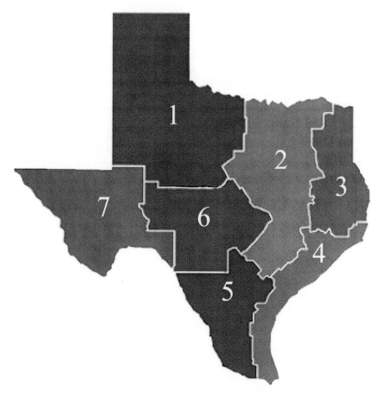

1 = Panhandle Plains Region
2 = Prairies and Lakes Region
3 = East Region
4 = Gulf Coast Region
5 = South Region
6 = Hill Country Region
7 = West Region

Introduction

Need to get away from the office-meetings-kids-housework? If only you had a few days of stress-free relaxation or spiritual renewal. Maybe you haven't spent time with your spouse or best friend lately. Maybe you need some quality time with the family. Or maybe you're thinking of taking a longer vacation closer to home this year.

But Texas is so big. Gas is so expensive. Time is so short. With the current economy, travel and relaxation may not be at the top of your priority list, but in these stressful times, getting away is one of the best things you can do for your health and family unity.

Texas Little Trips offers just what you need. Short trips where you can still feel like you're in a world apart from everyday chaos. Shop. Eat. Play. Couples may enjoy a romantic weekend to celebrate a special occasion or just for the fun of it. Girlfriends may shop and eat and talk. Families may play and enjoy quality time together.

No major cities are listed in this book because 1) you can read about those anywhere and they have far too many attractions to list here and 2) it's impossible to see a big city in a 2-3 day getaway. I've tried to find lesser known places or destinations that offer something different than amusement parks and shopping centers.

I list several B&Bs and Country Inns, since they're usually in historic homes or buildings and offer a totally different experience than staying in a hotel or motel. Individually furnished and often more "homey" than chain motels, most are owner operated by friendly folks who want to make sure you enjoy your visit. Families traveling with children would probably be more comfortable in a motel where they'll usually find a playground and swimming pool.

At the end of some regions is a listing of Distinctive Destinations. These special places are destinations unto

1

themselves. Some are secluded "in the middle of nowhere" and some are little oases near big cities. Not all offer meals, so you might need to venture out a bit, but for the most part you'll find all you need to enjoy a true getaway with no other "places to go or things to do" necessary. These are ideal for romantic getaways or honeymoons.

Texas boasts one of the best State Park systems in the country. I'll mention several of them as great places for inexpensive family outings, but you can find the entire list here: www.tpwd.state.tx.us

By no means are the listings in this book complete. I've had to leave out many interesting little towns throughout Texas. I would never get through writing the book and you wouldn't be able to hold it. But hopefully, it will start you on the road to discovering small towns and backroads of your own.

Texas Travel Information Centers

Professional travel counselors welcome visitors to Texas at eleven entry points across the state and in the state capital of Austin. They can provide travel and accommodations guides, maps, and information on points of interest, events, road conditions, and help with routing. The centers contain a plethora of brochures, booklets, maps, and other travel publications. Most offer free wireless internet access, covered picnic tables and 24-hour restrooms and security.

Hours of operation are 8 a.m. – 5 p.m. daily; 8 a.m. – 6 p.m. Memorial Day weekend through Labor Day. The Centers are closed New Year's Day, Easter, Thanksgiving, and Christmas Eve and Christmas Day.

Travelers may also call 800-452-9292 (toll-free) to speak with a travel counselor for travel assistance or road condition information from 8 a.m. to 6 p.m. daily; automated road condition information is available 24 hours a day. The same number provides a "hotline" for the best wildflower-viewing routes in the spring and fall foliage locations in autumn.

Travel Information Center Locations:

Amarillo
9700 E. I-40
Amarillo, TX 79118
806-335-1441

Anthony (El Paso)
I-10 @ New Mexico state line
Anthony, TX 79821
915-886-3468

Austin Capitol
11th St. and Brazos St.
Austin, TX 78701
512-463-8586

Denison
US 69/ US75 @ Oklahoma state line
Denison, TX 75020
903-463-2860

Gainesville
I-35 @ Oklahoma state line
Gainesville, TX 76240
940-665-2301

Langtry
U.S. 90 W. State Loop 25
Langtry, TX 78871
432-291-3340

Laredo
I-35 N. at US 83
Laredo, TX 78045
956-417-4728

Orange
I-10 @ Louisiana state line
Orange, TX 77632
409-883-9416

Texarkana
I-30 @ Arkansas state line
Texarkana, TX 75503
903-794-2114

Rio Grande Valley
US 77 @ US 83
Harlingen, TX 78552
956-428-4477

Waskom
I-20 E @ Louisiana state line
Waskom, TX 75692
903-687-2547

Wichita Falls
I-44/US 287
Wichita Falls, TX 76306
940-723-7931

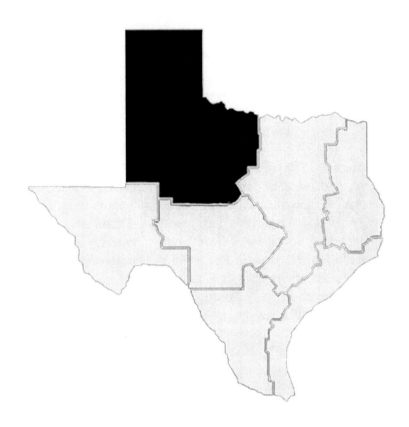

Panhandle Plains

Most folks think of a flat dusty landscape of the Texas Panhandle if they've seen too many old western movies. Dominated by agricultural and the petroleum industry, there are some fascinating attractions and striking geological features in this area.

Amarillo

Convention and Visitor Council
1000 S. Polk in the Bivins Mansion
806-374-1497; 800-692-1338
www.visitamarillotx.com

Amarillo (Spanish for "yellow") is the commercial, cultural, and recreational center for the vast region known as the Texas Panhandle. Wide-open spaces, breathtaking sunsets, friendly folks, and a rich western heritage are the characteristics loved by those hardy souls who call the Panhandle home. Historic Route 66 passes through town and attracts thousands of visitors who enjoy a nostalgic trip to that era of American history. Throughout the city are 56 parks that cover over 2,300 acres and offer recreational facilities such as swimming pools, tennis courts, playgrounds, fishing lakes, and a 36-hole municipal golf course. Amarillo is also the gateway to Palo Duro Canyon, America's second largest canyon and nearby, one of the finest museums in Texas.

Some folks might not have considered Amarillo a destination city in the past, but it's bursting with western heritage, outdoor activities, shops, restaurants, and an expanding art scene.

History & Museums

Remember "Get your kicks on Route 66?" Look for the "Old Route 66" highway signs marking the course through the city. Buildings that once housed theaters, cafes, and drug stores are now antique shops, specialty shops, boutiques, and restaurants along one mile of the historic route. Books and guides are available to lead you to the sights and memories along the route, or check it out online at www.amarillo66.com.

In the spirit of the Old West, start with the **American Quarter Horse Hall of Fame and Museum**. It offers hands-on and interactive exhibits, video presentations, and live demonstrations showcasing the history of the American Quarter Horse, the world's most popular breed, and the people who played a major role in its development. This world-class facility also includes educational opportunities, a vast research library and archives, meeting rooms, and an excellent gift shop.

www.aqha.com/foundation/halloffame/index.html
2601 I-40 East, 806-376-5181

The largest, and thought by many to be the best, history museum in Texas is in the small city of Canyon, about 15 miles south of Amarillo on the campus of West Texas A&M University. The **Panhandle Plains Historical Museum** has more than three million artifacts in its collection, depicting the courage, hardship, victory, and defeat of the early pioneer settlers. Actually five museums in one (heritage, paleontology, geology, transportation, and art/textile), its constantly changing exhibits and diverse array of educational programs and field trips draw visitors over and over. Built in 1933, the building itself bears a State Antiquities Landmark designation for its Art Deco architectural style.

www.panhandleplains.org
2503 4th Avenue, Canyon, 806-651-2244

Kids can explore, create, learn and play at **Don Harrington Discovery Center** with more than 100 exhibits and attractions that encourage hands-on activity. There are excellent activity programs and classes and a world-class digital planetarium. The six-story stainless steel time column adjacent to the Center was erected in 1968 to commemorate the world's greatest quantity of helium found here.

www.dhdc.org
1200 Streit Dr., 806-355-9547

Arts & Culture

The new (2006) **Globe-News Center for the Performing Arts**, a world-class performing arts venue featuring a 1,300-seat auditorium, is home to the Amarillo Symphony and Lone Star Ballet, as well as a variety of special events.

www.amarillo.com/globenewscenter
www.amarillosymphony.org
1000 S. Polk St., 806-376-8782
www.lonestarballet.org
ticket office: 401 S. Buchanan, 806-378-3096

The **Amarillo Museum of Art** exhibits a diverse collection of treasures and the Amarillo Little Theatre presents a rich variety of productions throughout the year.

www.amarilloart.org
2200 S. Van Buren, 806-371-5050
www.amarillolittletheatre.org
2019 Civic Circle, 806-355-9991

Palo Duro Canyon

Prairie grass and flatlands stretch as far as you can see, until the landscape breaks abruptly about 25 miles southeast of Amarillo into the vast chasm of Palo Duro Canyon. Walls plunge a thousand feet to the canyon floor, exposing brilliant multicolored strata and geological formations paralleled in beauty only by the Grand Canyon. The road into **Palo Duro Canyon State Park** offers only a taste of the rugged beauty of one of Texas' largest State Parks (more than 20,000 acres). It winds through a panorama carved by millions of years of wind and water erosion. To see more of the scenic landscapes, ride mountain bikes, hike trails or ride horses off the beaten paths. The park has first-class facilities, campsites for tents and RVs, picnic areas, miles of hiking trails; also riding stables and mountain bike rentals.

www.tpwd.state.tx.us/spdest/findadest/parks/palo_duro
11450 Park Road 5, Canyon, 806-488-2227

The best attended outdoor musical drama in the U.S., *"TEXAS"* is performed each summer in the 1500-seat Pioneer Amphitheatre in Palo Duro Canyon State Park. Horsemen carrying flags appear atop the 600-foot canyon bluff as colorfully costumed singers and dancers sweep across the stage below. A talented cast with vibrant voices and period costumes tell the settlers' stories of romance and humor, struggles and strengths. This musical extravaganza uses a professional cast and crew of more than 150 to recapture the drama of Panhandle history. Spectacular sound effects and remarkable lighting against a natural backdrop under the bright Texas stars add to the excitement. A steak dinner is served before every performance for an additional charge.

www.texas-show.com
tickets: 806-655-2181

As long as we're talking about the Canyon, the memorable Elkins Ranch **Cowboy Morning Breakfast** is an authentic chuckwagon breakfast experience. As you arrive at camp, a cup of fresh cowboy coffee brewed over the open fire awaits. The down-home tasty vittles are served up in a majestic setting with a backdrop of towering canyon cliffs. Then colorful characters will entertain you with some great boot-stompin' cowboy music and traditional storytelling. A family ranch comprised of thousands of acres, Elkins Ranch also offers a Cowboy Supper and Old West Show and Jeep tours into the scenic canyon.

www.theelkinsranch.com
806-488-2100

The imposing Lighthouse formation at Palo Duro Canyon.
(courtesy Texas Tourism)

Eat

Amarillo is in the heart of Texas beef country. Ask, "Where's the best steak in town?" and you'll cause an ongoing flap. Many locals frequent **The Country Barn** for great hand-raised, local beef, perfectly prepared over an open Mesquite fire. The extensive menu also offers fresh seafood (lobster, salmon, crab), barbecue (beef, pork, chicken), and excellent Mexican food (seafood enchiladas, quail, chile rellenos). The décor is authentic Western.

www.countrybarnsteakhouse.com

8200 I-40 W., 806-335-2325

David's Steaks & Seafood proudly serves Certified Angus Beef steaks, including their signature marinated filet. Seafood offerings include charbroiled salmon, shrimp scampi, and lobster. Go for a nice dining experience, fine wine list, and efficient service.

www.davidssteaks.com
2721 Virginia Circle, 806-355-8171

Still others will send you to **Outlaws Supper Club** for steak, chicken-fried steak and fried catfish. The prime rib sells out early.

10816 SE 3rd Ave., 806-335-1032

But indisputably, the most famous tourist place is **The Big Texan Steak Ranch & Horse Hotel** – part restaurant, part horse hotel, part motel, part gift shop, and all adventure. Want a free meal? The Big Texan is known far and wide for its 72-oz. steak dinner offered free to anyone who can eat the steak and all the trimmings in one hour. Well, some 40,000 folks have tried and more than 7,000 have succeeded. Not that hungry? Here's your chance to try rattlesnake or calf fries. The restaurant is chock a block with western memorabilia and is a fun place to people-watch, especially if you're near someone trying to eat the free dinner. If you don't get to watch an actual contestant, there's a video on their website.

www.bigtexan.com
7701 I-40 East, 806-372-6000

The **Nu-Castle Diner** is an Amarillo institution. It serves good ol' American cooking. Omelets and homemade cinnamon rolls are popular breakfast fare, while lunch (daily lunch specials) and dinner are for comfort food and very reasonable prices. Scrumptious homemade pies and cobblers sell out early. Good, friendly service.

518 E. 10th, 806-371-8540

The **Village Bakery Café** displays fresh artisan breads, pastries and desserts. Lunches are prepared with fresh, wholesome ingredients. Lunch specials may include Tuscan flatbread with grilled chicken, red peppers, spinach, mushrooms, and creamy basil spread or roast pork tenderloin on Foccacia with cranberry spread. Things like King Ranch chicken, meat loaf, or chicken pot pie may share the menu. Breakfasts are positively sinful, especially the French toast served only on weekends.

www.villagebakerycafe.com
2606 W. 22nd, 806-358-1358

Sleep

For a romantic retreat, stay in the "Heavenly Hideaway Suite" at **The Galbraith House**. Located on "Silk Stocking Row," the craftsman style home was built in 1912 by lumber merchant H.W. Galbraith. The wood work, mostly imported mahogany, throughout the home is almost beyond belief. The 650-square foot suite is located above the carriage house, separate from the main house and has an extra large Jacuzzi tub, walk-in shower, comfy king sized bed, and mini kitchen.

www.galbraithhouse.net
1710 S. Polk, 806-374-0237

Lubbock

Convention & Visitors Bureau
1500 Broadway, 6th floor Wells Fargo Center
806-747-5232; 800-692-4035
www.visitlubbock.org

The town that gave the world Buddy Holly has surprising diversity in its attractions – from world-class museums, theater and fine arts . . . to music and ranching history . . . to great eating and shopping . . . to the outstanding Texas Tech

University and Prairie Dog Town. Lubbock should be on the list of top destinations for families, couples, and girlfriends. It's hard to know where to begin.

Lubbock's tribute to native son, Buddy Holly
(courtesy Lubbock CVB)

Attractions

The city is probably best known as the home of the late, great Rock and Roll legend, Buddy Holly. Located in the Depot Entertainment District, the **Buddy Holly Center** contains, as you would expect, an excellent exhibit dedicated to the life and music of Buddy Holly. But it also contains the **Texas Musicians Hall of Fame** and the **Lubbock Fine Arts** Gallery, as well as offering first-rate music and arts programs.

www.buddyhollycenter.org
1801 Crickets Ave., 806-775-3560

The **West Texas Walk of Fame** began as a tribute to Buddy Holly in the late '70s. Some Nashville musicians were discussing ways to recognize Buddy when someone pointed out how many fine, talented musicians had come from West Texas. Interest grew, musicians and friends commissioned an enormous statue of Buddy, held a concert to raise money, and Lubbock's favorite native son was the first inductee of the "Walk of Fame," followed by such stars as Waylon Jennings, Mac Davis, Jimmy Dean, Tanya Tucker, Roy Orbison, and the Gatlin Brothers. Today, the Walk honors actors, artists, and entertainers as well as musicians.

www.civiclubbock.com/walk.html

The Ranching Heritage Center is a 30-acre museum.
(courtesy Lubbock CVB)

History & Museums

Without question, one of the most outstanding museums in Texas is the **National Ranching Heritage Center**. More than three dozen structures are displayed on the 30-acre complex –

from windmills to barns to a one-room schoolhouse – all authentically restored and furnished to tell the story of ranch life from the late 1700s through the early 1900s. Imagine a cabin made of cactus stalks and mud. Not only an extraordinary museum and historical park, it's an extensive reference library and treasure trove of educational and youth programs. Another gem is Cogdell's General Store that carries a nice variety of Western items, books and souvenirs.

www.nrhc.com
3121 Fourth St., 806-742-0497

One of the most fascinating stories of World War II is one seldom told. . . that of the U.S. Military Glider Program and its role in the war. The idea was to silently land behind enemy lines. This was a little known but valuable contribution to the Allies' invasion tactics. Since most of the American glider pilots received their wings at South Plains Army Airfield, now the site of Lubbock's airport, you can visit **Silent Wings Museum**. It features one of the few fully restored World War II gliders in existence. This powerful quote from the website says it all: "The one-way trip of the glider pilots became history and the Silent Wings Museum is their legacy."

www.silentwingsmuseum.com
806-775-3796

You'll find another interesting exhibit at the **American Wind Power Center and Museum**. More than 120 rare and fully restored windmills are displayed on 28 acres in an area known as Yellow House Canyon. Learn as much as you can comprehend at the interpretive center. The gift shop sells windmill-related items.

www.windmill.com
1701 Canyon Lake Dr., 806-747-8734

The American Wind Power Center & Museum
(courtesy American Wind Power)

With a first-class faculty and more than 28,000 students, **Texas Tech University** offers a varied academic curriculum and has a public art program ranked among the nation's ten best. Established in 1923, it's an outstanding university on a picturesque 1,850-acre campus. Internationally renowned, the **Museum of Texas Tech University** contains nearly 2 million objects and serves as the cultural, educational, scientific, and research environment of Texas Tech. Adjacent **Moody Planetarium** offers spectacular star shows and the **Lubbock Lake Landmark** interpretive center and archaeological site are open to the public.

www.ttu.edu
2500 Broadway, 806-742-2011
www.depts.ttu.edu/museumttu
3301 Fourth St., 806-742-2490

The **Science Spectrum and Omni Theater** is a novel, hands-on museum featuring interactive science exhibits dedicated to exhibiting educational science in an entertaining environment. Everyone will enjoy the Omni Theater with its advanced projector system and unique domed screen . . . you'll feel like you're a part of the movie.

www.sciencespectrum.com

2579 S. Loop 289, 806-745-2525

Prairie Dog Town. (courtesy Lubbock CVB)

Entertainment

The **Depot District** is the heart of Lubbock's revitalized Downtown scene. You'll find a wide range of music venues on weekends. Located here is the **Cactus Theater**, which operated as a movie theater from 1938-1958. Now beautifully redesigned, modernized, and equipped with state-of-the-art

17

sound and light equipment, the Cactus is considered by many to be the best live entertainment venue in West Texas.

www.cactustheater.com

1812 Buddy Holly Ave., 806-762-3233

Or pile the family in the car and take them to the **Stars and Stripes Drive In Theater**. Tell them how you used to take popcorn and blankets and . . . well, maybe not all the details. If you remember, take your sweetheart for old times' sake. It's open year-round and shows double features! Don't take your own popcorn though – you must visit the 50s Café for burgers, dogs and nachos. They also have popcorn and funnel cakes.

www.driveinusa.com

806-749-SHOW

Mention Lubbock to Texans and if they don't immediately say "Buddy Holly," they'll say **Prairie Dog Town**. Yes, of all the fabulous museums, cultural venues, art scene, and fine dining, folks remember Prairie Dog Town. So if you want to see it, take the kids to Mackenzie Park. Ok, they *are* fun to watch.

Wine

The Lubbock area has several award-winning wineries. Winner of the most accolades for their premium wines is the **Llano Estacado Winery**. Guided tours explain the art of winemaking and mention that most of the grapes used are grown within a 100-mile radius of Lubbock. And, of course, there's the tasting room and gift shop.

www.llanowine.com

3526 East FM 15895, 806-745-2258

Caprock Winery offers tours and tastings. (courtesy Lubbock CVB)

Caprock Winery offers tours, an elegant tasting room and gift shop. The magnificent tasting room is a favorite place for special events.

www.caprockwinery.com
408 E Woodrow Rd., 806-863-2704

Pheasant Ridge Winery, a family-owned, self-contained winery and vineyard operation, was one of the earliest wineries in Texas, planted in 1979.

www.pheasantridgewinery.com
3507 E. CR 5700, 806-746-6033

Shop

Another advantage of a college town is that you can find every kind of shop imaginable. It's especially fun to visit some of the outstanding Western Wear shops:

- **Hat Creek Trading Co.**, www.hatcreek.us, 10101 Slide Rd., 806-794-5404

- **Luskey's/Ryon's**, www.luskeys.com, 5035 Frankford, 806-795-7106
- **Cavender's**, www.cavenders.com, 5620 Loop 289W, 806-785-7400

Girlfriends will enjoy **Hollyhock's** or browsing the shopping center and outlet mall.
www.hollyhocksgifts.com
3521 34th St., 806-780-8787

Eat

Good places to eat abound in Lubbock. For Italian, try **Orlando's** for great food and good service. Both locations are popular with locals for lunch and dinner.
www.orlandos.com
24th & Ave. Q, 806-747-5998
and 70th & Indiana, 806-797-8646

For a more romantic setting, try **Stella's Restaurant & Deli** for authentic Italian cuisine and a nice wine list. They frequently have live music and host a wine club.
www.stellaslubbock.com
4646 50th St., 806-785-9299

Gardski's boasts an extensive menu, from great burgers, salads and sandwiches, to steaks and chops, chicken and seafood and a large assortment of side veggies. All excellently prepared and served in a lovely, comfortable setting.
www.gardskisloft.com
2009 Broadway, 806-744-2391

For outstanding steaks, even by Texas standards, go to **Cagle's**. Not a fancy place – in fact, the machine-made

Margaritas are served in styrofoam cups – just great steaks at reasonable prices.

www.caglesteaks.com

West 4th St. and FM 179, 806-795-3879

The **50 Yard Line** offers a variety of menu choices from lobster to salmon, but it's best known for excellent steaks. More upscale than most eateries in Lubbock, prices are a bit more, but portions are plentiful.

www.50-yardline.com

2549 S. Loop 289, 806-745-3991

For a special occasion that calls for a fine dining establishment, the **Double Nickel Steakhouse** is a great choice.

www.doublenickelsteakhouse.com

5405 Slide Rd., 806-792-0055

La Diosa Cellars, an eclectic, elegant restaurant in the winery offers a Bistro menu and coffee bar as well as a nice variety of Texas wines.

www.ladiosacellars.com

901 17th St., 806-744-3600

Café J is a special place for romance and haute cuisine, impeccable service, and an extensive wine list.

2605 19th St., 806-743-5400

Pedro's Tamales makes fine beef, pork, and chicken tamales using quality ingredients. Eat 'em there or take them home.

www.pedrosmarket.com

2309 N Frankford Ave., 806-744-5236, 800-522-9531

And last, but certainly not least – for good Texas BBQ, **Bigham's Smokehouse** serves excellent BBQ and plenty of it.

bighamsbbq.net
4302 19th St., 806-793-6880
and 3312 82nd St., 806-797-9241

As in most college towns, there's a huge variety of nightlife and intimate pubs and eateries. The **Depot Entertainment District** is the heart of it all.

Sleep

Dozens of hotels and motels line the major streets. For a romantic weekend, reserve the "Bali Hai" room at the comfortable **Broadway Manor**, a meticulously restored 1926 home just a few blocks from the Texas Tech campus. The owners are very knowledgeable about the city and its attractions and restaurants and offer warm hospitality and scrumptious breakfasts. They can also provide an "Enchanted Evening" package for sweethearts.

www.broadwaymanor.net
1811 Broadway, 806-749-4707

Or choose the President's Room at the **Woodrow House** directly across from the Tech campus.

www.woodrowhouse.com
2629 19th St., 806-793-3330

Abilene

Convention & Visitors Bureau
1101 N. First St.
325-676-2556; 800-727-7704
www.abilenevisitors.com

Abilene, named for Abilene, Kansas, the end of the old Chisolm Trail, has deep roots in the heritage of the Old West yet offers all the exciting benefits and activities of a thriving modern city. Although it may seem an unlikely destination for a Girlfriends Getaway or a romantic weekend, Abilene affords plenty of surprises. The Convention and Visitors Bureau is located in the restored Abilene Texas and Pacific Railroad Depot across the street from the Grace Museum, in the heart of Abilene's rejuvenated downtown.

History

Kids of all ages like **Frontier Texas!**, a 14,000 square-foot multimedia facility on over 6 downtown acres. Here you can relive the Old West with the help of state-of-the-art technology. Frontier Texas! introduces you to people who pioneered on the Texas frontier. Cutting-edge technology puts you in the middle of attacks by Indians and wolves, stampeding buffalo, a card game shootout and a prairie thunderstorm, even a lovely spring evening filled with fireflies.

www.frontiertexas.com
625 North First St., 325-437-2800

"Mature" visitors enjoy this nostalgic peek into the past. Listed in the National Register of Historic Places, The **Paramount Theater** has been restored to the grandeur of yesteryear. Inside the magnificent Art Deco building, you'll find drifting clouds and twinkling stars on a blue sky, neon and incandescent cove lighting, and domed turrets. Classic films, concerts, and special events are presented throughout the year.

www.paramount-abilene.org
352 Cypress St., 325-676-9620

About 15 miles south of Abilene, **Buffalo Gap Historic Village** is a must-see attraction interpreting the tumultuous history of the area from the 1870s to the 1920s. Did you know base ball was two separate words in 1883? Interactive audio tours and guidebooks explain the rich collections of frontier items and 21 meticulously restored authentic buildings, most of which are over 100 years old. For an even better experience, co-ordinate a visit to the Historic Village with lunch or dinner at Perini's (see Eat below).

www.buffalogap.com

133 N. William St., Buffalo Gap, 325-572-3365

Arts & Culture

The **Grace Museum** is actually three museums in one, housed in the historic Grace Hotel – The **Art Museum**, The **History Museum** and The **Children's Museum**. The Grace serves as a cornerstone for cultural arts and education.

www.thegracemuseum.org

102 Cypress St., 325-673-4587

The **Center for Contemporary Arts** is the setting for numerous artists, studios, and galleries.

www.center-arts.com

220 Cypress St., 325-677-8389

In Albany, about 35 miles northeast of Abilene, the acclaimed **Old Jail Art Center** has been called the best small-town museum in the state, exhibiting an outstanding collection of fine art.

www.theoldjailartcenter.org

201 S. 2nd, Albany, 325-762-2269

Outdoors and Critters

One of the five largest zoos in Texas, the **Abilene Zoo** is Abilene's top visitor attraction. Covering 13 acres and exhibiting more than 500 species of birds, mammals, reptiles, amphibians and invertebrates, it deserves the honor.

www.abilenetx.com/Zoo
2070 Zoo Ln., 325-676-6085

See part of the official Texas Longhorn herd at **Abilene State Park**. This 621-acre park is set on brushy prairie land with wooded valleys. Excellent facilities include a variety of campsites and RV accommodations and enough activities to entertain kids (of all ages) for days.

www.tpwd.state.tx.us/spdest/findadest/parks/abilene
150 Park Road 32, Tuscola, 325-572-3204

Shop

Historic Downtown Abilene is the place to shop. Dozens of specialty shops, galleries, and boutiques cluster along several blocks of North 1st, 2nd, 3rd, Hickory, Cedar, Cypress, and Pine Streets. **Texas Star Trading Company** is the quintessential Texas stuff store. **Under One Roof** is home to over 30 specialty shops offering a huge variety of items in a historic three-story building. And last, but certainly not least . . . literally dozens of antique shops call Abilene home. You'll need a map.

www.texasstartrading.com
174 Cypress St., 325-672-9696

Eat

As any city with well over 100,000 residents, Abilene has a plethora of eating establishments. For Texas' favorite meat, tender and juicy, smoked over Mesquite wood, **Joe Allen's Pit Barbecue** can't be beat anywhere.

www.joeallens.com
301 S. 11th St., 325-672-6082

While you girlfriends are making the rounds of downtown shops, a great lunch place is **Cypress Street Station**, offering a nice selection of delicious sandwiches, wraps, salads, pastas, and low-carb plates at reasonable prices.
www.cypress-street.com
158 Cypress St., 325-676-3463

Ask any local for the best steak in West Texas and he'll send you to **Perini Ranch Steakhouse** in nearby Buffalo Gap. Not just a restaurant, it's an experience. An event. Featured in nearly every publication from *Texas Highways* to the *New York Times*, the ranch is both famous and extraordinary. Even though Chef Tom Perini has cooked at the White House, he calls his fare "real Texas food – plain and simple."
www.periniranch.com
800-367-1721

Distinctive Destinations

Savor an unsurpassed Texas experience at the luxurious **Wildcatter Ranch & Spa**. A few miles south of Graham on a bluff above the Brazos River, this 4000-acre luxurious guest resort offers amazing panoramic views of the North Texas hills. Yes, it's a ranch and activities include horseback riding, canoeing, biking and hiking, hunting and fishing, but afterwards you can relax with a calming massage or in a Jacuzzi before you enjoy a fabulous dinner at the first-class steakhouse.

The historically themed rooms and suites are decorated and furnished with fine classic western décor and have every amenity you can imagine from 300-threadcount sheets to satellite TV with DVD/VCR player and internet access to a remote-controlled fireplace. Each cabin suite has porches with rocking chairs from which to enjoy morning coffee or an evening glass of wine under the stars. The hot tub is the place to be to watch the splendid sunsets – overlooking juniper and oak-covered hills and valleys near Possum Kingdom Lake.

www.wildcatterranch.com
6062 Hwy. 16 South, Graham, 940-549-3500, 888-462-9277

Chow time at Wildcatter Ranch. (courtesy Wildcatter Ranch)

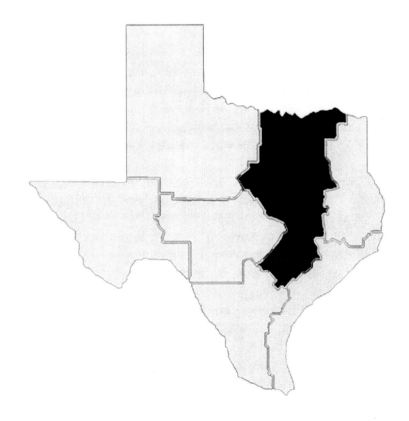

Prairies and Lakes

Extending from the Red River bordering Oklahoma to the border of the Gulf Coast region, this large area encompasses the huge Fort Worth-Dallas Metroplex as well as a multitude of delightful small towns, scenic state parks and picturesque rivers traversing the ever-changing landscapes.

Grapevine

Visitor Information Center in the Cotton Belt Depot
705 South Main Street @ the railroad tracks
817-410-8136
www.grapevinetexasusa.com
www.downtowngrapevinetexas.com

Texas-friendly folks and an enterprising hospitality industry celebrating history, vineyards, arts & culture, great shops and fine restaurants have all contributed to Grapevine's position as a major destination. Just minutes from the Dallas-Fort Worth International Airport, Grapevine claims to be the epicenter of the metro area. But this book is about small towns, so leave that be.

Historic Downtown Grapevine is far more than a destination – a walk down Main Street is a journey back in time. The entire district is listed in the National Register of Historic Places and boasts over 75 restored historic structures. From one end of downtown to the other, you'll find one-of-a-kind shops and eateries, a popular bakery, wine-tasting rooms, a restored theater, art galleries and studios, an old-fashioned barber shop, a restored vintage railroad, and on spring-to-fall weekends, a European-style open air market at the gazebo. In addition to all that, several whimsical sculptures enrich the streets of downtown. Note the night watchman atop City Hall, keeping vigil over the town. Look around to see if anyone saw you begin a conversation with that "guy" sitting next to you on the bench.

www.downtowngrapevinetexas.com

Picturesque as it is, Grapevine isn't some sleepy little town hanging onto dreams of the past – it's a vibrant, bustling center of modern galleries and boutiques, wine-tasting rooms and cafes, music and entertainment venues that appeal to the most sophisticated tastes.

The Skaters are one of the whimsical sculptures on Main Street.
(courtesy Grapevine CVB)

Events

And Grapevine knows how to celebrate! Chocolate Fest (March), Main Street Days (May), GrapeFest (September), Fireworks Extravaganza (4th of July), Butterfly Flutterby (October), and Christmas on Main Street (December) are only a few reasons to celebrate with live music, great food and drink in Historic Downtown Grapevine.

Entertainment & Culture

The renovated Art Deco **Palace Theater**, circa 1940, serves as the center of cultural and civic activity for the town, hosting theater, music, cinema, and the visual arts. Best known as the venue for the **Grapevine Opry**, a foot-stompin', hand-clappin' family country-Western show every weekend. Some of the biggest names in country music have performed on its stage and the Opry always serves up a G-rated show.

308 S. Main St., Theater 817-410-3100, Opry 817-481-8733

History

The **Grapevine Vintage Railroad** travels along 21 miles of the historic Cotton Belt Route between Grapevine and the Fort Worth Stockyards. Vintage engines and authentic 1920s and 1930s Victorian-style coaches let passengers experience train travel as it was in the glory days of the expanding west. In the Stockyards Station, you'll be right in the middle of the Old West environment of the Stockyards National Historic District and you'll have a few hours to explore before the return trip.

www.grapevinesteamrailroad.com
709 S. Main St., 817-410-3123

Grapevine Vintage Railroad travels along the historic Cotton Belt route.
(courtesy Grapevine CVB)

Outdoors

Water sports reign supreme on the 8,000-acre recreational **Lake Grapevine** in the summertime. With 146 miles of shoreline, the scenic lake is fabulous for boating, water skiing, and wind surfing. You can make arrangements for charter boating and fishing, horseback riding and bike rentals. Three top-rated golf courses and a unique indoor golf course should keep husbands busy while wives shop:

- **Grapevine Golf Course**
- **Cowboys Golf Club**, www.cowboysgolf.com
- **Bear Creek Golf Club**, www.bearcreek-golf.com
- **Texas Indoor Golf**, www.texasindoorgolf.com

Wine

Named for the native Mustang grape, it's no surprise that Grapevine has become a trendsetter in Texas, the fifth-largest wine-producing state in the U.S. It's currently home to eight wineries and tasting rooms, as well as the Texas Wine and Grape Growers Association. Tour the "Wine Trail" and check with the Visitor Center for special events at the wineries. Vineyards or tasting rooms in the Grapevine area are:

- **Cross Timbers Winery**, www.crosstimberswinery.com
- **Delaney Vineyards**, www.delaneyvineyards.com
- **D'Vine Wine of Texas**, www.dvinewineusa.com
- **Farina's Winery**, www.farinaswinery.com
- **Homestead Winery**, www.homesteadwinery.com
- **La Buena Vida Vineyards**, www.labuenavida.com
- **La Bodega Winery**
- **Su Vino Winery**, www.suvinowinery.com

Shop

Grapevine is a shopper's paradise! With huge retail centers, **Grapevine Mills Mall**, **Grapevine Towne Center** and **Grapevine Commons**, the area can satisfy the most avid shop-a-holic. **Historic Downtown Grapevine** is teeming with one-of-a-kind boutiques, antique shops, galleries, studios and specialty shops. And don't forget there are some fabulous shops at the **Gaylord Texan** (see Distinctive Destinations below).

A magic place to visit, **VETRO Art Glassblowing Studio** and Art Glass Gallery is a state-of-the-art facility where you can watch award-winning glass artists hand blow art glass into magnificent pieces during fascinating live demonstrations. The gallery is filled with amazing works of art and the studio offers ongoing classes, workshops, private tours and special events.
www.vetroartglass.com
701 S Main St # 103, 817-251-1668

Grapevine Mills Mall, one of the largest shopping centers in Texas, boasts over 1.6 million square feet of retail and outlet stores, restaurants, and arcades.
www.grapevinemills.com
3000 Grapevine Mills Pkwy, 972-724-4900

Downtown, one of the more unusual shops is the **British Emporium**, a premier British gift shop, tea merchant and grocer offering British specialties from teapots to Yorkshire pudding.
www.british-emporium.com
140 N. Main
817-421-2311

Schakolad Chocolate Factory is another favorite. They are internationally acclaimed for European-style chocolates.
www.schakolad.com
601 S. Main St. #103, 817-410-4720

Merry's Christmas and Clowns offers quite a variety, from gift baskets, to baby and children's apparel to home accents.

www.merryschristmasandclowns.com
309 S. Main St., 817-329-1431

Look for the Indian sitting in a rocker at the entrance to **Main Street Station**. With 45 vendors under one roof, you'll find a little bit of everything here.

www.mssgrapevine.com
337 S. Main St., 817-329-3684

Not all shops are geared towards women. **Bass Pro Shop** is the outdoor enthusiast's dream come true. Part store, part museum, part art gallery, part education center, Bass Pro Shop is really hard to describe. It's filled with waterfalls, aquariums, big game animal dioramas, a stocked fishing pond, and an archery and gun range. It also offers seminars and classes on everything from fly-fishing to hunter safety to golf.

www.basspro.com
2501 Bass Pro Dr., 972-724-2018

Eat

Most folks enjoy the traditional foods of Texas like Chili and Bar-B-Q, but an endless variety of other options abound in Grapevine. All the major chains from fast food to fine dining have a presence, most out on Highways 114 or 26.

Bartley's Bar-B-Que has been around forever, serving up great Texas Bar-B-Q to eat in or to go.

www.bartleysbbq.com
413 E. Northwest Hwy, 817-481-3212

A local favorite in historic downtown, **Big Fish** features seafood, but also offers delicious things that don't swim. Live music on Saturday nights.

www.bigfishonmain.com
414 S. Main St., 817-481-2010

A relaxed atmosphere, happy hour and foot-tappin' music welcome all to **Tolbert's Restaurant**. Native Texan, Frank X. Tolbert, Sr. was a co-founder of the original Terlingua Chili Cookoff in Big Bend in 1967 – now named for him and co-founder Wick Fowler. Frank and his son started this restaurant which features . . . drum roll . . . a Bowl of Red (chili). Steaks, burgers, salads, and other specialties are tasty, too. An aside: Frank was also a Texas historian and storyteller who made major contributions to Southwest literature with books and stories of Texas history.

www.tolbertsrestaurant.com
423 S. Main St., 817-421-4888

Main Street Bistro & Bakery uses the best ingredients, freshly milled flours, real butter and no preservatives to make their breads, pastries and scrumptious desserts. In addition to yummy croissants and muffins, the breakfast menu features omelets, eggs Benedict, breakfast tacos and migas, pancakes and specialty coffee drinks. The lunch and dinner menus offer some innovative sandwiches, salads, and entrées.

www.themainbakery.com
316 S. Main, 817-424-4333

The upscale **Tuscany Art in Dining** offers a fine dining experience, featuring excellent Italian cuisine, an extensive wine list and magnificent views from the rooftop Skybar.

www.tuscanygrapevine.com
1000 Texan Trail # 130, 817-328-6111

The **Gaylord Texan** (see Distinctive Destinations below) is home to some notable dining venues. For a truly special occasion, the posh **Old Hickory Steakhouse** serves Premium Black Angus Beef, artisan cheeses and boasts a remarkable wine list. The Chef at **Ama Lur** creates excellent Southwestern cuisine from a distinctive contemporary menu, and the open-air **Riverwalk Café** offers regional foods prepared with Texas flair and served on a patio reminiscent of San Antonio's Riverwalk.

The family-oriented Great Wolf Lodge. (courtesy Grapevine CVB)

Sleep

Nearly all the major hotel chains have a presence along Hwy. 114. Destinations unto themselves, the stupendous **Gaylord Texan** and the entertaining **Great Wolf Lodge** are listed in the Distinctive Destinations section. Many hotels have excellent spas and feature packages that include spa treatments, golf, or dining and wine. In historic downtown, a fabulous Bed and Breakfast offers deluxe accommodations.

Garden Manor Bed & Breakfast offers the only accommodations in the downtown historic district, within walking distance of its many shops, restaurants and music venues. An elegant Southern Georgian style home with only four bedrooms, it provides an intimate locale for romantic escapes or a convenient location for shopping girlfriends. Owner Judy describes the décor as "Country Chic," blending the charm of yesterday with the technology of today. In addition to the luxurious amenities you would expect, Judy pampers guests with such extras as nightly turndown service, chocolate truffles and early morning coffee before a full plantation style breakfast. She also offers some appealing specials like the "Wine and Roses Getaway and the "Will You Marry Me?" package.

www.gardenmanorbandb.com
205 East College St., 817-424-9177, 877-424-9177

Granbury

Convention & Visitors Bureau
116 W. Bridge St.
817-573-5548; 800-950-2212
www.granburytx.com

Granbury's historic town square was the first in Texas to be listed in the National Register of Historic Places. Today the square is lined with stores and boutiques of all descriptions, eateries and antique shops. You can have an old-fashioned soda or buy an authentic German beer stein. This town knows how to have fun and you'll probably find some kind of festival or celebration going on when you visit – General Granbury's Blazin' Beans Birthday Bash (March), the Brazos River Music Fest (March), Harvest Moon Festival (October), Civil War re-enactments, and a Candlelight Christmas Tour of Homes, to name a few.

Scenic Lake Granbury itself offers varied recreational activities – boating, fishing, water skiing, canoeing, and swimming. Several companies rent canoes, boats, jet-skis, and other water recreational equipment.

Entertainment

Some of the best entertainment in town is found at **Granbury Live**. This family friendly venue has been a mainstay for Granbury entertainment for the past decade. The All-American patriotic and nostalgic performances feature the area's top professional entertainers in lively productions suitable for all ages. The building's black and white Art Deco façade is stunning.

www.granburylive.com
110 N. Crockett St., 800-989-8240

Traveling vaudeville acts, minstrel shows, and melodramas are gone, but the **Granbury Opera House**, originally built in 1889, was meticulously restored and reopened in 1975. Today the Opera House presents plays, musicals, and comedy revues.

www.granburyoperahouse.net
133 E. Pearl St., 800-547-4697

After enjoying Granbury Live or the Opera House, stop in at the **Coffee Grinder** for a late night coffee.

129 E. Pearl St., 817-279-0977

Pile the family in the car and head for **The Brazos Drive-In**. One of the few remaining outdoor drive-in theaters in Texas, the Brazos has been lit up every season since it first opened in 1952. It still shows double features on Friday and Saturday nights and has a carload price (max. 6 folks in a car).

Couples, cuddle up and remember when. Families, show your kids what the drive-in experience was like!

www.thebrazos.com/home.htm

1800 W. Pearl St., 817-573-1311

Shop

Oh, the shops in Granbury! Girlfriends, you're in Heaven! Stroll around the square – all four sides – with your credit cards in hand. Some of the absolute "don't miss" ones are:

Dakota's Kabin, specializes in Western and rustic furnishings, home décor items, jewelry, candles, kitchen accessories, gourmet salsas and jams and on and on.

www.dakotaskabin.com

202 N. Houston St., 817-579-0275

Shopping on Granbury town square in the fall. (courtesy Granbury CVB)

Attention, Quilters! **Houston Street Mercantile** is one of the best quilting shops in Texas with a fabulous selection of fabrics, books, notions and chocolate. Girls, ask about the Quilt Inn, a restored 1895 farmhouse, fully equipped as a Quilting Retreat guesthouse that can accommodate up to 12 ladies. Quilt on . . .

www.houstonstmercantile.com
126 N. Houston St., 817-279-0425

The Pan Handle, an awesome kitchen shop chock a block with cookware, gadgets, custom gift baskets, gourmet food items, aromatic coffees and teas, cookbooks, and gifts. They also present fabulous gourmet cooking classes.

www.thepanhandle.com
106 N. Crockett St., 817-579-1518

Books on the Square has a nice selection of books, along with an extensive variety of gift items, party goods, games, greeting cards and souvenirs.

130 N. Houston St., 817-573-9672

Eat

With more than 70 restaurants in Granbury, you'll find anything your palate desires.

Girls, lunch at the **Merry Heart Tearoom** is mandatory. One of the favorites is the "trio" of mix-and-match salads (the chicken salad is made with yogurt instead of mayo) and soups. With a typical "tearoom menu" of quiche, fruit, stuffed avocados, salads, light meals, heavenly desserts, and raspberry tea, the food is good and the setting is even better – inside a Victorian gift shop.

www.granburyrestaurants.com
110 N Houston St., 817-573-3800

41

Everyone loves **Rinky-Tinks**, a combination ice cream parlor and sandwich shop. In addition to great sandwiches, cookies and pies, they make old-fashioned malts, shakes, floats, banana splits and hand-squeezed lemonade. Décor is '50s memorabilia.

www.rinkytinks.com
108 N. Houston St., 817-573-4323

Stringfellow's location, on the town square in a restored turn-of-the-century building, is one of the nicer dining venues in Granbury. The varied menu features light entrées as well as steaks, salmon, shrimp and chicken dinners. Open for lunch, they offer some nice sandwiches like a sautéed chicken avocado sandwich or a Southwest turkey and bacon wrap. Leave room for the Kaluha fudge pie. There's a tree-shaded courtyard if the weather is nice.

www.granburyrestaurants.com
101 E. Pearl St., 817-573-6262

In the renovated 1933 corner Sinclair Station, **Pearl Street Station** has an interesting menu of Cajun food and BBQ, with sandwiches served on toasted jalapeno/cheese buns. Boudreaux would be proud.

www.pearlststationgranbury.com
120 W. Pearl St., 817- 579-7233

About 15 miles southwest, toward Stephenville, in the tiny hamlet of Bluff Dale is **Let's Eat**, a hole-in-the-wall with a great chef. With an eclectic menu (mouth-watering steaks) on the blackboard and country music on the stereo, it's open for lunch and dinner. The food is outstanding and the place is small, so go early.

28602 US 377, 254-728-3635

If you have to wait, go over to the **Greenwood Dancehall & Saloon** – they'll call you when your table's ready. www.greenwoodbd.com

Sleep

Granbury offers a wide variety of accommodations. While most families with children will enjoy familiar-named motels, couples and girlfriends might enjoy some of the many B&Bs in town. Most are in restored historic homes within walking distance of the downtown square.

A great choice for a romantic getaway or for groups is the splendid **American Heritage House**. Innkeepers, Ron & Karen Bleeker, have created a warm, welcoming ambiance in an opulent Federal style Victorian mansion specifically designed for guests' comfort. Rooms and suites are tastefully furnished with heirlooms and period antiques and each has a luxurious private bath. Amenities include cable TV, irons and ironing boards, Turkish robes, WiFi and fresh roses and chocolates. A common room, fully-equipped with audio visual equipment, can hold up to 60 occupants for meetings, and could just as well accommodate girlfriend gatherings. A multi-course gourmet breakfast, served on fine china in the formal dining room, is bound to please the most discriminating guests. Ron & Karen will make arrangements for special occasion packages, picnics, and even a ride on their bicycle built for two.

www.americanheritagehouse.com
225 W. Morse St., 817-578-3768, 866-778-3768

For an ultimate romantic getaway, book a room or suite at **Inn on Lake Granbury**. It's like having a private lakefront home with beautifully landscaped grounds and a personal concierge service. Each guest room is luxuriously appointed with featherbeds and fine linens, remote controlled television

43

with cable, a CD/DVD player, desk, high-speed internet access and WiFi, and private bath with quality amenities. Some have a stone fireplace, others a porch or balcony. Each morning, you'll be served a delicious full breakfast.

www.innonlakegranbury.com
205 West Doyle St., 817-573-0046, toll-free 877-573-0046

Glen Rose

Visitor Center
1505 NE Big Bend Trail
254-897-3081; 888-346-6282
www.glenrosetexas.net

While Glen Rose is a super destination for families, it's also a pleasing little town for getaways, especially for nature lovers. Check to see if there's a performance, rodeo or concert at the gigantic multi-purpose Expo and Amphitheatre.

www.glenroseexpo.org
254-897-4509

Outdoors & Critters

The first sauropod tracks in the world were discovered in what is now **Dinosaur Valley State Park**. Sauropods were 60-ft.-long plant-eating reptiles that weighed up to 30 tons. Near Glen Rose, the Paluxy River flows over solid rock that contains the best-preserved dinosaur tracks in Texas. Now a picturesque state park occupies this scenic area of the Paluxy River with interpretive exhibits that offer a glimpse of how Texas might have looked 100 million years ago. The 1,524-acre park also offers camping, picnicking, and nature trails.

www.tpwd.state.tx.us/spdest/findadest/parks/dinosaur_valley
254-897-4588

At **Fossil Rim Wildlife Center**, one of the country's most renowned wildlife facilities, some of the world's most endangered animal species roam freely through 1,700 acres of unspoiled countryside. A 9.5-mile drive winds through the area so you can observe them. Fossil Rim has a world-famous breeding program for the Cheetah and White Rhino, the nation's second largest red wolf population, and more than 1,000 exotic and endangered animals. Other attractions include a petting pasture, café overlooking the valley, picnic area, nature trail, education center, and outstanding nature store. If you've got the time, inquire about the Foothills Safari Camp – a 3-day, 2-night behind-the-scenes adventure available only by advance reservations.

www.fossilrim.com
2299 CR 2008, 254-897-2960

For recreation, there's horseback riding, canoeing, kayaking, and swimming in the scenic Paluxy River, and **Squaw Valley**, a 4½-star golf course, named one of the top five municipal courses in Texas by the *Dallas Morning News*.

www.squawvalleygc.com/golf/proto/squawvalleygc
2439 E. Hwy. 67, 254-897-7956

Special Attraction

On Friday and Saturday evenings during September and October, people flock to Glen Rose for spectacular performances of ***The Promise***. Now in its 20th year, what began as a passion play has become a highly acclaimed live, epic drama of the life of Christ.

www.thepromiseglenrose.com
800-687-2661

45

Eat

You'll find most anything you like long Hwy. 67, from fast food to Mexican to barbecue. There's a casual restaurant at Fossil Rim if you plan to spend the day. Another good choice is **Ranch House Barbecue**.
1408 NE Big Bend Trail, 254-897-3441

For fine dining, there are two excellent options. **Inn on the River** is an upscale Bed & Breakfast Inn with an elegant dining room offering delectable four-course gourmet dinners on Friday and Saturday nights. You don't have to be a guest of the Inn but you must have reservations.
www.innontheriver.com
205 SW Barnard St., 254-897-2929, 800-575-2101

Rough Creek Lodge is an elite resort in the hills beyond Glen Rose. Unmatched service combined with an imaginative chef and exceptional gourmet cuisine has earned the dining room accolades from around the world. Reservations required.
www.roughcreek.com
800-864-4705

Sleep

Inn on the River, an upscale historic B&B along the banks of the Paluxy River, began as part of Dr. Snyder's Drugless Health Sanitarium. A Recorded Texas Historic Landmark marker is proudly displayed. With 22 luxurious rooms and an excellent chef, it's small enough to offer personal service for meetings and gatherings. The gourmet dinners are described above. Special B&B packages include a "Romantic Getaway," a "Couples Pampering Spa," "Bon Appetite," and golf and fishing packages, as well as a divine Wedding special.
www.innontheriver.com
205 SW Barnard St., 254-897-2929, 800-575-2101

Rough Creek Lodge – see Distinctive Destinations

Waxahachie

Chamber of Commerce
102 YMCA Drive
972-937-2390; 972-938-9617
www.waxahachiechamber.com
www.downtownwaxahachie.com

Designated in the early 1900s as Queen of the Cotton Belt, Waxahachie has grown to be known as the Gingerbread City for the ornate woodwork found on many of the historic homes. Also acclaimed as the Movie Capital of Texas, with more than 30 movies filmed in the area including three Academy Award winners (*The Trip to Bountiful*, *Places in the Heart*, and *Tender Mercies*), and the Crape Myrtle Capital of Texas. Quite a lot to live up to.

Antique shops, specialty stores, boutiques and eateries surround the picturesque Ellis County Courthouse, the hub of the community for over a century.

History

The **Ellis County Courthouse**, an elaborate structure of red sandstone and granite, was built in 1895 for the then outlandish cost of $150,000. Artisans were brought from Italy to do the exterior stone carving. The clock uses a windup mechanism that weighs 250 pounds and the bell-striker weighs over 800 pounds. The courthouse recently underwent a $15,000,000 facelift that was so detailed the county bought red sandstone for repairs from the same quarry that produced the stone used for construction in 1895 and matched the interior colors to the original ones. Listed in the top 100 most photographed structures in Texas, it stands proudly as an outstanding example of Romanesque Revival architectural style.

The Ellis County Courthouse in Waxahachie is one of the prettiest in the state. (courtesy Waxahachie CVB)

Arts & Culture

Waxahachie Community Theatre provides family entertainment throughout the year.

www.waxahachiecommunitytheatre.com

972-723-6976

Assuredly the major annual event is **Scarborough Faire Renaissance Festival**, open weekends from early April through Memorial Day. Featuring over 200 craft shops, food and drink booths and medieval entertainment – wizards, jugglers, jesters, jousters and puppets, costumes of royalty and rascals, poets and peasants – visitors are transported to a 16th Century English Village for fun and frivolity.

www.scarboroughrenfest.com

48

Nearby Ennis celebrates its Czechoslovakian heritage with a nice **Czech Museum** and shops in the historic downtown area specializing in Czech gifts, crystal, books and antiques. It also hosts the National Polka Festival each Memorial Day weekend.

www.nationalpolkafestival.com

Attractions & Events

The historical and cultural attractions of Waxahachie are many. Pick up a map at the chamber or commerce for a historic driving or walking tour, including such information as which building appeared in which movie. The annual Gingerbread Tour of Homes each June draws visitors from around the nation. The Candlelight Historic Home Tour during Thanksgiving weekend and into December is another way to see some of the magnificent homes, as is staying overnight in one of them that has been turned into a fine Bed & Breakfast establishment.

www.waxahachiedowntown.com/gingerbread.htm

Between Waxahachie and Ennis, the **Texas Motorplex** is a renowned NHRA Drag Racing facility, drawing some of the top names in racing.

www.texasmotorplex.com
972-878-2641

About 15 miles from Waxahachie, **Ennis** is noted throughout Texas for its springtime Bluebonnet Trails, sponsored by the Ennis Garden Club. Special events take place for weeks in April as tourists and photographers search the area for the most magnificent displays of Texas' state flower.

www.visitennis.org
972-878-4748, 888-366-4748

Shop

Numerous shops and businesses surround the historic courthouse. It's fun to just browse, but here are a few suggestions. A visit to the **Gingerbread Antique Mall** with its offerings of Victorian antiques and vintage collectibles will keep you busy for a while.

310 S. College, 972-937-0968

Mosaic Madness is North Texas' largest mosaic and stained glass studio. It's lots of fun checking out their selection of supplies and finished art pieces as well as the workshop and studio.

mosaicmadness.net
211 S. College, 972-937-5797

Find anything Western from "practical to posh" – jewelry, clothing and home décor – at **Buffalo Creek Cowgirls**.

207 S. College, 972-937-7490

If you're a quilter, you'll love **Common Threads Quilting**. Specializing in 19th century reproduction fabrics and 1930s florals, this is a gem for folks restoring historic homes.

www.commonthreadsquilting.com
315 S. Rogers St., 972-935-0510

Eat

Famous far and wide as a "haunted" restaurant, **The Catfish Plantation** has three friendly, resident ghosts, first-rate catfish, and great down-home Cajun food. Ghostly experiences don't occur on a daily basis, but there's always someone around to tell tales of prior incidents. Go for the food.

www.catfishplantation.com
814 Water St., 972-937-9468

The English-inspired **College Street Pub** makes a great meeting place to watch a game on TV, have a drink, snack or full meal. The creative menu offerings are far above what you think of as "pub grub," and daily specials are posted on a blackboard. Fries are awesome. So are the fish and chips. They serve the best Reuben in town! Desserts are to die for. 'Nuf said. Friendly, efficient service.

210 N. College St., 972- 938-2062

Part award-winning restaurant, part fine gift shop, part home furnishings store, part antique shop, **The Dove's Nest** is a "must" for you girls. The "New Southern" cuisine, under the eye of Executive Chef Aaron Neal, has won so many accolades in magazines, newspapers, and on TV that the restaurant now has its own cookbook. And the classy gift shop carries many of the same lines as chic big city boutiques.

www.thedovesnestrestaurant.com
105 W. Jefferson, 972-938-3683

Two Amigos Taqueria, a little café two blocks west of the courthouse, serves authentic Mexican food. The tortilla soup and nachos are awesome and prices are reasonable.

212 W. Jefferson, 972-923-3305

Sleep

Here's your chance to stay in one of those splendid homes! Only 35 minutes and 100 years from Dallas, **The Chaska House**, built in 1900 in the Revival Style, is listed in the National Registry of Historic Places. Reminiscent of a time when cotton was king and life was good, the home has been meticulously restored as a luxurious Bed & Breakfast. Showcasing original architecture, master craftsmanship, and imaginative interior design, the home blends the past with lavish amenities and modern comforts such as king-sized beds

51

with luxuriant linens, spacious baths with whirlpools-for-two, custom bath toiletries, individual temperature controls, LCD cable TV, DVD players and WiFi. The rooms and suites reflect the lives of well-known authors including Mark Twain, F. Scott Fitzgerald, Margaret Mitchell, William Shakespeare and Theodore Roosevelt. With warm Texas hospitality, gracious resident owners Louis and Linda will customize romance packages to make your special getaway memorable. They enjoy hosting girlfriend reunions, quilters, scrapbookers, and since their rooms are named for authors, the book club girls love it.

www.chaskabb.com
716 West Main St., 972-937-3390, 800-931-3390

The historic Chaska House is now a luxurious Bed & Breakfast.
(courtesy Chaska House B&B)

Waco

Travel Information Center
106 Texas Ranger Trail in Fort Fisher Park
254-750-8696; 800-922-6386
www.wacocvb.com

If you've never thought of Waco as a destination, think again. With more than a dozen major attractions, five historic homes, seven recreational venues, nine arts organizations and Baylor University, it truly does offer something for everyone. Named for the Huaco Indians, Waco has had a colorful and turbulent history of Comanche raids, frontier forts, cattle drives, railroads and cotton.

One of the impressive stained-glass windows
in the Armstrong Browning Library. (courtesy Waco CVB)

History & Museums

"How do I love thee? Let me count the ways." One of the best exhibits in town isn't the most well-known. Discover the love poetry and extensive works of British Victorian poets, Robert and Elizabeth Barrett Browning, at the **Armstrong**

53

Browning Library, located on the Baylor University campus. Containing the largest known collection of the Brownings' works, the library itself is a remarkable work of art with walnut paneling, marble columns and ornate ceilings. Inside, 62 magnificent stained glass windows illustrate passages from their poetry. Antique bookcases and memorabilia from the Brownings' home are also displayed. Romantics, take note.

www.browninglibrary.org
710 Speight, 254-710-3566

Dr Pepper Museum (courtesy Waco CVB)

A fountain drink mixed in The Old Corner Drug Store in the 1880s was dubbed a "Waco" by early patrons because Waco was the only place it could be found. Now known as Dr Pepper, the new drink was put on sale commercially in 1885, after two years of testing, blending, and processing. **The Dr Pepper Museum** is housed in the original 1906 bottling plant, now listed in the National Register of Historic Places. A recreated turn-of-the-century soda fountain serves up history and nostalgia along with Waco's favorite drink.

www.drpeppermuseum.com
300 S. 5th St., 254-757-1025

If you've got the family with you, plan to spend the better part of a day at the **Mayborn Museum Complex**. A wide spectrum of educational exhibits and programs encourage families to learn together. The **Jeanes Discovery Center** offers 16 hands-on, interactive discovery rooms. Fifteen wood frame buildings make up the 13-acre **Governor Bill & Vara Daniel Historic Village** to let folks see what life in Texas was like from the latter part of the 19th Century into the early 20th Century.

www.maybornmuseum.com
1300 S. University Parks Dr., 254-710-1110

In 1978, two guys were looking for arrowheads near the Bosque River when they discovered a large bone, creating lots of excitement when it was identified as a Columbian mammoth bone. After 30 years of careful excavation, the **Waco Mammoth Site** has revealed the remains of at least 22 Columbian mammoths and an indication of more. Bone casts were on display at the Mayborn Museum Complex (see above) until December, 2009 when the actual site was opened to the public. Visitors get an excellent view from an overhead walkway suspended over the dig shelter and the location in a stretch of woods along the river gives a glimpse into the time when the mammoths lived here.

www.wacomammoth.org
6220 Steinbeck Bend Rd., 254-750-7946

Waco boasts five grand historic homes, dating from circa 1868-1872. Four are managed by the Historic Waco Foundation and are open for tours, mostly on weekends.

www.historicwaco.org
810 S. 4th St, 254-753-5166

Few heroes from history books have ever captured our imagination as much as the notorious Texas Rangers. The

Texas Ranger Hall of Fame & Museum commemorates the history and lore of the legendary Texas Rangers, the oldest state law enforcement agency in the nation. See treasured collections of guns from the Old West, Texas Ranger badges, a Bowie Knife owned by Jim Bowie, and the weapons and possessions of Bonnie & Clyde. Lots of hands-on exhibits for kids encourage their interest in Texas history. Thirty-one Texas Rangers who gave their lives in the line of duty or served with utmost distinction are memorialized in the Hall of Fame. The museum store has officially licensed souvenirs and an exceptional selection of books. The Texas Ranger Research Center contains books, archives, photographs and oral histories related to the Texas Rangers.

www.texasranger.org
I-35 @ University Parks Dr., 254-750-8631

The **Texas Sports Hall Of Fame** is a special tribute to the pursuit of excellence and a showcase of legendary greats. Sports memorabilia highlight nationally known Texans, including Troy Aikman, Byron Nelson, Lee Trevino, Babe Didrikson Zaharias, George Foreman, and Nolan Ryan, to name a few. See the 1938 Heisman Trophy presented to TCU quarterback, Davey O'Brien, and game jerseys worn by Bob Lilly and Roger Staubach. Watch videos of historic sports events in the Tom Landry Theater and take home a souvenir from the gift shop.

www.tshof.org
1108 S. University Parks Dr., 254-756-1633

For those interested, the **Masonic Grand Lodge of Texas**, located in an impressive building in downtown Waco, displays items telling the story of Freemasonry in Texas.

www.grandlodgeoftexas.org
715 Columbus Ave., 254-753-7395

Arts & Culture

Home to **Baylor University** and **McLennan Community College**, you'll find no lack of music, nightlife, and top-rate entertainment venues in Waco. Performing Arts venues include the **Baylor Theatre**, which showcases productions of the Baylor Theatre department and **Waco Civic Theatre**, which presents several main season productions as well as special events.

www.baylor.edu/theatre, 254-710-1865
www.wacocivictheatre.org, 1517 Lake Air Dr., 254-776-1591

The **Waco Hippodrome Theater** has been the scene for everything from Vaudeville acts, road shows, movies, and local talent shows since it opened in 1914. With its ornate domed ceiling and gold leaf trim, the theater has been recognized as an architectural treasure and boasts both a Recorded Texas Historic Landmark and a listing in the National Registry of Historic Places. Now it hosts a wide variety of professional shows and great family entertainment.

www.wacoperformingarts.org
724 Austin Ave., 254-752-9797

McLennan Community College presents theater productions and concerts at three venues on the campus: the **Ball Performing Arts Center**, the **Fine Arts Theatre** and the **Bosque River Stage**.

www.mclennan.edu/bosque
1400 College Dr., box office 254-299-8200

Art Center Waco, an attractive Mediterranean-style building with beautifully landscaped lawns and sculpture garden, showcases a variety of art and photography exhibits.

www.artcenterwaco.org,
1300 College Dr., 254-752-4371

57

Outdoors and Critters

Cameron Park Zoo is a far cry from the cages of yesterday's zoos that most folks grew up with. This award-winning natural-habitat zoo gives the wild animals free-form surroundings, lush grasses and natural shelters. All exhibits are thoroughly explained by educational plaques. On 52 acres near the Brazos River amid huge pecans, elms, live oaks and mesquites, it's recreational as well as educational.

www.cameronparkzoo.com
1701 N. 4th St., 254-750-8400

Cameron Park itself covers 416 acres of limestone bluffs and wooded hills along the Brazos and Bosque Rivers. Picnic areas, nationally recognized bike trails and a challenging disc golf course draw locals and visitors alike. Kids can spend hours in play areas and the spray park– a view from the treehouse is a favorite.

The **Texas Ranger Hall of Fame** (above) is located in **Fort Fisher Park**, a scenic 35 acres along Lake Brazos, near the site of the original Texas Ranger fort established in 1837. Shaded riverside campsites, RV, and picnic sites are available.

Built in 1870, Waco's Historic **Suspension Bridge** provided cattle and cowboys following the Chisholm Trail the only pedestrian/wagon span across the Brazos River. Completed in January of 1870, the 475-ft. bridge required 2,700,000 bricks and cost $135,000 to build. Designed by the renowned New York firm that originated the suspension span bridge concept and later oversaw the building of the Brooklyn Bridge, it was the longest single-span suspension bridge west of the Mississippi at the time. Now it's the venue for many community festivals and events.

The bridge is flanked by two parks — **Indian Spring Park** on the west side, and **Martin Luther King, Jr. Park** on the east side. The River Walk on the west side of the river extends from Ft. Fisher Park, past the Historic Suspension Bridge and continues for an additional 1½ miles to the Herring Ave. Bridge, allowing walkers or joggers to enjoy the view from both sides of the river.

When it was completed in 1870, Waco's suspension bridge was the longest single-span suspension bridge west of the Mississippi.
(courtesy Waco CVB)

Special Attraction

One place almost everyone finds absolutely fascinating is **Homestead Heritage Traditional Crafts Village**, a Christian agricultural settlement in nearby **Elm Mott**, just north of town. Not a replica of a historic village, it truly is an authentic community where residents live and farm as their forefathers did generations ago. A Visitors Center provides information about seasonal activities and special events, including teaching seminars and workshops on agricultural skills like gardening, raising poultry, bees or goats, traditional crafts like pottery, woodworking, blacksmithing and basketry, fabric crafts like spinning and weaving, kitchen crafts like bread-baking, cheese making and soap making. The Visitors Center also houses the Homestead Farms Deli & Bakery, which features daily homemade lunch specials, deli-style sandwiches, and real homemade ice cream.

The 200-year old restored Barn showcases and sells the works of the village's craftspeople: handcrafted furniture, quilts, pottery, wrought iron, brooms and baskets, wooden cutting boards and spoons, oil lamps, beeswax candles, natural soaps, needlework, original watercolors and homesteading books, as well as Homestead specialty food items.

A visit here could be an eye-opening experience for those who are products of our urban, techno-industrial world.

www.homesteadheritage.com
Halbert Lane, Elm Mott, 254-754-9600

Shop

The **Shops of River Square Center**, located in historic downtown Waco, is a most wondrous collection of shops. Occupying 40,000 sq. ft. in the 100-year-old Waco Hardware building, "The Shops" include fabulous home furnishings, fashionable clothing, antiques, all kinds of gifts, jewelry, shoes, collectibles, souvenirs, a baby boutique and maternity shop. In the center of it all, **Simply Good Eatery**, a colorful café, serves great soups, salads and sandwiches and tasty hot lunch specials. Girlfriends, here's your all-day excursion!

www.shopsofriversquarecenter.com
2nd & Franklin Sts., 254-757-0921

Sironia is a great place to browse, with an eclectic collection of funky shops featuring jewelry, stylish clothing, antiques and collectibles, and a delightful tearoom for lunch.

www.shopsironia.com

1509 S. Austin Ave., 254-754-7467

Eat

As with any large college town, you can find dozens (probably hundreds) of restaurants, from fast food to ethnic to fine dining.

One Waco "institution" is the **Elite Circle Grille**. The first Elite Café opened downtown in 1919 and the second location opened in 1941 on one of the first traffic circles in Texas. It's had an interesting history, including a visit from Private Elvis Presley when he was stationed at nearby Fort Hood. Refurbished more than once, new owners in 2003 completely remodeled the Elite back to an ambiance of its original time and decorated it with historic memorabilia. Now, if only walls could talk!

www.elitecirclegrille.com

2132 S Valley Mills Dr., 254-754-4941

If you hang around Waco very long, you'll hear folks talking about the oriental fries at **Kitok's**. Great burgers and oriental food served in a funky hole-in-the-wall place.

1815 N 18th St., 254-754-1801

Many consider **Diamond Backs** the best restaurant in Waco. Several menu items sound tempting, but they specialize in steaks, and get rave reviews. Dessert is a toss-up between Bananas Foster and peach cobbler. It's a bit pricey, but the food, ambiance, service and nice wine list make it appropriate for a romantic dinner.

River Square Center, 254-757-2871

Sleep

You'll not find more gracious Southern hospitality than at the **Cotton Palace**. This 1910 Arts and Crafts style home showcases the exquisite woodwork and design of Waco's premiere architect, Roy Elspeth Lane. It's now an upscale Bed and Breakfast, where guestrooms are appointed with fine furnishings, luxurious linens, robes, toiletries, and marble whirlpool tubs. For romantic getaways, roses, champagne or chocolate-covered strawberries may be added for a nominal extra charge. Gourmet breakfasts are served on the antique dining room table. Comfortable, spacious common areas would be perfect for girlfriends to gather, around a stone fireplace, in rocking chairs on the front porch or sunroom . . . and then there's the bottomless cookie jar. Friendly innkeeper, Becky, would probably join you.

www.thecottonpalace.com
1910 Austin Ave., 254-753-7294, 877-632-2312

If you don't mind staying a few miles outside town, the suites at **Let's Go Country Bed and Breakfast**, are exceedingly comfortable. The tastefully renovated 1913 Victorian farmhouse is nestled on 127 acres of rolling farmland, affording marvelous countryside serenity. Hospitable innkeepers serve a hearty breakfast each morning.

www.letsgocountry.com
1182 Spring Lake Rd., 254-799-7947, 888-239-2517

Salado

Chamber Information
881 N. Main Street
254-947-5040
www.salado.com

The Village of Salado is an ideal place for a getaway, either with girlfriends or your sweetheart. Although fitting for romance and shopping sprees, there's little to interest children. Founded in 1859 by early Scottish settlers because of the plentiful springs and rich farmlands along Salado Creek, it quickly became a center of commerce and a stagecoach stop. Today the area around Main Street is a lively marketplace with more than 60 shops and galleries, offering everything from fine art to exclusive fashions to gourmet foods. Several Bed and Breakfast establishments offer accommodations from nice to extravagant.

Golf

Mill Creek Golf Club features three nine-hole courses designed by world prominent architect Robert Trent Jones, Jr. Weaving and flowing around Salado Creek amidst towering Oak and Elm trees, they offer a challenge to even the best golfer.

www.millcreek-golf.com/golf/proto/millcreek
1610 Club Circle, 254-947-5698, 800-736-3441

Arts & Culture

The **Silver Spur Theater**, in a converted granary, is a 150-seat theater that houses a unique blend of classic movies, Vaudevillian performances, and live music.

www.saladosilverspur.com
108 Royal St., 254-947-3456

Shop

There's no way any publication such as this could begin to list the shops and galleries in Salado. Suffice it to say you can find anything you need and several things you've never imagined. You'll have to "walk the streets" yourself.

Eat

Ambrosia Tea Room, inside the Salado Haus Gift Shop on Main Street, offers gourmet tea, sandwiches, homemade soups and tasty salads in a setting featuring antique furnishings.
102 N. Main St., 254-947-3733

A local favorite for over 20 years, **Browning's Courtyard Café**, located in the Salado Square shopping area, has a European flair. It serves great sandwiches on freshly baked bread, delicious soups, salads, and decadent desserts.
#4 Salado Square, Main St., 254-947-8666

The Range at the Barton House is an elegant eatery where Chef Dave Hermann prepares innovative and adventurous fare with a Mediterranean flair. Perfect for that romantic dinner.
www.therangerestaurant.com
101 Main St., 254-947-3828

The **Inn on the Creek** (see "sleep" below) serves a four-course gourmet dinner every Friday and Saturday evening by reservation only.

One of the oldest and most popular restaurants in Salado, **Stagecoach Inn**, is a historic inn and dining room.
www.staystagecoach.com/golf/proto/stagecoach
401 South Stagecoach Rd.
inn: 254-947-5111, dining: 254-947-9400

Sleep

At **Stone Creek Settlement**, owners Jill and Johnny have created a tranquil ambiance only minutes away from Salado's shopping and dining district. Individual cottages, each artistically decorated and created from architectural materials reclaimed from early Texas homes, are tucked into beautifully landscaped gardens with ponds, rose and herb gardens and walking trails (Jill is a Texas Master Gardener). Any of the cottages would be an excellent choice for a romantic weekend. Girlfriends like to gather around the fireplace or in the garden to visit before or after shopping.

www.stonecreeksettlement.com
714 College Hill, 254-947-9099, 888-777-8844

The Gazebo B&B Suite is the ultimate for romantic getaways or honeymoons! Originally built as an open-air gazebo and recently reconstructed, the luxurious B&B offers maximum seclusion overlooking the quiet waters of Salado Creek. In the heart of the village's historic district, it's within walking distance of the myriad shops, restaurants, and galleries. The Gazebo itself displays a unique architectural design, tastefully decorated in warm colors and the oversized windows provide stunning views of the pond and garden area. The bath features an awesome shower for two. In the Country French kitchen, you'll find wine glasses and corkscrews, and breakfast fixin's for a feast.

www.saladotex.com/gazebo.html
209 S. Main St., 877-947-5938

Inn on the Creek, an elegant 14-room Victorian inn offers gracious hospitality and seclusion in a beautifully landscaped setting along the banks of Salado Creek. Rooms reflect the simple elegance of a bygone era, yet with the conveniences of today's technical world. The Inn offers a Romantic Picnic package, a Sweetheart package, and a Golfing package, but the attentive staff can accommodate almost any request.

www.inncreek.com
602 Center Circle, 254-947-5554, 877-947-5554

The Rose Mansion, featured in *Southern Living* magazine, is an 1870 Greek Revival style mansion on two acres surrounded by a white picket fence. Brick paths wander through the beautifully landscaped grounds and reveal hammocks, swings and shaded seating areas nestled amid ancient trees and lovely flower gardens. The mansion has an elegant parlor and dining room in addition to four guest bedrooms. A cheery sunroom makes a great gathering place. Scattered around the grounds, several authentically restored early Texas dwellings – log cabins, cottages and stone homes – provide luxurious private accommodations. Each is superbly decorated and reminiscent of times long ago in Texas history.

www.therosemansion.com
903 Roseway, 254-947-8200, 800-948-1004

Bryan-College Station

Convention and Visitors Bureau
715 University Dr. East
979-260-9898; 800-777-8292
www.visitaggieland.com

Best known for Texas A&M University and the George Bush Presidential Library, Bryan-College Station has lots to offer. . . far too much to list here. If you need help, call the friendly and knowledgeable staff at the CVB (above). For non-college related getaways, here are some highlights.

History

The city of Bryan is in the process of revitalizing Historic Downtown Bryan to make it an attractive hub for shopping and dining. You'll find some fine old homes and buildings here, too.

www.downtownbryan.com

Built in 1903, **The Carnegie Center of Brazos Valley History** is the oldest existing Carnegie Library still used as a library in Texas. It contains a state-of-the-art history lab and an extensive genealogical collection.

www.bcslibrary.org/carnegie.html
111 S. Main, Bryan, 979-209-5630

Attractions

The state-of-the-art **George Bush Presidential Library and Museum** portrays and preserves official records, personal papers and memorabilia from the life and career of George Bush. One section is devoted to Barbara Bush's activities, from her promotion of literacy to her book about their dog, Millie. Everyone will find this both interesting and educational.

bushlib.tamu.edu
1000 George Bush Dr., College Station, 979-691-4000

Texas A&M University, renowned for its military Cadet Corps and ROTC, has outstanding research and experimental facilities in agriculture, animal pathology, salt and freshwater fisheries, engineering, and nuclear technology. Texas' first public institution of higher learning (1876) now has an enrollment of over 48,000 and is spread over 5,000 acres. Many A&M degree programs are ranked among the top in the country. Visitors are welcome – 90-minute walking tours and driving tours of the campus provide an overview of history, traditions, academics, and campus life. They begin at the Appelt Aggieland Visitor Center in Rudder Tower.

www.tamu.edu
979-845-3211, Visitor Center 979-845-5851

Veterans Memorial is an impressive tribute to America's military veterans. The centerpiece of the memorial is a massive bronze sculpture of a soldier carrying a wounded buddy and the

Wall of Honor lists the names of over 4,000 veterans. The Liberty Gardens were constructed in remembrance of those who lost their lives on 9/11/2001.

3101 Harvey Rd., College Station, 979-696-6247

Arts & Entertainment

The Arts Council of the Brazos Valley serves the arts, cultural and heritage needs of the area. The Council's extensive programs and services include rotating exhibits at several venues as well as classes, special events and professional development. The facility that houses the Arts Council is also home to the Texas Gallery and the Brazos Valley Art League.

2275 Dartmouth St., College Station, 979-696-2787

As for nightlife, you'll find a vibrant live music scene and an eclectic mix of restaurants in the **Northgate Entertainment District**, located on University Drive adjacent to the "north gate" of the Texas A&M campus.

Wine

The multi-award-winning **Messina Hof Winery & Resort** produces over 50 varieties of wine at their state-of-the-art facility. In addition to the winery tastings and tours, they host numerous special events throughout the year. The resort also includes The Vintage House, a first class, award-winning fine dining restaurant (Bananas Foster to die for) and The Villa at Messina Hof, an exceedingly romantic B&B (see Sleep below).

www.messinahof.com

4545 Old Reliance Rd., Bryan, 979-778-9463, 800-736-9463

Shop

Splurge with a visit to **Truman Chocolates**, where you'll find decadent, handcrafted gourmet chocolates created by master Chocolatier Mitch Siegert. The most sophisticated chocolate connoisseurs will find heavenly confections in this candy kitchen hidden in a strip shopping center.

www.trumanchocolates.com

4407 S. Texas Ave., Bryan, 979-260-4519

Catalena Hatters focus on one thing only . . . making fine quality custom hats. Not a Western wear store (no belts, boots or jeans), Catalena Hatters has made hats by hand, the "old fashioned way," one at a time since 1983.

www.catalenahats.com

203 N. Main St., Bryan, 979-822-4423

For eclectic treasures, visit the **Old Bryan Marketplace**. Browse through a 22,000 sq. ft. historical building filled with treasures from home décor to chic clothing, old and new.

www.oldbryanmarketplace.net

202 S. Bryan Ave., Bryan, 979-779-3245

The Benjamin Knox Gallery located in the historic 1900 College Station Depot, features fine art gifts and Texas scenes by renowned Texas Aggie artist Benjamin Knox '90, as well as custom framing, art classes, music, and a coffee & wine bar.

www.benjaminknox.com

405 University Dr. E, College Station, 979-696-5669

Brazos Glassworks Studio, a working stained glass studio and gallery, specializes in custom pieces and restoration work.

www.brazosglassworks.com

202 W. 26th St., Bryan, 979-823-0325

Eat

Award-winning **Christopher's World Grill** epitomizes exceptional food and service. A notable wine list complements the innovative menu, featuring such mouth-watering entrees as Raspberry Chipotle glazed Salmon and Thai Shrimp Fettuccini, as well as perfectly cooked Prime steaks. With consistently fabulous food and five professional chefs on staff, Christopher's is leading the way to developing a world-class dining scene in the Brazos Valley.

www.christophersworldgrille.com

5001 Boonville Rd., Bryan, 979-776-2181

Cenare serves excellent Italian food at reasonable prices with lunch specials and homemade pizza. At night, it morphs into a fine Italian restaurant with a more intimate atmosphere and sophisticated menu. The gnocchi gets rave reviews, as do all the desserts. A bit pricier than chain restaurants, it's not frequented by huge numbers of students.

404 University Dr. E, College Station, 979-696-7311

Located on the Messina Hof estate, **The Vintage House at Messina Hof** (see Wine above) pairs fine dining incorporating one of the vineyards' award-winning wines and is a perfect place for a special occasion celebration. For the utmost in extravagant dining, try the complete Chateaubriand Dinner for Two. Decadent Strawberries Romanoff, Bananas Foster or Cherries Jubilee are flambéed tableside.

Sleep

Like any large college town, Bryan-College Station has every imaginable type of accommodation. If you like B&Bs, **Aggie B&B Finder** will try to match you up with a B&B that fits your requirements. A wide range of distinctive accommodations are offered, all have been carefully inspected.

www.aggiebnb.com; 866-745-2936

Ten guest rooms at **The Villa at Messina Hof** are spacious with private balconies overlooking the estate (see Wine above). Incredibly romantic, The Villa pampers guests with richly appointed guest rooms, evening wine and cheese, a complimentary winery tour and tasting, and a European-style champagne breakfast. Several romance packages offer treats from in-room massages to chocolate and dining, but if you can't decide, they'll create a package just for you.

www.messinahof.com

4541 Old Reliance Rd., Bryan, 979-778-9463

The **7F Lodge & Spa** offers "romance in the country." Carefully hidden among live oaks and yaupon thickets are eight amazing secluded cottages. Each cottage is individually decorated and carries out a Texas theme or one of a country that flew a flag over Texas like France, Spain, or Mexico. Each provides indulgent comforts, elegant décor, a Jacuzzi tub, luxurious amenities and . . . remember, this is for a romantic getaway . . . no televisions or phones. Just the two of you.

www.7flodge.com

16611 Royder Rd., College Station, 979-690-0073

Brenham – Washington County

Washington Country Convention & Visitors Bureau

314 S. Austin Street

979-836-3695

www.brenhamtexas.com

Brenham is the heart and soul of Washington County. It's a charming little town with a downtown historic district listed in the National Register of Historic Places. Streets are lined with delightful and diverse specialty shops and eateries.

www.downtownbrenham.com

71

According to the July, 1992 issue of *Texas Highways* magazine, Washington County is the "best place in Texas to see wildflowers." Early March through late April is bluebonnet season and the visitor center distributes free "Bluebonnet Trails" maps that follow the most scenic routes. In May and June vibrant colors from Indian Paintbrushes, Black-eyed Susans, Thistles, Evening Primroses, and Coreopsis cover nature's canvas – the rolling hills of Washington County.

Washington-on-the-Brazos, the site of the signing of the Texas Declaration of Independence, is revered as the "Birthplace of Texas."

Fair warning: One getaway won't be enough to discover all the attractions of the Brenham – Washington County area.

History

The Brenham Heritage Museum, located in a revamped 1915 U.S. Post Office, is listed on the National Register of Historic Places. Permanent and special exhibits depict the history of the area. Adjacent to the museum, see the Silsby steam-powered, horse-drawn fire engine, purchased by the City of Brenham in 1879 for $3,000, a fortune in those days.

www.brenhamheritagemuseum.org
105 S. Market St.; 979-830-8445

Washington-on-the-Brazos State Historic Site is revered as the "Birthplace of Texas." This 293-acre complex is located on the original town site of Washington, which served as the capital of the Republic of Texas from 1842 to 1846. Everything tells about the beginning of Texas – a state-of-the-art Visitors Center with hands-on interactive exhibits and Independence Hall, where the Texas Declaration of Independence was drafted and signed on March 2, 1836, declaring its independence from Mexico. The Washington Emporium, located in the Visitors Center, is a premiere Texas gift shop. The Complex includes a

Conference Center, Education Center and Pavilions that are available for special occasions. Open year-round, the Park offers hiking trails, picnic areas with tables, grills, shelters, all free of charge.

www.birthplaceoftexas.com
936-878-2214

The exceptional **Star of the Republic Museum**, located within the Washington-on-the-Brazos State Historic Site (above), is in the shape of the five-pointed Texas star. Experience the rich history of the Republic of Texas which existed as a separate and independent nation from 1836 to 1846. With interactive exhibits, audiovisual presentations and educational programs, the Museum presents the story of the heroes and legends and cattlemen and farmers who settled and fought for Texas. It also contains an extensive research library and archives.

www.starmuseum.org

Barrington Living History Farm, encompasses the 1844 home of Anson Jones, the last president of the Republic of Texas and represents daily life on a working cotton farm of the 1850s. Interpreters in period clothing demonstrate 19th-century skills and crafts like blacksmithing, spinning & weaving and candle-making.

Arts & Culture

The Unity Theatre, a non-profit, professional live theatre located in historic downtown Brenham offers a variety of plays and musicals throughout the year in an intimate 125-seat restored warehouse theatre.

www.unitybrenham.org
300 Church St., 979-830-8358

The renowned **International Festival-Institute** at Round Top (see Round Top below) performs orchestral and chamber music concerts for six weeks each summer, as well as presenting diverse concerts throughout the year.

Attractions

The **Antique Rose Emporium** is one of the area's most popular attractions and beckons gardeners from far and wide. Located on the grounds of an early homestead in historic Independence, the gorgeous garden paths wander around restored buildings including an 1855 stone kitchen original to the site, an 1850 salt box house and an early 1900 Victorian home. The eight-acre retail display garden center is beautifully landscaped featuring romantic old garden roses, native plants, old-fashioned cottage garden perennials, herbs and wildflowers. What a wedding destination!

www.wearerose.com

10,000 FM 50, 979-836-5548, 800-441-0002

Everyone loves Blue Bell ice cream. (Washington County CVB)

A "must-see" for everyone is **Blue Bell Creameries**, home of the celebrated Blue Bell ice cream. Kids of all ages may take a 45-minute tour to see how the ice cream is made – and get a scoop of your favorite flavor at the end of the tour. This revered Texas treat began in 1911 when the Brenham Creamery Company supplemented its butter production by making a few gallons of ice cream. And, as they say, the rest is history. The name was changed to Blue Bell Creameries (for the wildflowers that covered the hillsides in spring), but otherwise little has changed. Although thousands of gallons are now made hourly, quality ingredients still make up the ice cream considered the absolute best by most Texans. The Blue Bell Country Store specializes in logo items and country gifts.

www.bluebell.com
1101 South Blue Bell Rd, 800-327-8135

The **Monastery of St. Clare Miniature Horse Ranch** is home to a group of Franciscan Poor Clare Nuns who support themselves by raising the miniature horses and by selling handmade ceramic wares, handpainted gifts, and horse-related items in the "Art Barn" gift shop.

www.monasteryminiaturehorses.com
9300 Hwy. 105, 979-836-9652

Outdoors

Originally an Indian trail, the scenic **La Bahia Road** stretched from western Louisiana into southeast Texas, passing Washington-on-the-Brazos and Independence and extending to Goliad, once known as La Bahia. Designated the first scenic highway in Texas, Hwy. 390 follows the historic route through rolling meadows past picturesque horse ranches and country estates from Burton to Washington. The delightful drive will lead you to **Independence** where Texas history abounds. Visit the Independence Baptist Church where Sam Houston was

75

converted and baptized and the graves of his wife and mother-in-law in the small cemetery across from the church. If you're a Baylor University graduate (or not), it's interesting to see where it was organized in 1845 as two separate schools – one for women and one for men, located at opposite sides of the town. Explain that to your modern-day child.

Lake Somerville State Park has 85 miles of shoreline and a great variety of birds and other wildlife. Two major recreation areas on the 11,640-acre Lake Somerville offer camping areas, horseback riding, hiking and biking trails, swimming, and great catfish and bass fishing. Access the Birch Creek Unit recreation area from the north and the Nails Creek recreation area from the south. The U.S. Army Corps of Engineers also operates two nice campgrounds on the south side of the lake.

www.tpwd.state.tx.us/spdest/findadest/parks/lake_somerville
979-535-7763

Windy Hill Winery offers tours and tastings.
(courtesy Washington County CVB)

76

Wine

Pleasant Hill Winery offers nice tours on weekends. Beginning in a "barn," the tours take you through the entire process of winemaking, from the grape to the wine to the tasting room. A gift shop features wine and "great grape gifts."

www.pleasanthillwinery.com
1441 Salem Rd., 979-830-VINE

Windy Hill Winery, a small, family winery on a lovely hillside overlooking the surrounding countryside, claims to be one of the few Texas wineries that uses only Texas grapes and bottles 100% of the wine on site, assuring a high quality Texas product. Enjoy browsing the gift shop and tasting the wine in the scenic setting.

www.windyhillwinery.net
4232 Clover Rd., 979-836-3252

Shop

This is going to sound like a cop-out, but historic downtown Brenham has a plethora of shops to keep everyone busy for days. You'll find exquisite antiques, fashionable clothing, gifts, jewelry, lamps and shades, home décor, furniture, party supplies, flowers, books, fine art, dolls and Texas souvenirs. There's no telling what fabulous find is hidden under the lace bonnet in one of the co-op antique malls. Take a break at one of the fine downtown coffee shops or restaurants. The "big box" stores are out on the highway.

www.downtownbrenham.com

A few favorites include **Nellie's**, an emporium of clothing, jewelry, gifts, art and home accessories.

200 W. Alamo, 979-830-1756

Antique Gypsy is chock a block with an eclectic mix of shabby chic and fine antiques, vintage jewelry, lamps, and decorative items.

204 W. Alamo, 979-251-7788

Hermann Furniture, "The oldest family owned and operated furniture store in Texas" has been displaying fine home furnishings, decorative accessories, gift items and furniture since 1876.

213 W. Alamo, 979-836-7231

Beadboard UpCountry carries a good selection of European linens, bath products, tableware, and home accessories.

www.beadboardupcountry.com
101 S. Baylor St., 979-830-8788

Eat

For a romantic dining experience, enjoy **Volare Italian Restaurant** where Chef Silvio DiGennaro prepares delicious authentic Italian and Mediterranean recipes. The innovative menu features fresh veal, chicken, seafood and pasta, scrumptious desserts and Italian wines and beers.

www.volareitalianrestaurant.com
205 S. Ross St., 979-836-1514

The **Brazos Belle** in a restored 1870s general store in nearby Burton, is open only on weekends. Chef Andre Delacroix trained at some of the finest restaurants in France before coming to Texas. He prepares a versatile menu of what he calls Country French cuisine with only the freshest ingredients. Another fine location for that romantic dinner.

www.brazosbellerestaurant.com
600 Main St., Burton, 979-289-2677

A popular lunch spot is the **Funky Art Café & Coffee Bar** where diners are surrounded by fun, quirky artwork and fanciful décor. The creative menu offers fresh salads, soups and sandwiches with innovative spreads and sauces.
202 W. Commerce St., 979-836-5220

Girlfriends, when you can't shop any more, stop at **Must Be Heaven** for lunch. Must Be Heaven has been serving great sandwiches, soups, salads, homemade pies and Blue Bell ice cream in Brenham for over 20 years. They've added a full-service cappuccino/espresso bar.
www.mustbeheaven.com
107 W. Alamo St., 979-830-8536

The New Orleans room at the Ant Street Inn in Brenham.
(courtesy Ant Street Inn)

Sleep

For the finest in Southern hospitality and elegance, stay at **Ant Street Inn**. This first-class boutique hotel makes an ideal destination for romantic getaways and honeymoons, although anyone would be comfortable in a rocking chair on the back veranda after a long day of sightseeing or shopping. Guest rooms with 12-foot ceilings are lavishly appointed with exquisite American antiques, Oriental rugs on polished hardwood floors, luxurious private baths and individual climate controls. Amenities include wireless high-speed internet and complimentary Blue Bell ice cream. The **Capital Grill** located in the Inn, is a full service restaurant and the location of breakfast, included in the B&B rate.

www.antstreetinn.com
107 W. Commerce St., 979-836-7393, 800-481-1951
Capital Grill 979-251-7800

Ingleside Bed & Breakfast, conveniently located near historic downtown, is a beautifully restored 1923 brick home with original Queen Anne and Chippendale furnishings in the formal living and dining rooms. Five spacious guest rooms are each tastefully decorated and include a private bath with fluffy robes, cable TV, wireless internet, and sitting area. Some rooms contain multiple sleeping accommodations (twin beds, sleeper sofas) perfect for girlfriend getaways. Help yourself to the 24-hour coffee bar, refrigerator, and ice machine. Rates include a full country gourmet breakfast.

www.inglesidebb.com
409 E. Main St., 979-251-7707

Texas Ranch Life – see Distinctive Destinations (Bellville)

Round Top

Chamber of Commerce
102 E. Mill Street
979-249-4042; 888-368-4783
www.roundtop.org

Once a part of the Austin Colony Settlement, Round Top claims to be the smallest incorporated city in Texas with a population of 77. Over 100,000 people invade the tiny town each April and October for one of the largest antique shows in the U.S.

Attraction

Founded by world-renowned concert pianist James Dick, the **International Festival Institute at Round Top** is an internationally acclaimed facility set on 210 scenic acres of central Texas. The landscaped campus features glorious gardens, historic buildings, and performance venues, including the European styled 1,100-seat Concert Hall. Various concerts are performed throughout the year, and in summer students in residence from throughout the world join the distinguished performers and teachers.

www.festivalhill.org

Hwy. 237 @ Jaster Rd., 979-249-3129

History & Museums

Winedale Historical Center is a restored 19th century farmstead is the Center for the Study of Ethnic Cultures of Central Texas, operated by the University of Texas. The property also serves as a site for seminars, arts & crafts festivals, and performances of Shakespearean dramas and special events.

www.cah.utexas.edu/museums/winedale.php

www.shakespeare-winedale.org

Henkel Square, an authentic restoration of German-American culture, was created to preserve representation of local life as it was in the 19th Century. Three of the square's structures stand where the owners built them. Most of the others were moved to Henkel Square from no further than 15 miles away. The Apothecary bookstore-gift shop serves as the entrance to the museum village.

www.texaspioneerarts.org

Eat

Located in the old tinsmith shop, **Klump's** is a dandy place for chicken fried steak, sandwiches, and great burgers.

www.klumpscafe.com
979-249-5696

Royer's Round Top Café is the quintessential small town café. Fame has made it as much a tourist attraction as an eatery. For a small town café, it serves a tremendous number of selections for lunch and dinner. The food is great and folks come from miles around for the good cookin' and down-home ambience. The café is widely acclaimed for homemade pies and fried chicken on Sundays. It's worth the trip just to read the menu . . . what a hoot!

www.royersroundtopcafe.com
979-249-3611

Sleep

There are several B&Bs in Round Top and dozens more in the surrounding countryside.

A fabulous destination, **Outpost @ Cedar Creek** is a complex of individual antique log cabins, cottages, bungalows and guesthouses offering luxurious amenities and modern conveniences. Owner Lenore exhibits a fantastic flair for decorating. Her bountiful breakfast, served in an elegantly rustic dining room, has received rave reviews from the most discriminating guests. The Outpost is perfect for romantic getaways! Ask about the "Romancing the Range" special.

www.outpostinn.com
5808 Wagner Rd., 979-836-4975, 888-433-5791

Bastrop

Old Town Visitor Center
1016 Main Street (lobby of the 1889 First National Bank Bldg)
512-303-0904
www.visitbastrop.org

Smithville

Information Center
First & Main Streets
512-237-2313
www.smithvilletx.org

Along the banks of the Colorado River, Bastrop's historic district and nearby neighborhoods contain more than 130 historic homes and buildings. You'll find small town friendliness in the district's shops, restaurants and B&Bs.

Only 12 miles away is the little town of Smithville, deeply rooted in the history of the Missouri Kansas & Texas (MKT or "Katy") Railroad. Recently it's become popular as a movie location with the filming of *Hope Floats* starring Sandra Bullock, Gena Rowlands, and Harry Connick, Jr. in 1997 and *The Tree of Life* starring Brad Pitt and Sean Penn in 2008.

History & Museums

The **Railroad Museum & Restored Depot** displays a nice collection of railroad memorabilia. An adjacent restored train depot provides a glimpse into the past.
102 W. First St., Smithville, 512-237-2313

The Central Texas Museum of Automotive History in nearby **Rosanky** features a collection of vintage automobiles.
www.ctmah.org
512-237-2635

Outdoors

The Colorado River meanders past pine covered rolling hills around Bastrop. Only a few minutes from downtown, one of the prettiest state parks in Texas, **Bastrop State Park** consists of 3,550 acres of rolling parklands shaded by the unusual "Lost Pines," an isolated area of stately Loblolly Pines far from the piney woods of East Texas. Fish, swim, hike, bike or picnic. Facilities include campsites, cabins and RV sites. A canoe or kayak trip down the Colorado River winds through stunning scenery and wildlife habitat; river access is also available at Fisherman's Park in the city.

www.tpwd.state.tx.us/spdest/findadest/parks/bastrop
3005 Hwy. 21 E., 512-321-2101

Inside the state park, the **Lost Pines Golf Club** is one of the finest and most scenic 18-hole golf courses in Central Texas and is playable year-round.

www.lostpinesgolfclub.com
512-321-2327, 512-303-1368

For a remarkably scenic drive, wander along Park Road 1C between Bastrop and Buescher State Parks and enjoy the serenity of the forest as you meander through the lofty Lost Pines of East Central Texas.

Buescher State Park, north of Smithville, has the same natural beauty as Bastrop State Park. Bicyclists love peddling along the wooded, winding roads. Pronounce it Bish-er.

www.tpwd.state.tx.us/spdest/findadest/parks/buescher
100 Park Rd. 1E, 512-237-2241

Shop

At **ROSCAR Chocolates**, Holland-born chocolatier Frans Hendriks makes, without a doubt, the richest, most extravagant, decadent, heavenly Texas-sized truffles on the planet. Fillings for the sublime treats include combinations like tequila and jalapeno, rum and lemon curd, triple dark blueberry, and cherry liqueur and pistachio. Frans' other specialties are his hand-crafted bon bons, blissful little filled, molded chocolates with names like Bailey's Silk, Crème Brulee, Brandy-Nog, New Orleans Punch, and Cabernet. Some are filled with lavender, ginger, or mint.

www.roscar.com
4501 Hwy. 71 E, Bastrop, 512-303-1500

Eat

Cedar's Mediterranean Grill features delicious, well-prepared Italian, Mediterranean and Lebanese dishes as well as steaks and seafood.

www.cedarsmedgrill.com
904 College St., Bastrop; 512-321-7808

Baxters on Main in historic downtown Bastrop, is a great place for that romantic dinner or special event. Exceptional steaks and creative seafood entrees are superbly prepared and the service is excellent.

919 Main St., Bastrop, 512-321-3577

Maxine's on Main typifies small town friendliness and good homestyle country cookin'. The award-winning chili has a huge following among locals. Chicken-fried steak, mashed potatoes and fried green tomatoes followed by a warm slice of homemade pie. Doesn't get much better than that.

www.maxinesonmain.com
905-Main Street, Bastrop; 512-303-0919

The Chef at the **Back Door Café** prepares totally awesome steaks. Food, service, and ambiance get rave reviews from locals and tourists alike.

117 Main St., Smithville, 512-237-3128

Try **Pocket's Grille** for great burgers, sandwiches, and hand-tossed pizza.

www.pocketsgrille.com
205 Fawcett St., Smithville, 512-237-5572

Sleep

In Smithville, **The Katy House** is named for the old "Katy" (Missouri Kansas & Texas) railroad line that runs through town. Built in 1909, the stately home's interior features long-leaf pine floors, pocket doors, and lovely antiques. Its historic character is complemented with all the modern conveniences. Owners Bruce and Sallie are railroad buffs extraordinaire and have displayed a fabulous collection of railroad memorabilia throughout the Inn. For special occasions, The Romance Package includes fresh flowers, chocolates, a snack basket and dinner for two. Sallie serves a scrumptious breakfast on reproduction Bluebonnet China from the railroad and her chocolate chip cookies are to die for.

www.katyhouse.com
201 Ramona St., Smithville, 512-237-4262, 800-843-5289

Loblolly Pines Village is a meeting, lodging, and recreational center set on 38 acres just two miles from Lake Bastrop. Landscaped grounds surround a pool, tennis courts and walking trails. Rooms are clean and comfortable, the hosts are friendly and helpful and the scenery can't be beat.

www.loblollypines.com
1128 TX Hwy. 21 E, Bastrop, 512-321-2499

Distinctive Destinations

Bellville

One of the most distinctive B&Bs in the state is probably **Texas Ranch Life**. In the scenic rolling hills between nearby Chappell Hill and Bellville, the working 1400-acre Lonesome Pine Ranch is home to quarter horses, bison, and one of the largest registered Texas Longhorn herds. The owners are history buffs and have authentically restored and furnished seven historic homes dating to the 1850s, some with original paint and German stenciling, each luxuriously appointed. Scattered across the ranch, these individual homes are available for guests who want a "real Texas Ranch experience." Participate in activities like horse-drawn wagon rides, campfires, or hike, bike, watch birds and wildlife or just relax and enjoy the peace and quiet of country life. The owners care deeply about Texas and enjoy sharing their passion with guests and they custom design packages that include ranching activities, cattle drives, fishing, dove and quail hunting, or horseback riding. Texas Ranch Life has been rated one of the ten 5-star Texas B&Bs by *Frommers*. Great for getaways of all kinds, the ranch can accommodate up to 45 people with conference facilities at ranch headquarters.

www.texasranchlife.com
866-TEXASRL

Grapevine

The **Gaylord Texan Resort and Convention Center** is an award-winning, Texas-sized, state-of-the-art resort boasting Texas hospitality and the best of the Lone Star State. Overlooking Lake Grapevine, the first-class resort features 4½ acres of lush indoor gardens and winding waterways under its signature glass atria. Spend your entire getaway here . . . you may sleep, dine, shop, and visit a nightclub, spa, or fitness center without ever leaving.

First things first – the luxurious hotel boasts more than 1500 guest rooms including 127 suites providing every comfort and modern convenience from high-speed wireless internet access and two-line phones with voice mail and data ports to refrigerators and coffee makers. Accommodations are comfortable with a Southwestern ambiance, oversized furnishings, custom mattresses and deluxe amenities.

The magnificent Gaylord Texan. (courtesy Grapevine CVB)

Shopping is fantastic in the more than 10,000 square feet of retail shops within the resort. In distinctive boutiques, art galleries and clothing stores, you'll find everything from Texas souvenirs and exquisite jewelry to authentic Texas art and fashionable western wear. After a morning of shopping, pamper yourself in the 25,000 sq.-ft. **Relache Day Spa** and adjacent 4,000 sq.-ft. state-of-the-art Fitness Center.

For fine dining, the posh **Old Hickory Steakhouse** serves Premium Black Angus Beef and fresh seafood, artisan cheeses and boasts an extensive wine list. The Chef at **Ama Lur** creates excellent Southwestern cuisine from a distinctive contemporary menu, served in a festive courtyard setting to the music of a lively Salsa band. The open-air, market-style **Riverwalk Café** features six "eating stations" serving regional foods prepared with Texas flair on a patio reminiscent of San Antonio's Riverwalk. Murder Mystery Dinner Theater productions are offered in the Riverwalk Café on weekends. The **Texan Station Sports Bar & Grill**, with its 30' high, 52' wide TV screen, serves bar snacks, burgers and great Texas barbeque along with a huge selection of brews. After hours, the **Glass Cactus Nightclub** features a state-of-the-art sound stage and 39,000 sq.-ft. of floor space including four bars plus another 13,000 sq.-ft. of outdoor deck space overlooking Lake Grapevine.

www.gaylordtexan.com

1501 Gaylord Trail, Grapevine, 817-778-2000

Grapevine

For an unsurpassed destination for family fun, choose **Great Wolf Lodge**. This first-class, full-service family resort is designed to capture the atmosphere and adventure of the North Woods. The main attraction is the 98,000 square foot indoor entertainment area that features an 80,000 square foot indoor waterpark, one of America's largest. Retail stores sell all sorts of essentials, swimwear, gifts and souvenirs. Kids can even create their own stuffed wolf to take home. Adults can enjoy facilities like the full service Spa and Starbucks®.

Several choices of themed suites offer a variety of accommodations. With names like KidKamp™ Suites or KidCabin® Suites, they feature Northwoods Log Cabin décor and bunk beds and TVs in the kids sleeping room. The adult part of the suite has a queen bed and full sized sleeper sofa, separate TV, coffee maker, WiFi, mini-fridge and microwave – all the amenities of a fine hotel. Grizzly Bear™ Suites have two private bedrooms and two full baths. All rates include passes to the water park.

Dining can be great fun – the **Loose Moose Cottage**™ offers a giant breakfast buffet for those who wake up hungry as a bear. The dinner buffet is loaded with nightly specials and kids' favorite dishes. **Camp Critter Restaurant**™ is on the 4th floor overlooking the lodge lobby while an outdoor patio overlooks Raccoon Lagoon. The **Bear Claw Café**™ offers a healthy alternative with lighter fare, salads and fresh fruit. But it also serves pastries, ice cream and fudge. Huh?

www.greatwolflodge.com/locations/grapevine
100 Great Wolf Dr., Grapevine, 800-693-9653

Glen Rose

Rough Creek Lodge advertises "rustic comforts." To describe this elite resort as "rustic" seems almost blasphemous. Well, it is a lodge – a very upscale, luxurious lodge with a full service spa and every amenity in the universe. Made of native stone, with 60-foot ceilings and a large outdoor terrace with magnificent views, it's perfect for grand events or a romantic weekend for two. What a great place for a proposal. Guests may choose from an amazing assortment of recreational opportunities like swimming, tennis, basketball, rock climbing, zip lining, fishing, bird hunting, deer hunting, kayaking, biking, hiking, golfing (driving range), paddle boating, horseback riding and four wheeling. Whew! Are you supposed to do that much over a relaxing weekend? You can just relax, read, or stroll around the 11,000-acre ranch. Oh, and you can even go fly a kite. See "eat" above for dining at the lodge.

www.roughcreek.com
800-864-4705

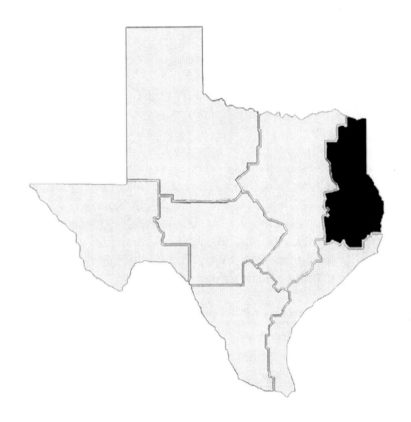

East Texas

First-time travelers to Texas usually have two big surprises – how far it is from one side to the other, and how East Texas doesn't look like the dusty, cactus-covered flat plains they've seen in western movies. In the Piney Woods of East Texas, great green trees and forests dominate the landscape, abundant lakes spot the countryside and gently rolling hills lead from one delightful small town to another.

Jefferson

Marion County Chamber of Commerce
101 N. Polk St.
903-665-2672; 888-GO RELAX
www.jefferson-texas.com

Girlfriends, Jefferson was made for you! Romantics, Jefferson was made for you! Visit an era when Jefferson was a major Texas river port. Tour a Victorian home, take a riverboat tour of Cypress Bayou where steamboats once arrived from New Orleans, ride through town in a horse-drawn carriage. The history of this charming little town is evident everywhere. Several grand homes offer tours. Check with the Visitor Center for special events or festivals during your visit.

History & Museums

Jefferson Historical Museum displays interesting collections of memorabilia from the city's history.
www.jeffersonhistoricalmuseum.com
223 Austin St., 903-665-2775

Jefferson's **Carnegie Library**, built in 1907, is one of only a few remaining Carnegie libraries still serving its original purpose. One of the most outstanding doll collections in Texas is displayed here.
301 Lafayette St., 903-665-8911

Railroad tycoon, Jay Gould, played a significant part in Jefferson's history. Tours of his private rail car are available.
903-665-2513

Scarlett O'Hardy's *Gone With the Wind*™ **Museum** is truly one-of-a-kind. The 1,700 sq.-ft. museum is dedicated to *Gone With the Wind*, the epic tale of the South, and exhibits one of the largest private collections of GWTW memorabilia in existence. It's well worth a visit. And you may continue the ambiance in **Scarlet O'Hardy's Bed & Breakfast** (see Sleep below), next door.

www.scarlettohardy.com
408 Taylor St., 903-665-1939

Tour **The Grove**, a historic home built in 1861. Other than joining the detached kitchen to the house in 1870 and adding an indoor bathroom in the 1930s, the house looks much like it did originally. A Recorded Texas Historic Landmark and listed in the National Register of Historic Places, it is said to be one of the most haunted locales in Texas with tales of supernatural experiences going back to 1882.

www.thegrove-jefferson.com
405 Moseley St., 903-665-8018

The Grove, one of Texas' most haunted locations
(courtesy Mitchel Whitington)

Outdoors

Caddo Lake, the only natural lake in Texas, lies only a few miles from Jefferson. Thriving aquatic plants, lush vegetation, and hanging Spanish Moss characterize this maze of bayous, bogs, sloughs, and ponds, more like Louisiana than Texas. It offers some of the best fishing in East Texas. Because of this, most folks don't go on the lake without a guide so guide services and boat tour operators are plentiful.

Turning Basin Riverboat Tours – Captain John Nance gives narrated riverboat tours of Big Cypress Bayou.

www.jeffersonbayoutours.com

903-665-2222

Caddo Lake Steamboat Company offers guided tours on an authentic replica of a paddlewheel steamboat, the Graceful Ghost.

www.uncertain-tx.com/gracefulghost

328 Bois D'Arc Ln., Uncertain, 903-789-3978

Several fishing guides offer boat and barge tours of Caddo Lake. Billy Carter (not that one) runs **Caddo Lake Guide Service** for fishing, duck hunting, birding, and sightseeing.

www.caddoguideservice.com

168 Mossy Brake Rd., Uncertain, 903-789-3268

Oodles of recreational activities are available at Caddo Lake State Park. Another gem in the State Park system, it offers campsites, cabins, day use facilities, a little museum, nature trails, a boat launch, and canoe rentals.

www.tpwd.state.tx.us/spdest/findadest/parks/caddo_lake

903-679-3351

Every Friday and Saturday night in season, the **Jefferson Ghost Train** departs the depot for a ride through the Piney

Woods along the Big Cypress Bayou. The conductor entertains with ghost stories while riders watch for supernatural activity.

www.jeffersonrailway.com

400 E. Austin St., 903-665-6400

The only natural lake in Texas, Caddo Lake looks like it should be in Louisiana swamp country. (courtesy Texas Parks and Wildlife)

Entertainment

Even though Jefferson is a peaceful little town, a few venues offer evening entertainment, community theatre, or live music. One such is **Auntie Skinner's Riverboat Club**.

www.auntie-skinners.com

107 W. Austin St., 903-665-7121

For a romantic carriage ride, the **Lone Star Carriage Company** will accommodate you.

www.geocities.com/thelonestarcarriage/LoneStar1.html

903-926-8216

Shop

Girlfriends, get ready! Literally dozens of antique shops, specialty shops, and boutiques line Austin Street and side streets for blocks around. Happy Shopping! A few of the more unusual ones include **Beauty and the Book**, a unique beauty shop-bookstore. And proprietor, Kathy, is one-of-a-kind!

www.beautyandthebook.com

608 North Polk St., 903-665-7520

Jefferson General Store and Old Fashioned Soda Fountain is more than a store, it's an incomparable experience.

www.jeffersongeneralstore.com

113 E. Austin St, 903-665-8481

For souvenirs, visit **Texas Treasures** or **Yesteryear Nick Nacks**.

www.txstrsrs.com

214 N. Polk St., 903-665-3757

www.ynntx.com

102 S. Polk St. 903-665-8692

Eat

For fine dining, the **Stillwater Inn** has been serving discriminating diners since 1984 in an 1890s-era Victorian house. The chef-owned restaurant has an innovative menu and an extensive wine list.

www.stillwaterinn.com

203 E. Broadway, 903-665-8415

LaManche's Italian Restaurant in the historic Jefferson Hotel, serves excellent seafood and classic Italian dishes from old family recipes.

www.lamache.com

124 W. Austin St., 903-665-6177

Kitt's Kornbread Sandwich & Pie Bar serves delicious sandwiches on cornbread buns.

www.kittskornbread.com

125 N. Polk St., 903-665-0505

The Bakery Restaurant serves great breakfasts and lunches – homemade soups, salads, sandwiches and burgers, and baked potatoes with assorted toppings. They serve dinner on Saturdays. But the bakery . . . oh, the bakery with its homemade breads, cookies, decadent brownies and pastries . . .

www.thebakeryrestaurant.net

201 W. Austin St., 903-665-2253

Swampi's Cajun Restaurant serves up tasty Cajun specialties like crawfish etouffe and scrumptious gumbo. Here's your chance to try alligator tails.

109 N. Polk St., 903-665-8040

Sleep

Jefferson is the Bed & Breakfast Capital of East Texas! With more than 30 B&Bs and two historic hotels, choosing one isn't easy.

Rooms at **Claiborne House** are named for the great romantic poets – how idyllic is that? In addition to all the amenities you would expect from a luxurious B&B, a framed poem and book of the poet's work are in each room. Gracious hosts have thought of everything to ensure guests' comfort.

www.claibornehousebnb.com

312 S. Alley St., 903-665-8800

A fabulous choice for a romantic getaway, the **Benefield House** is a Queen Anne Victorian Painted Lady and a Recorded Texas Historical Landmark property built in 1895. A front porch and side deck overlooking the lush lawns invite total relaxation. The Drawing Room and the Back Parlor are exquisitely furnished in 1890s Victorian style, yet cozy and welcoming. Each of the three spacious, luxuriously appointed guestrooms (pardon me, bedchambers) features a king-size bed with Egyptian cotton linens and fluffy pillows, bedside chocolates, a private bath with thick towels and Terry robes and quality toiletries. Begin each morning with a scrumptious full gourmet breakfast. Delightful hosts offer several romance packages and extras (candlelight dinner, special occasion cakes, roses, chocolate covered strawberries and bubbly, etc.) with advance notice.

www.benefieldhouse.com

1009 S. Line St., 903-665-9366

Located in the Historic District, **Falling Leaves Bed and Breakfast** is a Recorded Texas Historical Landmark and listed in the National Register of Historic Places. Nestled amid century-old magnolia and pecan trees, the gracious antebellum Greek Revival home, built in 1855, features high ceilings, hardwood floors and fabulous period antique furnishings. Four guest rooms offer elegant accommodations and massage packages are available to help you relax even more. Congenial owners pamper guests with Southern hospitality, afternoon refreshments and a full Southern breakfast.

www.fallingleavesinn.com

304 E. Jefferson St., 903-665-8803

Scarlett O'Hardy's Bed & Breakfast is next door to the *Gone With the Wind*™ **Museum**. The home, reminiscent of Southern mansions in Natchez, is opulent and elegant; the guestrooms are lavishly decorated. What a great place for a girlfriend Slumber Party! Or an exceptionally romantic weekend!

www.scarlettohardy.com/bandb.htm

410 Taylor St., 903-665-1939

Experience the charm of a bygone era at the **Historic Jefferson Hotel** in the heart of the Riverfront District. Built as a cotton warehouse in 1851, it's one of the oldest buildings in Jefferson and has led a colorful life since then. Allegedly, several spirits still hang around and haunt the halls.

www.historicjeffersonhotel.com

124 W. Austin St. 903-665-2631, 866-334-6835

Longview – Marshall

Longview Convention and Visitors Bureau
410 N. Center Street
903-753-3281
www.visitlongviewtexas.com

Chamber of Commerce
213 West Austin
903-935-7868; 800-953-7868
www.visitmarshalltexas.org

The Longview – Marshall area is one too often driven "through" on the way to Louisiana. But, whoa! There's plenty to do whether you like to shop or eat or drive scenic back roads.

In December, **Marshall's Wonderland of Lights** is a world-renowned Christmas extravaganza. From Thanksgiving to New Year's Eve, the Harrison County Courthouse is wrapped in more than 125,000 lights and businesses and neighborhoods decorate and celebrate with special events.

Attractions

Because Harrison County is home to abundant supplies of red clay and springs, folks have been making pottery in this area since 1891. Today, eight pottery manufacturers are located here.

One of the oldest potteries in the country, **Marshall Pottery** has over 100,000 square feet of retail display space for its pottery, housewares, gadgets, and gifts. It's still possible to see local craftsmen hand-turning pieces on the potter's wheel. Marshall Pottery remains the largest manufacturer of red clay pots in the U.S.

www.marshallpottery.com
4901 Elysian Fields Rd/FM 31, 903-938-9201

History & Museums

The **Gregg County Historical Museum**, housed in the historic Everett Building in downtown Longview, preserves artifacts and exhibits illustrating the history and development of the area. The Everett Building is a Recorded Texas Historical Landmark and is listed in the National Register of Historic Places.

www.gregghistorical.org
214 N. Fredonia, Longview, 903-753-5840

Harrison County Museum maintains extensive genealogical records as well as good exhibits of local history. It's located in the historic Ginocchio Hotel adjacent to the **T&P Depot Museum**.

www.marshall-chamber.com/pages/museum.php
707 N. Washington Ave., Marshall, 903-938-2680
www.marshalldepot.org
903-938-9495

The **East Texas Oil Museum** in nearby Kilgore is built around a full-scale boomtown from the 1930s using dramatic presentations to depict the sights and sounds of the oilfields.

www.easttexasoilmuseum.com
US 259, Kilgore, 903-983-8295

The **World's Richest Acre Park**, at Main and Commerce in Kilgore across from the railroad depot, marks the spot where the greatest concentration of oil wells in the world once stood. One original derrick and 36 new ones, along with a historical marker stand in tribute to the oil boom of the 1930s.

Also in Kilgore, is the **Rangerette Showcase**. Every young Texas girl wants to be a member of this world-famous precision drill and dance team. Formed in 1940 as halftime entertainment for local football games, it eventually brought international attention to Kilgore College. The museum features films and displays of props, costumes, uniforms, awards, and mementos.

www.rangerette.com
Kilgore College Campus, 903-983-8265

Shop

Marshall's most eclectic shopping area is **Washington Square**, centered in the 200 block of North Washington in downtown. A diverse collection of shops, mainly in renovated storefronts, are owned by friendly locals and offer goods from funky to traditional.

Eat

Bodacious Barbecue has scrumptious ribs, brisket, and pork – and there are four locations in Longview.

2227 S. Mobberly, 903-753-8409

Johnny Cace's has served top quality New Orleans-style seafood since 1949. Although they have excellent steaks, the specialty is seafood and they have several good combinations, including the "King O' the Sea" and the "Queen of the Sea" platters. Gumbo to die for.

www.johnnycaces.com
1501 E. Marshall Ave., Longview, 903-753-7691

Neely's Brown Pig serves the best pork BBQ in the whole world, according to those who are supposed to know. Their Frito Pie and fries get great marks, too.

1404 E Grand Ave., Marshall, 903-935-9040

Mineola

Chamber of Commerce
101 E. Broad Street
903-569-2087
www.mineolachamber.org/outside_home.asp

Mineola is the quintessential small town destination. A Texas Main Street City in 1989 and a National Main Street City in 2000 – handsome historic buildings, specialty shops, home furnishing & antique shops, artist studios and galleries fill the revitalized downtown. Girls, one of the biggest draws is superb antiquing!

Amtrak stops at the recently restored Texas & Pacific train station at 115 E. Front Street. In the glory days of railroads past, Mineola was a terminal for crews and had two railroad hotels, one on each side of the tracks.

Outdoors

In the middle of the excellent fishing lakes of East Texas, including **Lake Fork**, the "Big Bass Capital of Texas," it's a great getaway for guys, too. Now there's an acclaimed golf course on the world-class lake. The Piney Woods offer multitudes of water sports, hiking, birding, nature trails, and spring flower trails, throughout the area. A new nature preserve is at the south end of town.

www.ets-systems.com
www.mnpfriends.org

Arts & Culture

Lake Country Playhouse offers first-run movies and community theater productions, summer musicals, and concerts in the historic **Select Theater**.

www.lakecountryplayhouse.org
114 N. Johnson St., 903-569-2300

East of town, the studio and showroom at **Pine Mills Pottery** exhibits a collection of exceptional wood-fired pottery designed and handmade by artists Daphne and Gary Hatcher.

www.pinemills.com
5155 FM 49; 903-857-2271

Shop

The revitalized downtown area is lined with specialty shops, home furnishing & antique shops, artist studios and galleries. Mineola is known for its antique shopping and here are a few places to begin:

- **Karen's Korner**, 102 S. Johnson, 903-569-0127
- **Serendipity Home Furnishings**, 110 S. Johnson, 903-569-0820
- **Somewhere in Time Antiques Market**, 433 W. Broad, 903-569-8990
- **Broad Street Mall**, 118 E. Broad, 903-569-1686
- **Cottage Antiques**, 111 E. Broad; 903-569-5801
- **Uniques & Antiques**, 124 S. Line; 903-569-1133

AND . . . Mineola is only 30 miles from **Canton**, home of the most enormous, incredible flea market imaginable where thousands of vendors display their wares over the weekend of the first Monday of each month.

www.firstmondaycanton.com
www.cantontradedays.com

Blueberry Ridge Farm, about 5 miles east of Mineola, is the oldest certified organic blueberry farm in Texas. When the berries are ripe, it's a U-pick farm. Shop in the Country Store for blueberry products, local honey, molasses, old-fashioned candies, goats milk soap and all sorts of gifts and garden décor.

www.blueberryridgefarm.com

2785 E. Hwy. 80, 903-569-1550, 903-569-9800

Eat

Eat at a hardware store – huh? **Kitchen's Hardware & Deli** serves great sandwiches, salads and soups made fresh with locally produced ingredients. Their peppered bacon has become so famous, it's sold mail order around the country. The turn-of-the-century Hardware Store is a trip back in time, from the pot-bellied stove to the 1903 hand-operated Otis rope elevator in the back. Shelves groan with items your children have never seen.

119 E. Broad St./Hwy. 80, 903-569-2664

East Texas Burger Co. serves some of the best burgers on the planet. An eclectic hole-in-the-wall kind of place (look for the big red awning) with big, juicy burgers, sweet potato fries, curly fries, chicken fried steak, catfish, fried pies, homemade peanut butter pie, oh my. The owner, Ken, is usually on site to talk about baseball or Mineola history.

www.easttexasburger.com

126 E. Broad St/Hwy. 80, 903-569-3140

Sister restaurant, **La Waffalata**, next door, is owned by Ken's wife Debbie, a local celebrity as the food expert on the ABC affiliate news channel. La Waffalata can host private parties and meetings in a separate dining room. Their Reuben sandwiches are voted "Best Reuben" year after year. Another favorite is the roast beef sandwich on homemade jalapeno cheese bread. Finish it off with apricot bread pudding with amaretto sauce.

Sleep

Munzesheimer Manor has consistently been voted among the Best B&Bs in the U.S. and Texas by *Inn Traveler* magazine, *Arrington's B&B Journal*, and the *Dallas Morning News*. A visit here will truly transport you to a splendid 19th century Victorian manor. Pamper yourself with a bubble-bath in a claw-footed tub with your own rubber ducky, relax and sip lemonade on wrap-around porches, awake to freshly-brewed coffee before the full, gourmet breakfast served on china in the formal dining room. You get the idea – absolutely perfect for romance. Even though the picturesque manor could rival a museum with its fine period furnishings, the ambiance is casual and would make a great place for a girls' slumber party. Two rooms in a separate cottage are decorated with a railroad theme to reflect the association between Mineola and the "iron horse" which dates back to 1873. The friendly owners have been in business since 1987, so they know all the places to shop. If you're really lucky, you may get Bob's German pancakes for breakfast.

www.munzesheimer.com
202 N. Newsom; 903-569-6634

Fall Farm – see Distinctive Destinations

Tyler

Convention & Visitors Bureau
315 N. Broadway
800-235-5712
www.visittyler.com

Tyler lies in the heart of Northeast Texas with its rolling hills, creeks and lakes, and thick piney woods. Azalea and Dogwood trails are splendid in springtime and the Rose Festival in the fall draws thousands, but Tyler has plenty of things to do year-round.

Tyler's spectacular Rose Gardens bring thousands of tourists in spring and fall. (courtesy Tyler CVB)

Attractions

A large majority of tourists come to Tyler to see the **Tyler Municipal Rose Garden**. "America's Rose Capital" boasts more than 38,000 rose bushes of over 500 varieties displayed in a 14-acre park, the largest rose garden in the U.S. Commercial growers around Tyler ship hundreds of thousands of rose bushes to nurseries throughout the U.S. and 25 foreign countries.

www.cityoftyler.org/Visitors/RoseGardenCenter/tabid/168
420 Rose Park Dr., 903-531-1212

Lovely any time of year, it's especially striking in the spring and in mid-October. Thousands of tourists come during the Rose Festival in October to see the gardens in full bloom.

www.texasrosefestival.com

The **Tyler Rose Museum** is located in the Rose Garden Center and chronicles the rose industry as well as past festivals, Rose Queens and their gowns. Other memorabilia is displayed in the "Attic of Memories" and rose-themed items are plentiful in the gift shop.

903-597-3130

History

The Tyler area boasts some of the finest restored mansions from the 19th century in East Texas. An outstanding example of Eastlake Victorian is the **McClendon Historic Estate**, elegantly furnished to depict Tyler's political and cultural history after the Civil War. Now, it's an exquisite setting for weddings and special events. Guided tours are available by reservation.

www.mcclendonhouse.net
806 W. Houston, 903-592-3533

The **Dewberry Plantation** in nearby **Bullard** provides a glimpse into life in Antebellum East Texas. The house is listed in the National Register of Historic Places as well as being a Texas State Historical Landmark, and is available for tours and special events.

www.dewberryplantation.com

14007 FM 346 West, Bullard, 903-825-9000

Roseland Plantation in nearby **Ben Wheeler** offers tours and Bed & Breakfast accommodations in the opulent Windsor House.

www.roselandplantation.com

2601 Hwy. 64, Ben Wheeler, 903-849-5553

History buffs will enjoy the **Smith County Historical Society Museum** housed in the 1904 Carnegie Library building, listed in the National Register of Historic Places.

www.smithcountyhistoricalsociety.org/carnegie.php

125 S. College, 903-592-5993

The **Cotton Belt Depot** was built in 1905 and began serving passengers on the Cotton Belt Line in 1907. Inside the historic building is a model train collection on permanent display.

210 E. Oakwood St., downtown

The **Historic Aviation Memorial Museum** at the airport exhibits vintage aircraft and aviation memorabilia as a tribute to pioneers of flight.

www.tylerhamm.com

150 Airport Dr., 903-526-1945

Arts & Culture

Ballet Tyler is made up of East Texas dancers from 11 to 20 years old. The UT Tyler **Cowan Fine & Performing Arts Center** provides performing arts and educational programs for East Texas.

www.ballettyler.org
4703 D.C. Dr., Suite 105, 903-596-0224
www.cowancenter.org
3900 University Blvd. on the university campus; 903-566-7424

The **East Texas Symphony Orchestra** performs classical music concerts each year in the community.

www.etso.org
522 S. Broadway Ave, Ste 101, 903-526-3876

The **Tyler Museum of Art** features a 700-piece permanent collection as well as an array of traveling exhibitions.

www.tylermuseum.org
1300 S. Mahon Ave. adj to Tyler Jr College; 903-595-1001

Outdoors and Critters

Caldwell Zoo houses more than 2000 animals representing 250 species from around the world live in natural habitats. The first-rate regional zoo, designed especially for children, began in 1937 as a backyard menagerie. Seasonal presentations, children's programs and classes, and special exhibits ensure there's always something new and exciting at the zoo.

www.caldwellzoo.org
2203 Martin Luther King Blvd., 903-593-0121

Tiger Creek Wildlife Refuge is an "Incorporated Animal Shelter" for big cats. Not a zoo, the refuge welcomes visitors and explains the rescue and rehabilitation programs. The big cats here have been abused, neglected, or displaced. The facility had a moment of fame when Animal Planet filmed *Growing Up Tiger* featuring two resident Siberian tiger cubs.

www.tigercreek.org
17544 HWY. 14, 903-858-1008

Brookshire's World of Wildlife Museum & Country Store features more than 450 mounted specimens of wildlife in dioramas and exhibits. A replica 1920-era fully stocked grocery store and a 1926 Model T Ford delivery truck are reminders of the past. Outside, an antique fire truck and restored caboose sit near the playground and picnic area. It's all free!

www.brookshires.com/museum
1600 WSW Loop 323, 903-534-2169

Tyler State Park is one of the gems in the Texas State Park system. The 995-acre scenic playground in one of the most lush forests of East Texas offers fishing, camping, boating, swimming, nature trails, hiking, canoe and paddleboat rental.

www.tpwd.state.tx.us/spdest/findadest/parks/tyler
789 Park Road 16 (FM 14 North), 903-597-5338

Moore Farms is an unusual, but extremely interesting, attraction. A 5th generation farm family operates a 300-acre facility to educate the public about agriculture and farm life. There's always something going on – hayrides in the fall, a corn maze, pumpkin patch fun and other events. Visitors may buy fresh organic produce, cut flowers, and homemade goodies.

www.moorefarms.com
22142 County Rd. 181, Hwy. 344 W, Bullard, 903-894-1030

Try the new adventure sport that's sweeping the country! In nearby **New York**, Texas, **Zip Line Adventures** offers guided zipline adventures through the lush East Texas countryside. Zip high above the hillside for magnificent views.

www.goziptexas.com

7290 CR 4328, New York/LaRue, 903-681-3791

If you're fishing folks or have kids with you, a short drive will take you to the **Texas Freshwater Fisheries Center** near Athens. This innovative complex features more than 300,000 gallons of aquarium exhibits, and visitors can see nearly every major species of freshwater fish found in Texas in its recreated habitat. Explore the Hill Country Stream, East Texas Farm Pond, or go below the surface of a Texas Reservoir. Gaze into the eyes of an American alligator in a natural wetland environment. Wander through showcases that feature replicas of most state record fish caught in Texas, and even talk to divers as they hand feed the largest largemouth bass in captivity in a 26,000 gallon dive tank. Go to the Angler's Pavilion and Casting Pond for a hands-on experience catching rainbow trout or channel catfish. A 14,000-sq.ft. Conservation Center provides space for meetings and special events.

www.tpwd.state.tx.us/spdest/visitorcenters/tffc

5550 FM 2495, 903-676-2277

Special Place

Girlfriends! Whether you have green thumbs or not, head a few miles west of Tyler to **Blue Moon Gardens**. Flowers and herbs and garden gnomes . . . and so many exciting craft workshops, you'll wish you lived close enough to attend all of them. Mary, Sharon and Connie are so knowledgeable and helpful and the gift shop is filled with delightful goodies.

www.bluemoongardens.com

13062 FM 279, Chandler, 903-852-3897

Wine

Kiepersol Estates winery, nestled in a tidy 51-acre vineyard, has won wide acclaim for its fine wines. In addition to tours and tastings, the lovely setting itself is worthy of a visit. For the two of you, Kiepersol Estates offers luxurious Bed & Breakfast accommodations in five rooms featuring fine linens, king beds, and private baths. Three have private porches with hot tubs. The outstanding restaurant on premises serves an upscale menu using only perfectly-aged beef and the freshest seafood available.

www.kiepersol.com
3933 FM 344 E, 903-894-8995

Be sure to see some of the other wineries in the area. East Texas is becoming the best-kept secret in the Texas wine industry with about ten different wineries in the local area. See Palestine and Rusk for more.

Eat

For a romantic dinner, fine food and wine, and exceptional surroundings, visit the restaurant at **Kiepersol Estates** (see Wine above). **Bernard Mediterranean Restaurant** offers some delicious veal and steak entrees, as well as pasta.

www.bernardsintyler.com
212 Grande Suite C-106, 903-534-0265

For upscale French cuisine, it's **Currents Restaurant**. *Texas Monthly* said, "The companionable dining room of this off-the-beaten-path restaurant is both a go-to spot for lunch and a reliable special occasion place."

www.currentstyler.com
1121 E. 2nd St., 903-597-3771

For fun, good food and live music on weekends, visit **Mario's Italian Restaurant & Club.**
7916 S. Broadway, #200, 903-581-2309

In nearby Edom, the **Shed Cafe** is legendary. Serving genu-ine home-cooked meals for 37 years, it's been voted the #1 café in East Texas by *Texas Highways*, *Texas Monthly*, and *Ride Texas* magazines. The menu is strictly down-home, the pies are world class, and the staff is East Texas friendly.
www.theshedcafe.com
8337 FM 279, Edom, 903-852-7791

Girlfriends, you can shop and eat at the same time at **Potpourri House.** Dine on a strawberry spinach salad and homemade desserts while you admire the lovely gifts surrounding you in the boutique. Not just a girl's place, the menu offers steak and seafood dinners and live music entertainment on weekends.
www.potpourrihouse.com
3320 Troup Hwy., 903-592-4171

Just off the square, the **Downtown Soul Food Café** serves, as you would expect, sweet potatoes, black-eyed peas, and hot water cornbread – divine comfort food. On or off the menu, the offerings are reflective of owner Phil's Southern roots. It's a busy place at lunch and the cobbler sells out early.
403 N. Spring, 903-533-8897

Sleep

All the major chain motels have locations in Tyler. **Kiepersol Estates** (see Wine above) and **Roseland Plantation** (see History above) offer Bed & Breakfast accommodations.

Rosevine Inn offers five tastefully decorated guest rooms, each with a private bath, television, telephone, and wireless internet. Extra insulation in the walls prevents the noise problem common in older houses and motels. Spacious grounds include a small back courtyard with a stone fireplace that invites outdoor gatherings, and the Barn common area has a pool table, games, cards, and a fireplace.

www.rosevine.com
415 S. Vine Ave., 903-592-2221

The **Woldert-Spence Manor** is a magnificently restored landmark property in the historic Brick Street District. Nestled under Pecan, Sweetgum, and Magnolia trees, the manor offers seven elegant guest rooms, six in the main house and one in the carriage house. The innkeepers serve a full, freshly cooked breakfast in the dining room each morning.

www.woldert-spence.com
611 W. Woldert, 800-965-3378

Palestine – Rusk

Palestine Convention & Visitors Bureau
825 Spring Street
903-723-3014; 800-659-3484
www.visitpalestine.com

Rusk Chamber of Commerce
415 N. Main
903-683-4242; 800-933-2381
www.rusktexascoc.org

Whether making a day trip from Tyler, or spending a few days, the Palestine-Rusk area is home to the Texas State Railroad, a fun-for-all attraction and some good wineries.

History

The **Texas State Railroad** was established in 1881. Historic trains (both steam engines and diesel) wind 25 miles through the rolling hills and dense piney woods of East Texas. Passengers may depart from depots in either Palestine or Rusk for the nostalgic excursions. Both terminals are in park-like settings and built to resemble turn-of-the-century depots, but with modern full service facilities. Excursions operate year-round; check for dinner trains or special events.

www.texasstaterr.com
903-683-2561, 888-987-2461

Palestine is second only to Galveston in number of historic buildings, many in downtown housing antique shops and eateries. The **Anderson County Courthouse** features beautiful stained glass and a double spiral staircase inside the Neo-classical building. Just two blocks west of the Courthouse is **Old Town Palestine**, a pleasant green space with nice shops, a coffee house and restaurant.

Outdoors

Davey Dogwood Park just north of Palestine on N. Link St. is an exceptionally beautiful park, especially during late March and early April during the annual Texas Dogwood Trails. Paved roads wind through the 200-acre park of rolling hills, clear flowing streams, forests and meadows.

A day trip to the **Freshwater Fisheries Center** (see "outdoors" Tyler) near Athens is educational and fun for all.

Wine

Sweet Dreams Winery in Palestine. This family-run winery makes excellent fruit wines, as they say "in the tradition of times past" such as Strawberry, Blackberry Grape, Peach Blackberry, Honey Raspberry, and Jalapeno Wine (if you're that adventurous). Visit their large, covered porch for tastings every Saturday.

www.sweetdreamswinery.com
2549 ACR 441, Palestine, 903-549-2027

Maydelle Country Wines in Rusk. This small winery produces award-winning Grapefruit Wine and Creole Blush as well as wines made from other local fruits. It's a friendly place to visit – they even have root beer on tap for the kids.

www.maydellewines.com
175 CR 2108, Rusk, 903-795-3915

Nacogdoches

Visitor Center
200 East Main
888-653-3788
www.visitnacogdoches.org

Claiming to be the oldest town in Texas, history is a major attraction – folks come to see **Oak Grove Cemetery**, the **Old Stone Fort Museum**, **Sterne-Hoya House Museum**, and the **Old University Building**, the only original building of a university chartered by the Republic of Texas still standing and listed in the National Register of Historic Places.

Home of **Stephen F. Austin State University**, this college town offers lots of shopping, dining, and a hodgepodge of entertainment venues. There's a thriving arts community and festivals throughout the year.

History & Museums

Legend has it that the town was founded when a Caddo chief sent his twin sons to establish settlements – one 3 days to the east, the other 3 days to the west. The established settlements were Nacogdoches, Texas and Natchitoches, Louisiana.

Millard's Crossing is a first-rate reconstructed historic village that portrays East Texas as it was in the 19th century, from simple log cabins to Victorian homes.

www.millardscrossing.com

6020 North St., 936-564-6631

Outdoors

In this part of Texas, it's all about nature. Popular fishing and birding sites attract folks year-round. More than a dozen parks around Nacogdoches offer golf, volleyball courts, picnic areas, hiking trails, and places to simply relax and enjoy the great outdoors.

Texas' largest azalea garden boasts one of the most diverse collections in the nation, featuring more than 7,000 azaleas spread over eight forested acres. Each March, the Ruby M. **Mize Azalea Garden** is the center of the annual Azalea Trail. Ablaze with brilliant blooms of red, pink, white, yellow, orange, and purples, the garden is located just south of the SFA Coliseum on University Drive.

If your quest for natural beauty and outdoor recreation takes you to nearby **Lufkin**, visit the **Texas Forestry Museum**. The only museum of its kind in Texas has permanent and temporary exhibits telling the story of the people, places, and products of the Piney Woods. Exhibits include an old sawmill town, forest flora and fauna, early logging machinery, wildland fire fighting equipment and a forest fire lookout tower, and a paper mill room. Special events and educational programs are offered throughout the year, many for kids.

www.treetexas.com

409-632-9535

Shop

Nacogdoches has a large number of locally-owned specialty and antique shops, selling everything from vintage jewelry to gourmet kitchen items to fiddles. Watch the artists at a stained glass studio or get a hair cut at an old-fashioned barber shop. The Visitors Center has a free shopping guide and map or you may download it from their website so you can have your itinerary mapped out before you go.

Eat

As you would expect in a college town, fast food and pizza places are all over the place. Dozens of casual, family restaurants and a few fine dining establishments offer a vast selection of cuisines.

The **Garden of (Good) Eatin'** is a few miles out of town, but well worth the short drive for a weekday lunch of some of the best country cookin' you've ever had the pleasure of eatin'. The menu changes daily with specials like chicken and dumplings or smothered pork chops. Everything is made fresh and you can see the garden from the windows. Homemade pies to die for!

4781 Hwy. 21 W
936-560-2030

Butcher Boys Smokehouse serves up great burgers and even better onion rings. The old-fashioned meat market and deli also offers a full menu of fresh sandwiches, chicken fried steak, giant stuffed potatoes and party trays.

www.butcherboysnac.com
603 North St., 936-560-1137

Sleep

Set in a 200-acre woodland in lush Texas pine forest country surrounded by bountiful natural resources, a special place draws couples for honeymoons, romantic getaways and all kinds of groups for reunions and gatherings. **Stag Leap Country Inn** overlooks Bonaldo Creek and offers miles of nature trails for exploring. Tastefully decorated individual cabins and cottages are scattered around the retreat, each offering seclusion and all the amenities and conveniences you could ever want.

www.stagleap.com

2219 FM 2782, 936-560-0766

In nearby **Lufkin**, choose **Wisteria Hideaway**. This 1939 Colonial-style home with its heirloom gardens and lush green lawn provides an oasis of Southern hospitality. The four-acre estate is an ideal setting for weddings and parties. For "just the two of you," the Master Suite is large, private, and features an adjacent sunroom with a hot tub. The accommodating owner will even serve breakfast in the sunroom overlooking the back lawn. The outside patio area features a Wisteria-laden pergola that's glorious when covered with large purple blooms. An outdoor fire pit makes a nice place for evening gatherings. A large upstairs common area can accommodate girls chatting or watching TV.

www.wisteriahideaway.com

3458 Ted Trout Dr., 936-875-2914

Distinctive Destinations

Mineola

A superb destination for couples or girlfriends, **Fall Farm** offers a wide variety of comfortable accommodations. Mike and Carol Fall have created a luxurious country retreat on ten acres of beautiful East Texas countryside near Mineola.

Rooms and cottages are exquisitely decorated and furnished with heirlooms and antiques, have private baths, sitting areas, fine linens, and all the amenities you can think of plus some. Carol's decorating talent and attention to detail are evident throughout the premier inn and grounds. At the 6,000-sq.-ft. main inn are a swimming pool and spa, spacious common areas, and lovely pastoral views. Owner Carol is an outstanding cook and serves a mouthwatering "Gourmet Texas Breakfast." The kitchen has nibbles and beverages available all the time. She can arrange massages and facials or "special touches" like roses or chocolates, with advance notice. Check the website for specials – currently there are five romance packages offered. About a mile from the main inn, Harvest House is a delightful 5-bedroom house, decorated in "Casual Americana," that would be ideal for reunions, scrapbooking or quilting parties, or any gathering of giggling girls.

www.fallfarm.com
2027 FM 779; 903-768-2449

Relax at Fall Farm Country Inn (courtesy Fall Farm Country Inn)

120

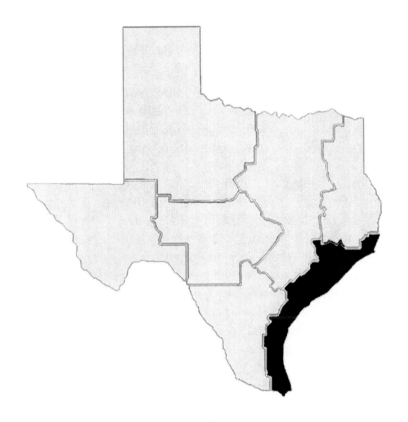

Gulf Coast

The Texas Gulf Coast is one of the best places in the state for a getaway, be it romantic celebration, a girlfriend reunion, or a family vacation. You'll find friendly towns, sandy beaches, oodles of birds, great fishing, funky art, and an easygoing lifestyle.

Rockport-Fulton

Chamber of Commerce
404 Broadway, Rockport
800-242-0071; 361-729-6445
www.rockport-fulton.org
www.txcoastalbend.org

The Chamber of Commerce has a brochure entitled "51 Things To Do in Rockport/Fulton," but the best thing to do is enjoy the beach and the glistening bay waters . . . and relax . . . and do as little as possible. That's hard to do here because this charming little community is paradise for nature lovers and birders, offering some of the best birding in the nation. And superb fishing. And, if nature isn't your thing, Rockport boasts the largest per capita percentage of artists in the country, resulting in a fine collection of galleries and studios.

The same seascape that attracts visitors and artists also attracts the area's most famous winter visitors, the Whooping Cranes. Standing over five feet tall, these majestic birds are endangered and nearby Aransas National Wildlife Refuge (see "outdoors" below) is the winter home for the only natural wild flock in the world.

History

Experience the rich maritime heritage of Texas at the **Texas Maritime Museum**. Learn how Texas has relied on the sea throughout history with changing exhibits, interactive displays and educational public programming.

www.texasmaritimemuseum.org
1202 Navigation Circle, 888-729-AHOY

Fulton Mansion State Historic Site was indeed a magnificent mansion for its time (1874-77). Even more impressive were the latest technological conveniences including modern plumbing, central heat and a gas lighting system. Call for tour times.

www.thc.state.tx.us/hsites/hs_fulton.aspx

317 Fulton Beach Rd., 361-729-0386

Birders flock to Aransas National Wildlife Refuge to see the only wild flock of Whooping Cranes in the world. (courtesy Al Buckner)

Arts & Culture

The **Rockport Center for the Arts** lies between scenic Rockport Harbor and Aransas Bay, showcasing three galleries and a sculpture garden. Check to find out what's going on in town as far as exhibits, concerts, classes and workshops.

www.rockportartcenter.com/main

902 Navigation Circle, 361-729-5519

Outdoors and Birding

Renowned as the principal wintering ground for the endangered Whooping Crane, the **Aransas National Wildlife**

Refuge sits on a broad peninsula across the bay northeast of Rockport. A Wildlife Interpretive Center features mounted specimens, a slide show and literature. This is a great place for observing nature, hiking, and photography. The story of the Whooping Cranes is one of survival – when the Refuge was established in 1937, the wild flock numbered only 18. Today, with successful conservation efforts, it now numbers over 250 and attracts visitors from around the world. The entire complex is comprised of over 115,000 acres that provide vital resting, feeding, wintering, and nesting grounds for migratory birds and native Texas wildlife.

www.fws.gov/southwest/REFUGES/texas/aransas
361-286-3559

The Whooping Cranes are not the only feathered visitors to the area – on any given day over 75 different species can be spotted in the marshes and along the sandy beaches. The climate and geography draws thousands of birds as the seasons change, many arriving from Central and South America to nest during the summer. September is the perfect time to see hundreds of migrating hummingbirds on their way through town. The informative, educational, fun Hummer/Bird Celebration is held the second weekend in September.

Goose Island State Park is home to the "Big Tree," an immense live oak certified as the largest in Texas, estimated to be 1,000 years old. On a peninsula between Copano and St. Charles Bays, this park offers a children's play area, restrooms, showers, picnic sites, fishing pier, fish cleaning table, boat ramp and unsupervised beach for bay swimming.

www.tpwd.state.tx.us/spdest/findadest/parks/goose_island
361-729-2858

Don't miss one of Captain Tommy's tours at **Rockport Birding & Kayak Adventures**. This family run business

124

provides delightful nature tourism experiences. The Skimmer was built to navigate shallow waters and is powered by quiet outboards so it's ideal for birding cruises. Knowledgeable guides are educational and helpful, ensuring you'll have lots of fun and learn something, too. The Dolphin watching cruises are great fun and the sunset cruises are awesome.

www.whoopingcranetours.com
361-727-0643
877-892-4737

Shop

Downtown Rockport has dozens of interesting shops and some first-class art galleries. Popular shops include:

- **Comforts of Home**, 103 S. Austin, 361-727-1471
- **New Beginnings**, 410 S. Austin, 361-729-8778
- **Hidden Treasures**, 207 N. Austin, 361-729-5177
- **Connections**, 209 S. Austin, 361-729-4298
- **Austin St. General Store**, 502 S. Austin; 361-790-7493
- **Bay Window**, 705 Hwy. 35 N, 361-790-7025
- **Shop the World**, 2955 Hwy. 35 N, 361-729-5165

All are filled with amazing arrays of delightful items.

Galleries include:

- **Austin Street Gallery**, 501 S. Austin, 361-790-7782
- **Coastal Creations**, 415 S. Austin, 361-790-8101
- **Salt Flats Gallery**, 415 S. Austin, #9, 361-288-2752
- **Gallery of Rockport**, 503 S. Austin, 361-729-2900

Eat

As you would imagine, the Rockport/Fulton area has some excellent seafood restaurants. But many other good restaurants offer a wide variety, from fast food to home cooking to gourmet.

125

Latitude 2802 Coastal Cuisine & Fine Art offers fine dining and an excellent wine list in the heart of historic Rockport, with European influenced cuisine served in an art gallery atmosphere. They specialize in presenting fresh seafood in creative ways and the crab dishes are to die for. So is the stuffed shrimp and the service is excellent.

www.latitude2802.com
105 N. Austin, Rockport
361-727-9009

Crab N in nearby **Aransas Pass**, will prepare your fresh catch (cleaned and filleted) to your liking, but you don't have to bring your own dinner. This popular restaurant overlooks a canal leading to the bay and offers an innovative menu featuring fresh seafood (shrimp, crab, oysters, scallops, fish) with savory sauces and well-prepared steaks. The crab bisque is awesome and so popular it's sold by the quart. They offer decadent desserts if you still have room – or get them to go.

210 Gulf Gate, Aransas Pass
361-758-2371

Los Comales serving authentic freshly prepared Mexican food, seafood and steaks is popular with locals.

431 Hwy. 35 S, Rockport
361-729-3952

Sleep

Perfect for that romantic getaway or relaxing weekend, **Hoopes' House** commands a panoramic view of Rockport Harbor. Listed in the National Register of Historic Places, the house (circa 1890) has been meticulously restored to its original splendor. Within walking distance of the beach and downtown shops, galleries, eateries, and the Maritime Museum, the cheerful yellow B&B consists of four luxurious guest rooms in the main house and four additional rooms in a poolside wing. The Victorian-era main house exhibits fine stained glass, pocket doors, broad pine floors and a fireplace in the parlor. A large pool, hot tub and gazebo on the beautifully landscaped grounds afford more places to relax. Friendly, long-time innkeepers Paula and Mike know Rockport and can offer helpful recommendations.

www.hoopeshouse.com
417 N. Broadway, Rockport, 800-924-1008

In Fulton, **Pelican Bay Resort** is a small "village" consisting of several free-standing New England-style cottages and mini-suites nestled among shady live oaks, along with a spacious clubhouse/meeting room, gazebo, outdoor grills, swimming pool and hot tub. Each Cottage has a fully equipped kitchen, cable TV, queen sofa bed, and porches with rocking chairs. A lighted fishing pier with a fish cleaning area gives access to Aransas Bay.

www.pelicanbayresort.com
4206 N. Hwy. 35, Fulton
361-729-7177, 866-729-7177

Port Aransas

Convention & Visitors Bureau
403 W. Cotter
800-452-6278
www.portaransas.org

Beach, Sun, and Family Fun! On the northern tip of **Mustang Island**, Port Aransas offers the natural serenity of a stroll on the beach or an endless array of activities and adventures.

Getting to Port A, as locals call it, from the north is part of the fun – kids of all ages love the free ferry ride across the

Corpus Christi ship channel from Aransas Pass where you're likely to be accompanied by Bottle Nose Dolphins or pelicans.

Beach vacations are always fun for everyone. (courtesy Texas Tourism)

The bays, jetties and deep Gulf waters offer the finest fishing around. Launch your own boat and find a spot or choose from several experienced guides or charter boat services. Or fish from dry ground on area lighted piers.

More than 500 species of birds visit annually, making the area one of the most popular birding destinations in North America. The island's Visitor Center is "bird-friendly" and can provide information about birding sites and check lists for Port Aransas and Mustang Island.

The Trolley travels daily through the city, transporting folks in air-conditioned comfort. Main streets and several side streets leading to the beach are on the route that repeats every hour, passing RV parks, birding areas, the city marina and the Mustang airport. And it only costs 25¢.

www.cityofportaransas.org/Transportation.cfm

Attractions

The **University of Texas Marine Science Institute** offers a great introduction to oceanography. The Institute is dedicated to research, education, and outreach as they apply to the Texas coastal zone and other marine environments. The Visitor Center promotes interest in Marine Science with self-guided tours and educational movies. Seven aquaria display typical Texas coastal habitats and the organisms that live in them. The 83,000 sq. ft. central complex is located on 72 acres of beachfront land and consists of a series of laboratories, classrooms, offices, a library, museum, exhibit halls, visitor's center, auditorium, seminar rooms, and workshops. Over 40,000 visitors tour the facility annually.

www.utmsi.utexas.edu

Outdoors

The 18 miles of uncrowded public beaches on Mustang Island are great for strolling, shelling, sunning or playing. You may see folks windsurfing, parasailing, kiteboarding, kayaking or surfing. Rent a bike or buggy to zip around. Play a round of golf. About 15 miles south of town, the popular **Mustang Island State Park** encompasses nearly 4,000 acres of sand dunes, sea oats, and five miles of Gulf beach frontage.

www.tpwd.state.tx.us/spdest/findadest/parks/mustang_island
361-749-5246

Some annual events draw enormous crowds. The **Texas SandFest** (www.texassandfest.com) in April has become one of the biggest beach festivals in the state. More than a hundred participants from across the nation, including world-class master sculptors, create unbelievably detailed, amazing sand sculptures. In addition to the sand sculpting contests, the free festival features vendor tents of all kinds, arts & crafts, sand sculpting lessons, music and entertainment.

129

SandFest is one of the biggest events in Port Aransas with competitors from around the world. (courtesy Al Buckner)

The **Celebration of Whooping Cranes & Other Birds** the last weekend in February celebrates all things "bird-y" – from lectures and workshops by world-renowned experts to guided trips to the Aransas National Wildlife Refuge (see Rockport) to see the Whooping Cranes in their winter home. Narrated bus and boat tours, seminars, demonstrations, photo opportunities and a first-rate trade show make this an impressive event.

Shop

For fine or funky art, peruse the area galleries – take home the work of a local artist as a special treasure. Search the plethora of gift shops and boutiques to find nautical décor and island fashions. You'll find gifts, clothing, jewelry, toys, and just plain "stuff" at these stores:

- **Gratitude**, 316 N. Station St., 361-749-0302
- **Pretty Dam Cute**, 1007 Hwy. 361, 361-749-0824
- **Stephanie's Stuff**, 710 Alister, 361-749-4422

- **Winton's Island Candy Co.**, 509 Alister, 361-749-4773

Eat

There's no lack of places to eat in Port Aransas – fresh seafood, pasta, steaks, barbecue, pizza, burgers, Mexican, Italian and Cajun food and more. A favorite is Shell's Pasta & Seafood, serving up great pasta, homemade bread, and fresh fish at reasonable prices. The choices are almost overwhelming for such a small, casual bistro; service is excellent.

522 E. Avenue G, 361-749-7621

Cancun Grill & Cantina offers fantastic homemade Mexican food, reasonable prices and a friendly staff.

445 W. Cotter Ave., 361-749-5596

A good family restaurant is **Seafood & Spaghetti Works**, serving up pizza and pasta as well as delicious specialty seafood dishes. Generous portions, reasonable prices, and friendly, efficient service.

710 S. Alister St., 361-749-5666

South Padre Island

Visitor Center
600 Padre Blvd.
800-SO-PADRE
www.sopadre.com

With its alluring beaches, warm Gulf waters, fine dining, and a vast diversity of outdoor activities, South Padre Island makes a great getaway destination, but for heaven's sake, don't go in March over Spring Break! The Island is also ecologically significant with 34 miles of sand dunes, water birds, shrimp, and the best deep-sea fishing in Texas.

One of the premier playgrounds in Texas, this 34-mile long barrier reef island at the southernmost tip of the Texas Gulf Coast boasts more than 300 days of sunny weather a year. Surrounded by the warm waters of the Laguna Madre Bay to the west and the Gulf of Mexico to the east, South Padre Island is a coastal resort town with five miles of seashore fun and 29 miles of pristine beach.

Once on South Padre Island, transportation around the island is free via the WAVE Shuttle.

Outdoor Activities

First things first – water sports. Dozens of companies offer boat tours, fishing charters, dive charters, beach buggy rentals, parasailing, scuba and snorkeling lessons, windsurfing lessons and kayak rentals. Laguna Madre bay, separating South Padre Island from the mainland, is recognized as one of the world's top windsurfing destinations. Kiteboarding is fast becoming the most popular new water sport and certified instructors will teach you how. Or learn to surf, scuba dive or snorkel in the warm, clear water. Take Sandcastle building lessons. Now, that's fun!

Ride horseback on the beach! Across the dunes and into the sunset . . . The **Island Equestrian Center** has horses appropriate for all riding levels.

www.horsesonthebeach.com
956-761-4677

Eco Tourism and Birding is huge here. The **South Padre Island Birding & Nature Center** at the southern tip of the island, is part of the **World Birding Center** providing nature adventures in every season. South Padre Island is a crucial first landfall for birds making an arduous cross-Gulf migration from Southern Mexico and northern Central America. Several companies offer bay cruises and dolphin-viewing cruises and bird-watching expeditions.

www.worldbirdingcenter.org/sites/spi/index.phtml

Next to the Convention Centre, the **Laguna Madre Nature Trail** is a 1,500-foot boardwalk that extends across four acres of wetlands.

Sea Turtle, Inc. was founded in 1977 by Ila Loetscher, better known as "The Turtle Lady of South Padre Island" to assist in the protection of Kemp's Ridley Sea Turtle and to ultimately restore the Ridley population to a level that will ensure its survival.

Over time, the non-profit organization has expanded its scope to support the conservation of all marine turtle species. By providing educational programs to schools, civic organizations and media, Sea Turtle Inc. hopes to ensure the rehabilitation of injured sea turtles for their return to the wild.

www.seaturtleinc.com

6617 Padre Blvd., 956-761-4511

If you have the kids with you, take them to **Schlitterbahn Beach Waterpark** to splash, slide and tube.

www.schlitterbahn.com/spi/default.asp

956-772-7873

Shop

A stroll down Padre Blvd. will lead you past shops and boutiques selling every type of T-shirt, souvenir or knick-knack you can imagine.

Eat

Dirty Al's must be the most popular eatery on the island, judging by the lines. No white tablecloths, just sizeable portions of shrimp and fries to die for. Other awesome choices include burgers, onion rings, po'boys, crab legs, and fish tacos. Casual, friendly place with fantastic food.

www.dirtyals-daddys.com/dirtyals/menu.htm

33396 State Park Rd. #100 at Sea Ranch Marina

956-761-4901

If you want to take that special someone to a fine restaurant, try the **Palms Resort Café on the Beach**. With lovely views and covered deck dining areas, the Café serves excellent offerings for breakfast (exceptional eggs Benedict), lunch and dinner. Although the food is outstanding, it's still a laid-back beach café with great service.

palmsresortcafe.com/cafe.htm

3616 Gulf Blvd., 800-466-1316

For amazing gourmet sandwiches, go to **PsychaDeli.** All sandwiches are loaded with quality meats and cheeses and fresh veggies on homemade Artisan breads – you may create your own from an enormous list of choices or order a "Groovy Creation" like a Marvelous Muffaletta (veggie available) or a Ravin' Reuben. They make Espresso drinks and smoothies and shakes – ever have a chocolate peanut butter shake? Definitely not a typical sandwich shop – the service is friendly, prices are reasonable and the menu is extensive.

www.psychadeli.biz

2500 Padre Blvd. Ste. 2

956-772-9770

The **Sea Ranch Restaurant & Bar** has been around a long time because its efficient staff serves excellent seafood and well-prepared steaks.

searanchtx.com

1 Padre Blvd., 956-761-1314

Sleep

South Padre Island has literally thousands of rooms in hotels, motels, B&Bs, condos and vacation homes on the island. One nice B&B for a romantic getaway is **Casa de Siesta**, with the architectural style and ambiance of Old Mexico. Owners, Lynn and Ron, designed and built it as a B&B, bringing Ponderosa Pine from New Mexico and Saltillo tiles from Mexico. Rooms surround a courtyard with a hand carved Mexican stone fountain. Only one block from the beach and one block from the bay, Casa de Siesta is convenient to everything in town.

www.casadesiesta.com

4610 Padre Blvd., 956-761-5656

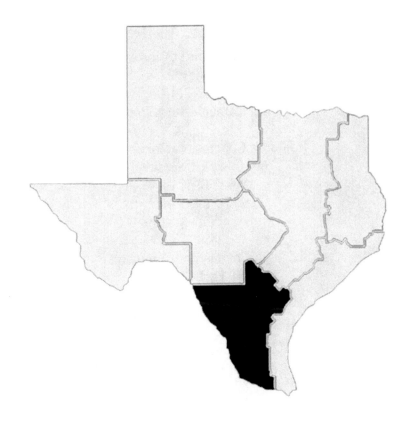

South Texas

Much of South Texas still has a deep connection with its south-of-the-border blend of history and culture. Visitors begin to appreciate the intertwined heritage as they explore the missions and small villages of the region (as well as San Antonio, the top destination in Texas). For a real getaway, surround yourself with nature – exotic birds, swaying palm trees and brilliant bougainvillea – in the lower Rio Grand Valley.

Rio Grande Valley

Alamo Chamber of Commerce
130 S. 8th St.
956-787-2117
www.alamochamber.com

Edinburg Chamber of Commerce
602 West University
800-800-7214
956-383-4974
www.edinburg.com

Hidalgo Chamber of Commerce
611 East Coma
956-843-2734
www.hidalgotexas.com

McAllen Chamber of Commerce
1200 Ash Ave.
877-622-5536
956-682-2871
www.mcallenchamber.com

The Greater Mission Chamber of Commerce
220 E. 9th St.
800-580-2700
956-585-2727
www.missionchamber.com

Pharr Chamber of Commerce
308 West Park
956-787-1481
www.pharrchamberofcommerce.com

San Juan Chamber of Commerce
1006 S. Standard
956-783-9957
www.cityofsanjuantexas.com

Weslaco Chamber of Commerce
301 West Railroad
888-968-2102
956-968-2102
www.weslaco.com

Blue Herons are a common sight along the wetlands of the
Rio Grande Valley. (courtesy Al Buckner)

The **World Birding Center** is a unique network of nine
sites, encompassing more than 10,000 acres spread along 120
miles of south Texas' river road from Roma to South Padre

Island. Each is an ecological treasure, dedicated to protecting native habitat and conservation as well as education to promote bird and wildlife appreciation. This massive project involves Texas Parks & Wildlife, U.S. Fish & Wildlife Services and nine valley communities.

www.worldbirdingcenter.org
2800 S. Bentsen Palm Dr., Mission, 956-584-9156 Ext. 221

- **Bentsen-Rio Grande Valley State Park**:
  www.worldbirdingcenter.org/sites/mission/
- **Edinburg Scenic Wetlands**:
  www.worldbirdingcenter.org/sites/edinburg/
- **Estero Llano Grande State Park**:
  www.worldbirdingcenter.org/sites/weslaco/
- **Harlingen Arroyo Colorado**:
  www.worldbirdingcenter.org/sites/harlingen/
- **Old Hidalgo Pumphouse**:
  www.worldbirdingcenter.org/sites/hidalgo/
- **Quinta Mazatlan**:
  www.worldbirdingcenter.org/sites/mcallen/
- **Resaca de la Palma State Park**:
  www.worldbirdingcenter.org/sites/brownsville/
- **Roma Bluffs**:
  www.worldbirdingcenter.org/sites/roma/
- **South Padre Island Birding and Nature Center**:
  www.worldbirdingcenter.org/sites/spi/

The **Museum of South Texas History** is an exceptional museum presenting the rich heritage and blended cultures of the Rio Grande Valley. Originally located in the **1910 Hidalgo County Jail**, the museum underwent a $5.5 million expansion in 2003 that added 22,500 sq.-ft. including a grand lobby, gift shop, and room for several permanent exhibits, yet still incorporating the old jail. Several enthusiastic docents make the exhibits fascinating with their storytelling.

www.mosthistory.org

200 N. Closner Blvd., Edinburg, 956-383-6911

An observant osprey. (courtesy Al Buckner)

One of the top-rated zoos in the country, the **Gladys Porter Zoo** in Brownsville exhibits more than 1,600 specimens representing some 337 species, many of which are listed as endangered. Well known for its conservation and breeding programs, the zoo is a visitor-friendly park. There's a downloadable map on the website so you can plan your visit to the 31-acre facility in advance. Also an online calendar lets you see what's happening – the dedication to education is evident by the number of special events and "safaris" for kids.

www.gpz.org

500 Ringgold St., Brownsville, 956-546-7187

A South Texas resident. (courtesy Al Buckner)

For a bit of nostalgia, visit **Smitty's Jukebox Museum** housed in an historic building by the railroad tracks. Leo Schmitt Sr., who passed away in 2000, assembled and lovingly restored an impressive collection of vintage jukeboxes spanning the entire era of the music machines. Now "Junior" Schmitt works in the little museum, restoring old Wurlitzers and Rock-Olas found in basements and garages. The workshop/museum displays about 60 antique jukeboxes, the oldest built in 1926 – a song cost a nickel. If Junior has time, he'll entertain you with fascinating stories.

116 W. State St., Pharr, 956-787-0131

Pepe's on the River is an extremely popular restaurant, bar and entertainment venue with a patio right on the Rio Grande. All-you-can-eat catfish on Fridays, happy hours and great entertainers draw huge crowds.

www.pepesontheriver.net

4 miles South Conway, Mission, 956-583-3092

Visitors enjoy a boat tour of the Rio Grande. (courtesy Al Buckner)

Distinctive Destinations

Tucked away amid 40 acres of countryside, **The Inn at Chachalaca Bend** provides visitors a hidden paradise. Natural lake frontage and abundant wildlife draw fishermen and birdwatchers. Luxurious accommodations and the secluded location attract those looking for peace and quiet. A warm year-round climate allows for golfing on some great nearby courses. Relax in the spacious wood and leather appointed reading room or take your coffee and binoculars through the French doors to the wrap-around balcony overlooking beautifully landscaped grounds and gardens. A 40-foot observation tower affords outstanding views. The gracious innkeepers offer warm hospitality and tons of knowledge about the area and its flora and fauna.

The luxurious inn has six individually decorated guest rooms, each with private bath and Jacuzzi, and first-class amenities. Separate from the main inn, The Lodge has a fireplace and large meeting room with a covered patio as well as a one bedroom, one bath suite with a private balcony, making it perfect for gatherings. All rates include refreshments and delicious breakfasts.

www.chachalaca.com
20 Chachalaca Bend Dr., Los Fresnos
956-233-1180, 888-612-6800

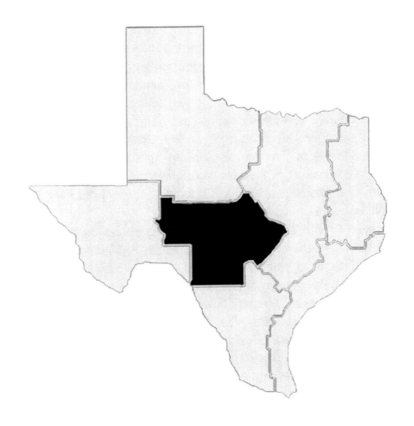

Texas Hill Country

The enchantment and scenic beauty of the Texas Hill Country is legendary, its quiet splendor created by Mother Nature about 15 million years ago. An upheaval of the earth formed the Edwards Plateau rising above the fault line in tiers, which the Spanish named balcones (balconies), thus the Balcones Escarpment. Centuries of water erosion across the plateau formed a patchwork quilt of lush green valleys and limestone hills. Known as the Texas Hill Country, this is a scenic land of sparkling rivers and streams, magnificent live oaks, and pastoral villages.

From the underground springs and limestone cliffs flow the clear rivers of the Texas Hill Country, making their way through canyons and scenic countryside for eons, providing life-sustaining water for animals and humans from early times and a paradise for outdoor enthusiasts today.

The spirit of helping each other and hospitality are deep-rooted in the Hill Country. Today, descendents of hardy German settlers live in charming, artsy little towns and welcome travelers to their laid-back way of life. Fifth and sixth generation ranchers share their cowboy culture with visitors on dude and guest ranches.

You'll find the seven beautiful Texas show caves in the Hill Country; they are: Cascade Caverns at Fair Oaks Ranch, Cave Without a Name at Boerne, Caverns of Sonora at (of course) Sonora, Innerspace Cavern at Georgetown, Longhorn Cavern at Burnet, Natural Bridge Cavern at New Braunfels, and Wonder Cave at San Marcus.

Folks visit the Hill Country for a variety of reasons, but most include some form of nature appreciation. They go to see splendid wildflowers in the spring, eat succulent peaches in the summer, tube, kayak or fish in the clear rivers, or hike in the scenic state parks. Some go simply to escape the bustling cities for a weekend of peace and quiet and romance. For whatever reason you find yourselves there, enjoy the charm, the history, and the hospitality of the people as well as its beauty.

The Hill Country has so much to offer, it boasts its own superb magazine: www.hillcountrymagazine.com.

Highland Lakes

www.highlandlakes.com
www.lakesandhills.com

A chain of six scenic recreational lakes wandering northwest from Austin includes **Lake Austin, Lake Travis, Lake Marble Falls, Lake LBJ, Inks Lake,** and **Lake Buchanan**—each with its own distinct personality. Lady Bird Lake (formerly Town Lake) is not technically one of the Highland Lakes and Lake Austin is generally considered in the city. Any of the other lakes would make a perfect weekend getaway, but it's easy to spend much more time in the area.

The lakes were created when the Lower Colorado River Authority (LCRA) built a series of dams along the **Colorado River** during the Depression of the 1930s and 1940s. The construction of the two-mile long Buchanan Dam was the first, completed in 1937. Built before the super computer age, the dam is an engineering marvel. Still managed by the LCRA, the lakes provide flood control, water, and electricity for the Hill Country.

The lakes vary immensely in size and degree of development, but they all focus on water activities like swimming, boating, and fishing. You can rent a boat, pontoon, or take a guided cruise on most of the lakes. You can even rent a houseboat on Lake Buchanan. Camping is extremely popular. Ever so many places attract families—state parks, LCRA parks, and private campgrounds, with an abundance of recreational activities and facilities. Small towns around and between the lakes offer interesting stores, art galleries, and farmers markets. The Highland Lakes area is home to a huge population of white-tailed deer as well as many other species of cute critters.

Pick up a copy of one of the maps of the lake area available anywhere in the area. An excellent map is available from the LCRA (Lower Colorado River Authority). Another essential publication is the outstanding *101 Fun Things To Do in the Highland Lakes*. It's a 100-page magazine provided free at tourist/visitor centers throughout the area.

Lower Colorado River Authority
www.lcra.org
P.O. Box 220, Austin, TX 78767-0220
800-776-5272, 512-473-3366

Burnet

Chamber of Commerce
229 S. Pierce
512-756-4297
www.burnetchamber.org

"Burnit, durnit!" NOT Burn-ETT or you'll be corrected quickly by locals. At the edge of the Hill Country, amidst the beautiful Highland Lakes, lies the historic community of Burnet.

Today, antique shops, boutiques, galleries, and eateries line the streets surrounding the Burnet County Courthouse. Historic homes are being restored as shops and Bed & Breakfast Inns. In late March and April, some of the most beautiful bluebonnets in the state bloom along the rural roads around Burnet, especially towards Lake Buchanan. **Hamilton Creek Park** is a beautifully landscaped area along the creek where you can go for a walk, have a picnic or just sit and people-watch. It's attractive with a walkway, plants, and bridges within walking distance of the downtown square.

A town of about 5,000 friendly folks, Burnet has a challenging 18-hole golf course, a fitness center, riding stables, two museums and other attractions and activities. Only a few minutes away are Inks Lake and Lake Buchanan, with oodles of water sports, recreational opportunities and camping facilities.

Attractions

In a large hanger at the Burnet Airport, The **Highland Lakes Air Museum** displays the results of painstaking work by members of the local **Squadron of the Commemorative Air Force** who collect, restore, and maintain vintage aircraft from WW I and WW II. Exhibits also include military vehicles and wartime memorabilia. Some of the CAF members are usually on hand to answer questions and tell war stories.

www.highlandlakessquadron.com/museum.html
Burnet Airport, southwest on Hwy. 281, 512-756-2226

Longhorn Caverns State Park is estimated to be a million years old and has one of the most fascinating histories of all the Texas caves. Prehistoric cavemen were probably the first to use it as their home. Then, since bat guano was an ingredient of gunpowder, Confederate armies used it to manufacture gunpowder during the Civil War. Off and on, it was used as an outlaw hideout—legend has it that Sam Bass hid $2 million in the cave. During Prohibition, it was used as a dance hall or "speakeasy" and a restaurant where food was passed through a hole in the ceiling. More recently, it functioned as a church, and finally, a State Park. Visitors can tour about two miles of underground fantasy. At eleven miles, Longhorn Cavern is considered the largest cave in Texas. A little museum displays Indian artifacts, frontier and Civil War items.

www.longhorncaverns.com
11 miles southwest of Burnet
830-598-CAVE, 877-441-CAVE

The scenic state park covers 650 acres in the heart of the Highland Lakes region, near four different lakes and communities that offer camping, fishing, and hunting. The observation tower offers spectacular panoramic views of the Hill Country. Guided tours of the 68-degree cavern last approximately 1½ hours. There's a gift shop, snack bar and deli, picnic area, and a few hiking trails. In the Visitor Center, see the CCC exhibit—if you don't know about the work done by the CCC (**Civilian Conservation Corps**) in the Texas Park Systems, make it a point to learn – it's a significant, rich part of Texas history.

Eat

Girls, **Tea-Licious** is too cute for words! But the "little tearoom on Burnet's historic square" is as popular with guys as it is with girls at lunchtime – local businessmen like the large specialty sandwiches, loaded baked potatoes and scrumptious desserts like individual Chocolate Volcano cakes. Vicki strives for high-quality, healthy food and good service. Her gourmet sweet pickles have become famous and are now shipped all over the U.S. Tea-Licious does catering and since the tearoom closes at 5:00, it's a great venue for private parties and any after-hours special event. And there's more. The "Giftique" displays an amazing array of unusual gifts, ladies accessories, quilts and teapots.

www.tea-licious.com
216 S. Main, 512-756-7636

Sleep

Canyon of the Eagles Lodge and Nature Park – see Lake Buchanan below.

Lake Marble Falls

Lake Marble Falls is more like a river that wanders for about six miles below the town, offering a pretty paradise for boaters and fishermen. The town of Marble Falls has grown with the popularity of the lake. A huge country club and numerous parks and resorts offer a multitude of recreational activities. **Johnson Park**, an 18-acre free park, provides a public boat ramp, a playscape for children, picnic area, and restrooms.

Marble Falls

Marble Falls/Lake LBJ Chamber of Commerce
916 2nd St.
830-693-8215
www.marblefalls.org

Marble Falls' name originally came from a 20-foot waterfall in the Colorado River over marble ledges. The falls are now covered by Lake Marble Falls. But **Granite Mountain**, a huge stone monolith on the western edge of town is what secured Marble Falls' place in Texas history—it was here that the famed sunset red granite of the State Capitol Building was quarried. The age-old granite formations attract rock hounds from all over.

Today, the Marble Falls/Lake LBJ area is one of the most popular in Texas. The natural beauty and serenity of the area and the friendly hospitality of the local folks are two of the big draws. It's a huge year-round recreation area, too – golf, tennis, horseback riding –and the lakes offer tons of water activities.

Marble Falls has a very active Chamber of Commerce, which sponsors numerous activities and events throughout the year. One of the most spectacular is the Christmas Walkway of Lights—over a million lights strung along Lake Marble Falls. Others include a Fine Arts & Wine Festival (April), Mayfest

Carnival (May), Independence Day Celebration with fireworks at Lakeside Park (July 4th) and the crowd-attracting Lakefest Drag Boat Race (August),

The historical marker (on a granite monolith) on the western edge of town commemorates the 866-foot dome of solid pink granite known as **Granite Mountain**. The formation covers 180 acres and contains the largest quarry of its kind in the country. A railroad line was built especially to haul the granite to Austin when the rock was used to build the state Capitol. The tracks and quarry activity can be seen from the roadside park on RR 1431.

Zip through the trees for an exciting adventure.
(courtesy Cypress Valley Canopy Tours)

Activities and Adventures

Fly through the canopy of old growth Cypress trees at **Cypress Valley Canopy Tours** in nearby Spicewood. Steel zip lines lead from platform to platform, affording magnificent views of the Hill Country. A spectacular tree top adventure!

www.cypressvalleycanopytours.com
1223 Paleface Ranch Rd., Spicewood, 512-264-8880

A 4-acre hay maze in the shape of Texas! The object is to enter at Brownsville and find 11 cities throughout Texas. It's just for fun although the winners do get a free soft drink. **Sweet Berry Farm** is really a pick-your-own farm with fresh strawberries and blackberries in the spring and a fall pumpkin harvest. The farm hosts lots of school field trips, so don't be surprised to find little ones learning about farm life.

www.sweetberryfarm.com
1801 FM 1980, Marble Falls, 830-798-1462

Wine

Flat Creek Estate Vineyard and Winery sits amidst 80 acres of lush, verdant rolling hills between Marble Falls and Austin. Proprietors, Rick and Madelyn are committed to producing fine handcrafted Texas wines. If the many awards and accolades are any indication, they're doing a fine job. An imposing special event center and tasting room offers a spectacular view of the vineyards.

www.flatcreekestate.com
24912 Singleton Bend East Rd., Marble Falls, 512-267-6310

Family owned **Spicewood Vineyards** won a silver medal in a national competition with its first Chardonnay. It's yet another scenic location and another fine vineyard and winery.

www.spicewoodvineyards.com
419 Burnet County Road 409, Spicewood, 830-693-5328

Stone House Vineyard produces grapes of excellent quality. The first wine, Claros, won a gold medal and "best of class" in an international wine competition. As they continue to win awards, the vineyard and winery continue to grow.

www.stonehousevineyard.com
24350 Haynie Flat Road, Spicewood, 512-264-3630

Shop

Marble Falls is the shopping hub of the Highland Lakes area. The historic downtown Main Street area has several one-of-a-kind specialty stores. **The Book Shop** has a great selection of books about Texas and nature, children's books, hard-to-find books, flags and gifts.

www.thebookshoptexas.com
212 Main St.; 830- 693-7276

Several of the stores are in a little courtyard area called **The Shops at Old Oak Square: Three White Doves** features quality Native American handcrafted jewelry, silver and turquoise.

www.3whitedoves.com
309 Main St. #1, 830-693-5253

Sakow Cards showcase unique, original hand-painted or hand embellished cards.

www.sakowcards.com
309 Main St., #4, 830-693-2627

Zoo La La, a gourmet kitchen, gift, and wine boutique is chock-a-block with really cool stuff for cooking and baking, entertaining, and gourmet foods and specialty items.

www.zoolala.com
309 Main Street, #6, 830-798-0161, 877-ZOO-LALA

Eat

The **Blue Bonnet Café** has been a favorite with both locals and tourists since 1929. Well-known as a place to get good, inexpensive home-style meals and breakfast any time of day. The menu lists eight different kinds of omelets as well as several traditional breakfasts, including steak and eggs. Choose from daily specials like chicken-fried steak, pot roast, fried chicken livers, chicken and dumplings, fried catfish, and more. And oh, those yeast rolls! It's consistently a blue-ribbon winner in magazine polls and especially acclaimed for the homemade pies to die for. Customers like the friendly, homey atmosphere as much as the scrumptious pies. And that's saying a lot.

www.bluebonnetcafe.net
211 Hwy. 281, 830-693-2344

Overwhelming aromas lure folks to **Brothers Bakery & Café**. Breads, muffins, cookies, pies, pastries, and fabulous French-style croissants will tempt you to forget that diet completely. The lifetime dream of CIA-degreed Chef Ryan, it's a busy place at lunch when he serves made-from-scratch soups, salads, quiche, and sandwiches on freshly made artisan breads.

www.brothersbakery.com
519 Hwy. 281, 830-798-8278

For a romantic dinner on a hill overlooking the lake, try **Russo's Texitally Café**. The cuisine is described as "Texas Fare with an Italian Flair," thus the unusual name. The innovative menu offers an abundant selection of steaks and seafood, chicken and veal, as well as a few classic Italian dishes. A bit pricey for dinner, several scrumptious lunch selections are quite reasonable.

www.texitally.com
602 Steve Hawkins Pkwy., 830-693-7091

Doc's Fish Camp & Grill is one of the best steak and seafood restaurants in the Hill Country, if not the state. From fried catfish to boiled shrimp to scrumptious steaks, everything is tasty. The menu lists appetizers as "Fish Camp Bait" and offers a huge selection of soups (awesome gumbo), salads, great lunch baskets and burgers, too.

www.docsfishcamp.com
900 FM 1431 West, 830-693-2245

Ok, it's a fast food restaurant. But **Storm's** is legendary in central Texas. Serving great burgers for over 50 years, there are locations in Burnet and Kingsland also.

www.stormsrestaurants.com
1408 W. Hwy. 1431, 830-693-0012

Kingsland

www.kingslandchamber.org

This beautiful spot was popular even before the lakes were built. At the turn of the last century, tourists and fishermen came on trains from Austin. The scenic area is still popular with fishermen and a haven for water sports enthusiasts. It's an active community and the chamber sponsors events all year long, but life is a slower pace and the focus is on relaxation. There's a lot to enjoy and explore in the area.

The casual, friendly community of Kingsland is a blend of local residents, tourists, Winter Texans, and retired folks. Many people from big cities own weekend homes in the Highland Lakes area and eventually retire there. As a matter of fact, Kingsland is listed as one of the top three retirement areas in the U.S.

Attractions

Nightengale Archaeological Center. Ever wonder how people lived 10,000 years ago? Before computers? Located near Kingsland, on the shores of Lake LBJ, the LCRA Nightengale Archaeological Center was discovered in 1988 and soon recognized as a major archaeological discovery. Researchers have uncovered more than 170,000 artifacts revealing evidence that the site has been continuously inhabited possibly as far back as 10,000 years. A Visitor and Learning Center was opened in 1991.

www.lcra.org/parks/natural_resource/nightengale.html
830-598-5261

Designed by Tom Kite, Roy Bechtol and Randy Russell, **The Legends Golf Course** on Lake LBJ challenges golfers of all ability levels. Surrounded by Lake LBJ, it's a scenic course and facilities include a practice area and a grill serving breakfast and lunch. **The Villas at The Legends** offer deluxe overnight accommodations.

www.legendsgolftx.net
105 Range Way Cir., 325-388-8888
The Villas 325-388-8030

Sleep

Built by the Austin & Northwestern Railroad in 1901, **The Antlers Hotel** is listed in the National Register of Historic Places. The lobby still has the original train bulletin above the check-in desk and many of the original furnishings.

For a romantic getaway, choose one of the hotel's restored well-appointed guest rooms. For a gathering, select one of the comfortable cabins nestled in the woods near the waterfront or in the orchard. Cabins accommodate from 2-6 persons; each has a small kitchen, living area with TV/VCR, rocking chairs on the porch and an outdoor grill. Browse the excellent website to choose the one to fit your needs.

If you've got the kids with you, spend the night in a real, honest-to-goodness caboose! Three brightly colored historic cabooses have been redesigned as guest rooms for 2 adults and 2 children. Each caboose has a queen-sized bed and kid-sized bunk beds, an efficiency kitchen, bath with shower, and living/dining area with TV/VCR. Climb a ladder to the cupola and discover benches for watching the sunset. The cabooses bear the logos of railroads that have run on the tracks in front of the Antlers. Across the street, an 1890s wooden combination car offers luxury accommodations for four.

Enjoy the water and outdoors. Stroll through the 15-acre wooded grounds on Lake LBJ, swim along the granite-lined private waterfront, fish off one of the docks. Guest boat slips are available if you want to bring your own boat. The lovely landscaped lawns and gardens around the property provide a beautiful background for a wedding or other special event.

www.theantlers.com
1001 King St., Kingsland, 325-388-4411, 800-383-0007

Lake Lyndon B. Johnson (LBJ)

At 6,200 acres, Lake LBJ is not the largest, nor the smallest, and by most accounts not the prettiest, but it's probably the most popular of the Highland Lakes. Fed by both the Colorado and the Llano Rivers, it's normally a constant level lake, making it perfect for sailing, water skiing, boating and all water sports and activities.

Unlike Lake Buchanan and Inks Lake, Lake LBJ is becoming increasingly developed with resort communities and upscale homes with manicured lawns and boathouses lining its shores. Because of the residential development, rental units are not as numerous on this lake, although there are a few in the communities of Horseshoe Bay, Sunrise Beach, Kingsland, and Granite Shoals. Hundreds of folks from big cities around the state own weekend homes on the lake, and this area has been rated in the top three areas of the U.S. for retirement.

Inks Lake is one of the most popular state parks in Texas.
(courtesy Texas Parks and Wildlife)

Inks Lake

Lake Buchanan/Inks Lake Chamber of Commerce
512-793-2803
www.buchanan-inks.org

Inks Lake is thought by many to be the prettiest in the Highland Lakes chain, surrounded by rugged natural beauty—colorful outcroppings of pink granite, ancient oaks, and craggy bluffs. The smallest lake, at just 4.2 miles long and 0.6 miles at its widest point, it lends credence to the old saying about the best things coming in the smallest packages.

Enter at Park Road 4, just a few miles west of Buchanan Dam, and stop at the scenic overlook. Watch the sparkling waterfall cascade into the deep blue waters of the **Devil's Waterhole**, an awesome summer swimming hole framed by giant pink boulders.

But the Devil's Waterhole isn't the only attraction here—Inks Lake attracts nature lovers, campers, boaters and fishing enthusiasts year round. Covering only 800 acres, it's a constant-level lake and is also the site of one of the most popular state parks in Texas.

Inks Lake State Park extends along the entire eastern shore of the lake. Beloved for its pastoral setting amid granite rock outcroppings, rugged shoreline and thick oak and juniper woods, it's one of the most fully equipped parks in the region, offering a seemingly limitless array of recreational activities. Everyone should find something to do with two lighted fishing piers, a swimming beach, boat ramp, picnic sites, 8 playgrounds, amphitheater, 9-hole golf course (complete with carts and rental clubs), and a park store that rents canoes and paddleboats year-round. If you're not a camper, overnight accommodations are available in nice, new air-conditioned mini-cabins that sleep four (bunk beds).

www.tpwd.state.tx.us/park/inks
3630 Park Rd. 4 West, 512-793-2223

In addition to the infinite water fun, nature-lovers enjoy nature/geology walks with over seven miles of scenic hiking trails through pink granite boulders, woodlands, and rolling grasslands. Staff members lead several interpretive tours and conduct various Junior Ranger programs and nature activities during the summer. Cool off with a tour of nearby Longhorn Caverns State Park (see Burnet).

Lake Buchanan

Lake Buchanan/Inks Lake Chamber of Commerce
512-793-2803
www.buchanan-inks.org

The first and largest and deepest of the Highland Lakes is Lake Buchanan, pronounced buck-an-un. Don't make "buch" rhyme with puke or you'll identify yourself as not-from-around-here. Boating, water skiing, and sailing are popular water sports, although Buchanan's probably best known for its excellent striper bass fishing. Covering more than 23,000 acres, its nonetheless one of the most undeveloped of the lakes, retaining a laid-back, favorite-fishing-spot feeling. Several businesses around the lake rent fishing boats and pontoons, and guide services offer a variety of year-round fishing excursions.

Along the northeastern shore, where the Colorado River empties into the lake, the spectacular cliffs, rocky outcroppings, and scenic waterfalls provide one of the prettiest views anywhere. Wildlife is common and American Bald Eagles winter along the shoreline (see Vanishing Texas River Cruise below).

Stop at the **Buchanan Dam Museum and Visitor Center** right off Texas 29 at the dam. Museum displays portray the history and construction of the dam in 1937 with photographs, videotapes, and comments from many of the workers who helped build it. From May – September, volunteers offer free guided tours of the massive generating facility. An impressive walkway leads from the Visitor Center out to the spillway and offers a spectacular panoramic view of the lake. There's also an observation deck off the parking lot.

Museum 512-793-2803

The area around Lake Buchanan and neighboring Inks Lake has been designated "Bluebonnet Capital of Texas" by

161

the state legislature—aptly named for the spectacular spring wildflower displays throughout the area. The Chamber of Commerce, located at Buchanan Dam, operates a hotline of the best viewing locations in Burnet and Llano counties.

Buchanan Dam Chamber 512-793-2803

Special Attraction

Taking the **Vanishing Texas River Cruise** will undoubtedly be one of the highlights of any visit to the Texas Hill Country. On a 2½-hour narrated sightseeing cruise of the rugged Colorado River Canyon on Lake Buchanan, see wildlife and waterfalls cascading over dramatic limestone cliffs from the viewing decks of the *Texas Eagle II*, a 70-foot, enclosed three-deck boat.

In the spring, cruisers see vivid fields of Texas wildflowers, the summer season offers brings dinner and sunset cruises, and winter (November – March) is the time to see one of the largest colonies of American Bald Eagles that migrate to the Texas Colorado River Canyon for the winter. Imagine seeing these majestic birds in flight or sitting on treetop perches. Experienced guides will help you find them. Take binoculars and order a box lunch or bring your own picnic.

The cruise departs from **Canyon of the Eagles Lodge and Nature Park** (see Sleep below).

www.vtrc.com

512-756-6986, 800-474-8374

Wine

In nearby **Tow, Fall Creek Vineyards** was established in 1975 by Ed & Susan Auler, making it one of the first wineries in Texas. Named after the sparkling spring-fed Fall Creek, which flows through the Auler family ranch near the winery and empties into the Colorado River at the spectacular Fall Creek waterfall. In the last decade, a focus on red wines has led to the production of Meritus, a super-premium red wine, critically acclaimed by several noted wine critics. Many of their wines have won gold medals and awards in national and international competitions.

www.fcv.com

1820 County Rd. 222, Tow, 325-379-5361

Sleep

In the heart of the Hill Country lies a sparkling jewel. **Canyon of the Eagles Lodge and Nature Park** can be found at the end of RR 2341, on the northeastern tip of Lake Buchanan. This eco-friendly resort mixes recreation and relaxation with education and appreciation for nature and wildlife. Only open since 1999, it has already earned a reputation as one of Texas' most beautiful parks and nature areas, and has been certified a Texas Wildscape by Texas Parks & Wildlife.

Perfect for getaways of all kinds, Canyon of the Eagles offers tremendous diversity – miles of hiking trails, water and recreational activities, hikes and educational programs, weekend entertainment (maybe a cowboy poet or storyteller), areas for simply relaxing, watching sunsets, or stargazing, a restaurant, park store, lodge rooms and cottages and camping accommodations. The lodge was designed to fit in with natural surroundings and cottages are nestled among the trees.

Splash in two small, rock-lined swimming pools or on the swimming beach, rent canoes, play horseshoes or volleyball, or try your luck on the fishing pier. Inside the Eagle's Nest (the guest hospitality room), play dominoes, cards, or watch the large-screen TV.

www.canyonoftheeagles.com

16942 RR 2341, Burnet, 512-756-8787, 800-977-0081

For nature lovers, over 14 miles of hiking trails loop though the park along the shoreline of the lake. Detailed trail maps are available at Park Headquarters. Naturalists give presentations on topics like animal-track identification, insects, endangered species, and the highly popular reptile show. Some programs are held in the amphitheater; others take place on the trails. If you're lucky, you may spot a Bald Eagle between mid-Oct. and mid-March. Enhance your chances by taking the Vanishing Texas River Cruise, above.

The stars at night are big and bright all over the Hill Country, but you can see them intimately at the **Eagle Eye Observatory**. The Austin Astronomical Society holds monthly star parties, celestial viewing classes, and outings designed to introduce beginners to astronomy. But if that's too structured for you, just lean back and look up. There's minimal lighting around the lodge to maximize stargazing enjoyment.

Mason

Chamber of Commerce
Town Square
325-347-5758
www.masontxcoc.com

This area is noted for camping, hunting and fishing. In addition to deer, you may also find a javelina, raccoon, possum or fox. There's no telling what you might see since several ranches raise exotic species of antelope, Ibex, even buffalo. You'll see lots of birds for sure—mockingbirds (the state bird), golden eagles, hummingbirds, cardinals, scrub jays, dove, quail, and more. A profusion of wildflowers cover the surrounding hills and valleys during spring. Watch for the picturesque rock fences that partition the land.

Mason's historic town square exhibits some fine examples of sandstone architecture, now housing shops, galleries, and restaurants.

Blue Topaz, the state gem, is found only in Mason County. A few ranches allow visitors to hunt topaz and arrowheads for a nominal fee. Please don't go wandering across fences or stopping alongside creeks to hunt on your own, as folks can be a mite touchy about trespassers. For a listing of stores that carry topaz, a list of gemstone cutters, or the names and phone numbers of the ranches that allow topaz hunting, call the Chamber at 325-347-5758.

History

The restored 1928 **Odeon Theatre** shows first-run movies and often features special musical entertainment on weekends. Admission is much less than today's multi-screen theaters and the experience far more memorable.

Town Square, 325-347-9010

Now operated by the Mason Country Historical Society, reconstructed officers quarters mark the spot of the original **Fort Mason** atop Post Hill, a location that commanded a panoramic view of the surrounding countryside. The building was reconstructed on the original foundation using rock from the original fort buildings. Crumbling foundations indicate where about 23 other buildings once stood, including barracks, storehouses, stables, a guardhouse, and a hospital.

The **Mason County Memorial Museum** occupies the second story of the old Mason schoolhouse on the corner of Moody and Bryan and the **Mason Square Museum** exhibits well-done displays ranging from prehistoric times to current day. Learn about the rich, colorful history of Mason – the Mason County War, the establishment of Fort Mason, and the finding of the largest topaz found in North America. The Gift

Shop offers a nice selection of books, photos, artwork and related items.

www.masonsquaremuseum.org

103 Fort MacKavitt, 325-347-0507

Mason Characters

Mason's native son **Fred Gipson** wrote touching tales of animals and children and growing up in the beloved Hill Country where he was raised. His most famous book was undoubtedly *Old Yeller*, about a boy's love for a dog. It won awards and accolades around the world, was made into a Walt Disney movie, and is now considered a favorite classic. An excellent exhibit honoring Fred Gipson is on display in the main entryway of the M. Beven Eckert Memorial Library.

The board room in the home-owned Commercial Bank houses a personal collection of unique wood sculptures of **Gene Zesch**, Mason County's world-renowned artist. During banking hours, the public is welcome to come in and enjoy the humorous cowboy caricature carvings, portraying modern day cowboys trying to hold on to a vanishing way of life. The expressions on the faces of his characters are priceless. Born and raised on a ranch in Mason County, Gene Zesch gets ideas for his work from first hand experiences.

www.tcbmason.com

100 Moody St., 325-347-6324

Outdoors

An estimated 4-6 million Mexican free-tail bats call the **Eckert James River Bat Cave** their summer home. One of the ten largest populations of Tadarida brasiliensis in the world, the bats emerge from the cave about dusk each evening to feed on 10-20 tons of insects. Joint owners, The Nature Conservancy of Texas and Bat Conservation International, strive to protect the bats and their nursery and to provide access for the public to visit and safely witness the dramatic nightly emergence. The Conservancy's Preserve Manager is on site to provide information and assist visitors.

325-347-5970 during the season, 512-263-8878 off season

Eat

Cooper's Pit Bar-B-Q is the original Cooper's Pit Bar-B-Q, established in 1953 by the late George Cooper. By using the same recipe for over 50 years, this place has become a Texas institution. In 2003, when *Texas Monthly* magazine did a statewide review of the 50 best barbecue restaurants, Cooper's in Mason was among the top five. With rave reviews in newspapers all over the country, the original Cooper's Pit Bar-B-Q is without a doubt one of the best places to go for excellent barbecue.

Hwy. 87 South, 325-347-6897

A local favorite, **Santos Taqueria** serves authentic Mexican dishes in casual, comfortable surroundings. Owner, Santos Silerio cooks like her grandma did – preparing dishes and salsa from scratch using fresh ingredients. Dine indoors or outdoors on the covered patio from the extensive menu. Handmade gorditas with a choice of filling seem to be the specialty – try the shrimp ones. Everything is delicious here, probably one of the reasons *Texas Monthly* Magazine listed it as one of the 25 best places to eat in the Hill Country.

www.santostaqueria.com
205 San Antonio St., 325-347-6140

The **Coffee Mug N' More** is located in the historic Hofmann Building on the north side of the Courthouse Square. One of the most fascinating, entertaining, whimsical shops in Texas, it has comfortable sofas with books and magazines to read, games to play, tasty pastries, good music, WiFi, books and funny greeting cards and mugs and t-shirts to buy, and oh yes . . . great coffee. They offer a wide variety of the finest coffee beans in the world and serve great espresso drinks, homemade cinnamon rolls and kolaches, yummy Panini sandwiches for lunch, and gelato for dessert. Wow, what a place to hang out!

www.thecoffeemugnmore.com
220 Fort McKavett, 325-347-1600

Sleep

Over 3 dozen Bed and Breakfasts offer lodging in and around Mason. One of the best is **Raye Carrington on the Llano** River. Raye and her husband David have created a private retreat on the bank of the sparkling Llano River to offer guests seclusion, with only wildlife and birds and stars for company. The river is perfect for fly fishing, kayaking or canoeing and miles of country roads beckon bicyclists. Lodging is in a rustic tin-roofed inn with a porch overlooking the river, bird feeders and lovely gardens. Each guest room is air-conditioned and comfortably furnished with all the modern conveniences you would expect at a first-class bed and breakfast inn. David serves a delicious full country breakfast each morning.

www.llanoriver.com
8603 Lower Willow Creek Rd., 325-347-3474, 866-605-3100

San Angelo

Chamber of Commerce
418 West Avenue B
325-655-4136
www.sanangelo.org

Countless surprises await in this West Texas town between San Antonio and Midland . . . a refreshing mixture of arts and culture and family fun. Begin at the new state-of-the-art Visitor Center on the banks of the **Concho River**. The river, named for the mussels that produce the unique pink Concho Pearl, has always been the city's biggest treasure.

Walk along the **River Walk**, a beautification project featuring colorful gardens and waterfalls, a playground, plaza area, and River Stage to the revitalized downtown historic district. **El Paseo de Santa Angela** is a heritage trail linking the city's past and future. Pathways connect several attractions, restored buildings, the river, a restaurant, and open areas.

History

There's plenty of it in San Angelo, which literally grew up around **Fort Concho**, now the city's primary tourist attraction. One of the best-preserved forts of the Texas frontier, this 40-acre National Historic Landmark and its exhibits are not to be missed. If you're lucky, you might be in town during one of the living history demonstrations or other special events held at the fort.

www.fortconcho.com
325-657-4444

The restored **Orient-Santa Fe Depot**, built in 1909, now houses an excellent **Railway Museum**. In 1929, The **Cactus Hotel** was the largest, most ornate and most expensive of Conrad Hilton's hotels at the time. No longer open to overnight guests, it accommodates civic organizations, shops, galleries, and a café. Today, much of the city's colorful history is reflected in the eclectic shops and architecture along Concho Avenue, the first street in old "Santa Angela."

railwaymuseumsanangelo.homestead.com
703 S. Chadbourne, 325-486-2140

One more historical tidbit – ignore this if you're bringing the kids. The "Best Little Bordello Museum in Texas" exposes some of the more interesting aspects of the history of the Wild West. **Miss Hattie's** claims to be the most famous brothel in West Texas from the turn of the century until the Texas Rangers shut it down in 1946.

www.misshatties.com

18½ E. Concho Ave., 325-653-0112

Magnificent, historically correct murals record the city's history on buildings around town. Read the history, see photos, meet the artist and get caught up in the story of the murals at: www.historicmuralsofsanangelo.org. Technology even allows a "cell phone guide" to the murals.

The **Aermotor Windmill Company** has been making windmills since 1888 and claims to produce the best windmills in the USA.

www.aermotorwindmill.com

325-651-4951

Arts & Culture

The vibrant arts community here offers a symphony, classical ballet, civic theater, and a wide variety of fine arts venues. **Angelo State University** is a city treasure. Their **Planetarium** is one of the largest and technically sophisticated planetarium theaters located on a university campus. Programs are open to the public during the school term. The **ASU Theater** presents a first-rate variety of musicals and plays.

The new 30,000-square foot **San Angelo Museum of Fine Arts and Education Center** has attracted international attention and praise.

www.samfa.org

one Love Street, 325-653-3333

Art galleries abound around town. The **Old Chicken Farm Art Center** is an unusual compound of artists' studios, galleries and educational facilities.

www.chickenfarmartcenter.com

2505 Martin Luther King, 325-653-4936

Outdoors

The last thing you'd probably expect to find in West Texas has to be the **International Water Lily Garden** (325-657-4279). Located in the Civic League Park at West Beauregard and Park streets, this internationally recognized privately owned garden boasts the largest collection of water lilies in the world – more than 100 varieties, both day and night blooming. Elevated pools allow visitors to examine the fragrant blooms up close. The collection includes over 75% of all known species, and several exotic ones no longer found in the wild. The best viewing "season" runs from May to October. Other lovely gardens – Sunken Garden, Rio Concho Garden, Terrace Garden – appear as delightful havens around town.

The lakes surrounding San Angelo offer almost unlimited recreational activities. A great place for families is **San Angelo State Park** offering boating, fishing, swimming, hiking, biking, and horseback riding, as well as camping and picnic areas.

www.tpwd.state.tx.us/spdest/findadest/parks/san_angelo

325-949-4757

Birders love the area's varied habitat. It's far enough south to pick up many species usually associated with Mexico and located near the 100th meridian which means it has both western and eastern species. The San Angelo Nature Center offers displays and audiovisual educational programs for all ages, although it's especially geared toward kids. Paint Rock, approximately 22 miles east of San Angelo, is home to the Painted Rocks pictographs.

Shop

San Angelo offers an impressive variety of shopping, from a major mall to an assortment of small shops, galleries and boutiques to a summertime farmers' market. It's loads of fun browsing **Eggemeyer's General Store**, chock a block with everything imaginable.

35 East Concho Ave.

325-655-1166

Crosscutters features handcrafted crosses made from native Texas stone.

www.crosscutters.net

2678 W. Avenue N; 325-949-5156

Chester Dorner Jewelry is a third generation family-owned business offering a great selection of Concho Pearls.

219 S. Chadbourne, 325-655-4495

J.L. Mercer and Son Custom Boots have been making high quality custom boots since 1923. Customers include the late Lyndon B. Johnson, Billy Ray Cyrus, Lori Morgan, and the late John Wayne.

www.jlmercerboots.com

224 S. Chadbourne, 325-658-7634

Eat

A romantic, intimate, restaurant located in a former home near downtown, **Peasant's Village** gets rave reviews for the creative chef and attentive staff. Although recommended as a special occasion restaurant, the food is exceptional and the lunch menu is quite affordable.

www.peasantvillagerestaurant.com
3 South Park, 325-655-4811

Zentner's Daughter is practically an institution in West Texas, well known for their outstanding steaks.
www.zentnersdaughter.com
1901 Knickerbocker, 325-949-2821

Many locals prefer **Western Sky** for steaks and burgers. They give a military discount, too.
www.westernskysteakhouse.org
2024 N. Chadbourne, 325-655-3610

For romantics, several restaurants offer wine tastings paired with gourmet dinners. San Angelo is home to numerous other fine steakhouses, BBQ joints, and Tex-Mex restaurants, as well as all the usual chain and fast food places.

Sonora

Chamber of Commerce & Welcome Center
205 Hwy 277 North, Suite B
325-387-2880; 888-387-2880
www.sonoratx-chamber.com

Sonora is best known for the **Caverns of Sonora**, about 15 miles southwest of town. It's a great place to experience the wonders of nature. Bill Stephenson, founder of the National Speleological Society, sums it up this way: "Its beauty cannot be exaggerated, even by Texans!" Recognized as one of the most beautiful show caves in the world, it was designated a National Natural Landmark in 1965. It's also one of the most active caves in the world with more than 95% of its formations still growing in delicate crystal beauty and amazing profusion on ceilings, walls, and floors. Guided tours (limited to 12 people) cover 1.75 miles underground and take about two hours. If staying on a walkway sounds too tame, check out the website or call for information about the Discovery Challenge Adventure Tour.

www.cavernsofsonora.com
1711 RR 4468, 325-387-3105

History

A Texas Historical Commission Main Street City in 1994, the town itself is worthy of exploration. The **Bank Vault Park** off Main Street is a delightful place to relax. Historic buildings have been restored and preserved to manifest the heritage of Sonora and Sutton County. The first jail, once home to many frontier outlaws, now houses a museum. The magnificent **Sutton County Courthouse** is an imposing sight and a descriptive brochure "guides" you on a walking tour of the historic downtown. Don't miss the **Old Sonora Ice House Ranch Museum** near the courthouse – it's a nice exhibit honoring the courageous pioneer settlers and their livestock heritage.

Outdoors

Where the far western Hill Country and the Chihuahuan Desert meet, you'll find a diverse array of plants and wildlife. The best way to learn about the terrain is to visit **Eaton Hill Wildlife Sanctuary**, a 37-acre nature park with over 3 miles of hiking trails. Surprises await along the trails, and if you're hooked on geocaching, bring your GPS. The Sanctuary is paradise for birders since Sonora lies in a major migratory flyway. Painted Buntings, Ruby-crowned Kinglets, Black-capped Vireos, Bewick's Wren, and Hummingbirds are a few who make their homes at Eaton Hill.

Eat

By now, you'll need a place to eat. There are the ubiquitous fast food places on the highway, but locals recommend the **Sutton County Steakhouse**, offering a varied menu, including great steaks and homemade yeast rolls. Lots of folks choose the chicken-fried steak with cream gravy. Décor is "old Texan" with rifles and vintage photos on the walls.

1306 N. Service Rd,, 325-387-3833

Other favorites are **La Mexicana** for Tex-Mex and their fabulous salsa.

240 Hwy. 277 N., 325-387-3401

Rosa's Casita in nearby El Dorado, believed by many to have the best Mexican food around.

318 SW Main St., El Dorado, 325-853-2506

Sleep

For an authentic West Texas experience, stay at the **X Bar Ranch** about 20 miles north of Sonora near El Dorado. The Round House is the most private getaway in the middle of the 7,100-acre ranch offering star-filled night skies, scenic vistas, and splendid sunsets. For families or girlfriends, the Live Oak Lodge and cabins are perfect. Each lodge has a fully equipped kitchen and BBQ grill. A self-catered continental breakfast is included in the rates. Warm hospitality is evident here where Stan Meador's family has ranched for five generations. Stan encouraged opening the ranch to nature tourism about ten years ago and says, "Most folks come just to get away and enjoy the quiet." Outdoor enthusiasts may take advantage of a wide range of recreational activities like swimming, mountain bike riding, birding and nature photography.

www.xbarranch.com
325-853-2688

Frio Canyon

Billed as a "Vacationland for all Seasons," the Frio Canyon area from Leakey (pronounced LAY-key) to Concan has long been recognized as a premier destination for warm weather recreation. Beginning in northern Real County, the spring-fed **Frio River**, lined with centuries-old cypress trees, tumbles over limestone rock, past bluffs and live oaks on its way to Concan.

Along the way, campgrounds, lodges, vacation homes and rustic cabins offer accommodations and river front access, great swimming holes, tube rentals, and retail stores. It's an ideal area for fishing, hunting, bird-watching, camping, cycling, and spectacular scenery. Thousands of Texans have fond childhood memories of learning to swim, swinging off a rope into the frigid water, or days of splashing and tubing down the Frio.

The Frio River (Rio Frio means Cold River in Spanish) eventually flows into the Nueces River on its journey to the Gulf of Mexico. In this part of the Hill Country, three spring-fed rivers and river valleys parallel each other (Sabinal, Frio, and Nueces) and the area is known as the Tri-Canyon region.

Between Leakey and Garner State Park, RR1120 offers several picturesque river crossings and points of entry. You'll understand why the Frio is so enticing with its stone steps carved by nature, white pebbles, and crystal clear water. Cabins, lodges, vacation homes, camp stores and tube rental places line both sides of the road.

Leakey

Frio Canyon Chamber of Commerce
830-232-5222
www.friocanyonchamber.com

The hand cut, native stone **Real County Courthouse** still stands in Leakey, along with several other historic buildings and markers. At one end of the scenic route along FM 337 between Vanderpool and Leakey, the natural beauty of the Frio Canyon continues. The area offers great recreational opportunities, lodging, supplies, and restaurants.

Frio Pecan Farm is a working, award-winning pecan orchard right on the scenic Frio River. It also offers "rustic luxury" lodging with 16 two-bedroom air-conditioned log cabins, each with color satellite TV, VCR, fully-equipped kitchen, covered porch, BBQ pit and picnic table. Eight varieties of pecans are harvested annually in October and November. If the friendly folks have time, they'll give you a tour of the farm and answer questions. They usually have pecans available for purchase year around.

www.friopecanfarm.com
FM 337 at the river, 830-232-5294, 877-832-0674

Eat

Vinny's Italian Restaurant in Leakey is a cozy Italian restaurant where owners, Sal and Winnie, use family recipes passed down for generations to create mouth-watering veal, chicken and shrimp dishes, pastas and pizzas.

www.vinnysitalian.com
Hwy. 83 N., Leakey, 830-232-4420

The Leakey Feed Lot gets marvelous reviews from locals and visitors alike, raving about the "great grub" – best cheeseburgers, unrivaled fried chicken, steaks and shrimp and homemade mashed potatoes. But the chicken fried rib eye steak seems to hog the spotlight. The atmosphere is rustic junkyard . . . a casual, homey place.

www.leakeyfeedlot.com
547 U.S. 83 South, 830-232-5919

177

Garner State Park

234 Ranch Road 1050
830-232-6132
www.tpwd.state.tx.us/spdest/findadest/parks/garner/

This popular family-oriented park is located on the Frio River in an exceptionally scenic area seven miles north of Concan. Since Frio means "cold" in Spanish, the crystal clear water makes a terrific place to splash and play on a sizzling summer day. Tubing under an awning of bald Cypress trees is unparalleled. Others prefer canoeing, swimming, fishing, hiking, picnicking, seasonal miniature golf and paddleboat rental, and just enjoying nature at its best. More than 200 documented bird species make it a favorite destination of birders.

Garner is the most-visited State Park in Texas as families bring their offspring to share the traditions they remember from their childhood and adolescence. "Oldies" fill the jukebox and kids from 8 to 80 fill the dance floor. Since 1941, countless romances flourished at the park's historic CCC-constructed dance pavilion where generations have danced the nights away under the Texas stars. Country singer B. J. Thomas played here in the '60s and '70s and one of his band members wrote a song titled *Garner State Park*, still one of the park's most popular jukebox tunes. A fellow told of meeting his wife there as his father had met his mother and his grandfather had met his grandmother!

Limited accommodations are available in comfortable stone and timber cabins. A camping area provides shaded sites for tents or trailers, screened shelters, and restrooms with showers. There's also a grocery store and a snack bar/restaurant in the summer.

Concan

Northern Uvalde County including the Concan area and Utopia are marketed under the name **Texas Hill Country River Region**. Picturesque limestone hills and canyons carved by the crystal waters of the spring-fed Nueces, Frio, and Sabinal Rivers as they flow toward the Gulf of Mexico show off the natural beauty of the area. Stunning displays of wildflowers in spring and fall colors in autumn complement the abundant wildlife. World-class birding draws folks from across the nation to add the rare Golden-cheeked Warbler and the Black-capped Vireo to their life lists. The rivers offer fun for the whole family be it swimming, fishing, canoeing, kayaking, or tubing. Enjoy activities and special events throughout the year – horseback riding, bicycling, local festivals and rodeos.

www.thcrr.com

Folks have been coming to Concan, near the junction of FM127 and U.S. 83, since the 1920s to play in the clear waters of the Frio River. Cabins, cafés and restaurants, and a few shops supply tourists' needs; outfitters in the area rent tubes and kayaks. The Frio Canyon offers a near perfect environment for bird watching. The Audubon Society rates the area around Concan one of the best bird watching areas in the U.S. Approximately 200 species visit the area, including some listed as endangered. Bird watchers flock to the area in the fall and winter months.

Activities

Nature Quest, a celebration each April, offers seminars, workshops and field trips by noted experts in their fields – native plants, wildflowers, butterflies, insects, bats, and of course birds. Each October, the **Bicycle Classic** offers bicyclists a chance to see the rugged beauty up close.

Headquartered at Garner State Park, the Classic offers a choice of supported routes, from an enjoyable "scenic cruise" for families to challenging routes for serious cyclists. The **Utopia Arts & Crafts Fair** draws crowds the first Saturday in November.

Guides at **Hill Country Adventures** lead tours around this rugged, scenic area of the Edwards Plateau. Popular tours include "Nature by Kayak" on the Frio, the "Champion Big Tree" tour, and a variety of birding and nature tours around private ranches and state parks. But for an awesome experience of a lifetime, take the "Frio Bat Flight Tour." The world's second largest colony of Mexican free-tailed bats (10-12 million) leave their cave at dusk to gorge the night away on insects. Watch as hawks swoop in for a mid-air snack. It's a breathtaking sight!

www.hillcountryadventures.com

830-966-2320

Awesome Bat Show! (courtesy Al Buckner)

The **Club at Concan** is a surprisingly challenging golf course, 7,333 yards from the Championship tees (5187 from the forward tees) with panoramic views of the surrounding countryside. Stay and Play packages available.

www.concangolf.com
830-232-4471, lodging packages 888-926-6226

Eat

Neal's Dining Room serves up hearty breakfasts, great burgers, and country cooking with such favorites as chick fried steak, fried chicken, and barbecue. The place is usually packed on Fridays for the catfish special. The patio and deck offer a panoramic view overlooking the Frio River. **Neal's Lodges**, an "institution" founded in 1926, has been a favorite playground for decades. It's still family owned. Located on the Frio, the complex consists of 65 cabins, 10 RV hookups, a country store and gift shop, grocery, Laundromat, and restaurant.

www.nealslodges.com
Concan, 830-232-6118

Sleep

Whether you're looking for a romantic getaway or a family vacation, you'll have a great time in the Texas Hill Country River Region. Accommodations are plentiful, from motels to river cabins, guesthouses, Bed & Breakfasts, and RV and camping sites. **Rio Frio Lodging** is a reservation service for private vacation homes and cabins located throughout the Frio and Sabinal Canyon areas. Owners LeAnn and Anthony Sharp know the area and its flora and fauna and will offer helpful advice for area activities. Sharing an office with **Hill Country Adventures** (above), the headquarters boasts a new Nature Center with a delightful porch for bird watching.

www.friolodging.com
830-966-2320

Utopia

Located along the banks of the sparkling Cypress-lined Sabinal River, the quintessential small Texas community of Utopia is aptly named. Bring your fishing rod, swimsuit, golf clubs, camera or easel and leave the rest of the world behind.

A delightful gift/antique shop, **Main Street Utopia** is stuffed with a wonderful variety of quality decorator items, antique furnishings, lovely gifts, colorful dishes, jewelry, books, photographs by local artists, and more.

282 Main St., 830-966-5544

The **Sabinal Canyon Museum** showcases the history of the canyon, pioneer farm life, geology, and other memorabilia. Fifteen miles north is the spectacular Lost Maples State Natural Area (below). **Utopia Golf** is a nice, 9-hole course just south of town. A brand new clubhouse includes a café, rock patio, fitness room, and small pro shop.

www.golfutopiatexas.com
830-966-5577

Eat

Located in a cute little house next to the museum, **Utopia Joe's Coffee House** serves fresh coffee, tea, cappuccinos, lattes, and fruit smoothies in a comfortable atmosphere. The friendly folks also offer decadent pastries for breakfast and salads, soups and sandwiches for lunch . . . and free WiFi.

www.utopiajoes.com
655 Main St., 830-966-5656

Lost Maples Café is the oldest restaurant in town, located in a historic building built before 1904.

www.lostmaplescafe.com
384 Main St., 830-966-2221

Paradise Pizza makes great pizza with all of your favorite toppings, and while you're there try their delicious calzone.
283 Main St., 830-966-3392

The **Hicks House** serves delicious sandwiches, salads, and homemade lunch specials in a restored home. The "BLAT" (bacon, lettuce, avocado, tomato) is awesome and the homemade chicken & dumplings sell out fast. Part café, part bakery, they have luscious desserts and will package them to go for you.
128 W. Lee St., 830-966-2345

If you're around on a Saturday, make lunch or dinner reservations at the **Laurel Tree**, a European-style "Guest Table" just south of Utopia. Chef Laurel Waters has a long culinary pedigree that includes Le Cordon Bleu in Paris. Her innovative menu features seasonal cuisine using fresh herbs and vegetables from her garden adjacent to the restaurant. If the weather is nice, eat in the back yard dining area under a century old Live Oak.
www.utopiagourmet.com
18956 N. FM 187, 830-966-5444

Sleep

Two miles south of town, **Utopia on the River** nestles in a tranquil setting where deer feed and wild turkey roam. Spacious, well-appointed rooms have either a porch or balcony overlooking the deer-feeding area and a back window with a view of the pool or down the hill to the river. The inn has 1500 feet of river frontage. The isolated location makes it a great place to watch birds and hummingbirds zip around the feeders. And talk about a perfect place to stargaze. A large common room is an ideal gathering place to chat or play games. It's also where you will be served a country breakfast each morning, included in the rate.

www.utopiaontheriver.com

363 County Road 360, 830-966-2444

Vanderpool

Ranch Road 337 between Vanderpool and Leakey (see: Frio Canyon) is sometimes called the "Texas Alps." Dense stands of juniper and oak cover the steep canyons and rugged terrain with elevations as high as 2100 feet above sea level. Designated one of the most scenic highways in Texas, the winding roads make it extremely popular with motorcyclists and bicyclists.

The Lone Star Motorcycle Museum is a popular stop for bikers riding the Hill Country. (courtesy Al Buckner)

The **Lone Star Motorcycle Museum**, located on FM 187 about a mile south of the entrance to Lost Maples SNA, is in the heart of some of the best bike-riding roads in the state. Displaying a fabulous collection of vintage motorcycles dating from the 1910s to the present, the museum has been featured in several magazines. Biker buffs appreciate the exceptional variety and constantly changing array. In the back corner, the **Ace Café** offers gourmet hamburgers, Aussie meat pies, salads and desserts.

www.lonestarmotorcyclemuseum.com

Vanderpool, 830-966-6103

Most tourists visit Lost Maples in the fall, but it's pretty any time of year.
(courtesy Texas Parks and Wildlife)

Lost Maples State Natural Area is most popular in late October and November to see the blazing reds and golds of the bigtooth maples. But it's a lovely park the rest of the year, when the crowds are gone, the hiking trails almost deserted, and wildlife easier to observe. At the western edges of the Edwards Plateau, the **Sabinal River** has carved rugged limestone canyons creating a microclimate that makes a natural refuge for a remarkable diversity of plant and animal life, including more than 200 species of birds. To understand the park's geological history and find out why the bigtooth maple is found here, visit the interpretive exhibit in the park headquarters. The park has been minimally developed to protect its resources. Almost eleven miles of trails lead to scenic overlooks, spring-fed ponds, and several attractive primitive camping sites. An RV park near the entrance has 30 sites with water and electric hookups and restrooms.

www.tpwd.state.tx.us/spdest/findadest/parks/lost_maples
37221 FM 187, Vanderpool, 830-966-3413

Axis deer, known as "chital" in their native India, were introduced into Texas in the 1930s. (courtesy Al Buckner)

186

Sleep

Between Vanderpool and Leakey on scenic RR 337, the **Lodges at Lost Maples** offer comfortable cedar cabins with Texas décor, cathedral ceilings and hardwood floors; each accommodates 4-6 people and contains a fully equipped kitchen, casual dining area, fireplace and private porches with mountain views. Families like the bunk beds built into the walls and the baskets of toys and games by the fireplace. "The Sweetheart Suite" offers the perfect romantic getaway with a king size bed and two person Jacuzzi whirlpool tub. Owner Jeralyn adds thoughtful touches like birdseed and an information binder with information about the area. Enjoy spectacular sunsets from the hammock, then appreciate the non-city art of stargazing in the dark skies. Jeralyn will deliver breakfast – freshly baked pastries, fresh fruit, coffee and juice – to your door each morning.

www.lostmaplescabins.com
RR 337, Vanderpool, 877-216-5627

Bandera

Convention & Visitors Bureau
126 Hwy 16 South (½ block South of Main St.)
www.banderacowboycapital.com
830-796-3045; 800-364-3833

Self-proclaimed the **"Cowboy Capital of the World,"** Bandera keeps the frontier spirit alive with rodeos, western-wear stores, and a downtown area that looks like a movie set straight out of the Old West. On the courthouse lawn, a bronze monument honors the many National and World rodeo champions who call Bandera home.

Home to dance halls and dude ranches through the years, the cowboy culture and small-town hospitality is genuine. Established in the mid-19th century along the banks of the sparkling Medina River, today Bandera's population hovers right around 1000. Although the town gets an ample number of tourists, most of the shops lining Main Street sell western clothing and western art instead of antiques and fancy gifts. The saddle barstools and the "John Wayne Room" in the **O.S.T.** keep the memories of the cowboy era alive.

You can be a "dude" at a dozen or so working Dude Ranches and Guest Ranches in the scenic rolling hills around Bandera and get a taste of life in the Old West. Most activities involve the outdoors: horseback riding, swimming, golfing, fishing, hunting, hiking, and camping.

Riders in the "Celebrate Bandera" parade over Labor Day weekend.
(courtesy Al Buckner)

History

In 1853, a mill was established along the Medina River to saw the massive Cypress trees into shingles. Shortly after that, sixteen Polish families immigrated to Bandera to work at the shingle camp. A stunning reminder of their heritage is evident

in the **St. Stanislaus Catholic Church**, the second oldest Polish Catholic church in Texas. The adjacent Catholic Cemetery is a historical gem itself.
602 7th Street, 830-460-4712

Eclectic is the only word to describe the Recorded Texas Historic Landmark **Frontier Times Museum** with its diverse collection of relics. Historian/journalist J. Marvin Hunter founded the museum in 1927 when his collection of Western paraphernalia covered the walls and hung from the ceiling of his tiny office. Artifacts portray day-to-day life on the harsh frontier—clothing, tools, cooking utensils, firearms, saddles, and school books. As his friends found out about his growing museum, they began bringing their favorite "treasures" to add. So today you can see a Texas map made of rattlesnake rattles, a stuffed baby goat with two heads, an ornately-carved throne from a Venetian palace, shrunken heads from South America, and Englishwoman Louisa Gordon's collection of more than 400 bells from around the world. Photographs and Western art paintings hang in the gallery wing of the museum, a section devoted to local artists.
www.frontiertimesmuseum.com
506 13th St., 830-796-3864

Outdoors

The Cypress-lined **Medina River** flows through Bandera County and the City of Bandera. You can rent canoes, kayaks, and tubes to get an up-close view. Nearby **Medina Lake** is a popular boating and fishing lake. The scenic, 77-acre **Bandera City Park** provides picnic areas with barbecue pits and allows fishing and swimming in the Medina River. There's also a 9-hole Disc Golf Course in the park. Two 18-hole golf courses are open to the public: **Lost Valley Resort** and **Flying L Guest Ranch**. The countryside around Bandera is perfect for bicycling and horseback riding – more than a dozen ranches and stables offer horseback tours. More than 200 species of birds have been identified in Bandera County and excellent birding opportunities are available in the city park, Hill Country SNA and Lost Maples SNA.

Lost Valley Resort: 830-460-8008, 830-460-7958
Flying L Guest Ranch: 830-460-3001, 800-292-5134

Hill Country State Natural Area was opened to the public in 1984. Much of the nearly 5,400 acres of the most scenic Hill Country land was donated with the stipulation that it be preserved far removed and untouched by modern civilization. With its rugged canyons, rocky limestone hills, flowing springs, and majestic oaks, this undeveloped natural area protects a variety of wildlife and several species of birds. The recreational activities utilize the 36 miles of trails for horseback riding, hiking, and mountain biking. Limited camping, swimming, and fishing are allowed.

www.tpwd.state.tx.us/park/hillcoun
10600 Bandera Creek Rd., 830-796-4413

This guy's good! (courtesy Texas Tourism)

Scenic Drive

Probably the most scenic drive in the county starts in Bandera, goes west on Hwy. 16 along the Medina River through Medina where you pick up RR 337 to Vanderpool, then south on FM 187 through the Sabinal River Canyon to RR 470 northeast through Tarpley and back to Bandera. This loop allows you to cross the Medina and Sabinal Rivers often, and takes you to elevations with majestic panoramic views. For even more spectacular vistas, take RR 337 on west from Vanderpool to Leakey along hairpin curves through craggy canyons – one of the most dramatic drives in Texas. These trips show off some of the best natural scenery in the Hill County.

Night Life

Country Music, dancing and Honkytonks are an integral part of Bandera's history. The downtown area has several honky tonks, most with live music on weekends.

Established in the 1930s, **Arkey Blue's Silver Dollar Saloon** is probably the oldest honky-tonk in town. Entertainer/songwriter Arkey Blue has been performing since 1968 with the likes of locals Bruce and Charlie Robison and the legendary Ernest Tubb and Willie Nelson.

308 Main St., 830-796-8826

The **11th Street Cowboy Bar** is a popular destination for just about anybody. Touted as the "Biggest Little Bar in Texas," it always features first-rate live Country Western music, dance floor, patio, cold beer, and a lively crowd. Check the Events Calendar for frequent jam sessions, steak nights, special events, benefits and celebrations.

www.11thstreetcowboybar.com

307 11th St., 830-796-4849

Shop

Downtown Bandera is crowded with shops offering western wear, saddles and tack, antiques, fashion clothing and shoes, gifts, cedar and cypress furniture, and tons of cowboy themed souvenirs.

The Cowboy Store sells high quality Western wear, hats, boots and accessories for men and women.

www.thecowboystores.com

302 Main St., 830-796-8176

Gunslinger, a chic upscale Western Emporium, is the dream-come-true of Melissa Benge. Stuffed with an overwhelming selection of fabulous clothing, jewelry, and home décor, it's a special place for discriminating shoppers.

www.gunslingerofbandera.com

1107 Cypress St., 830-796-7803

Shoe Biz specializes in the latest fashion clothing and footwear. With an excellent selection and friendly sales ladies, it's a fun place to shop.

301 Main St., 830-796-8302

Eat

The O.S.T. has been a local hangout since it opened in 1921. Named for the **Old Spanish Trail** that passed through Bandera at one time, it's filled with authentic Western memorabilia like barstools with saddle seats, a wagon wheel chandelier, and a salad bar inside a covered wagon. The walls of the John Wayne dining room are. . . well, predictably lined with posters and photographs of the Duke and other cowboys. Some photos show John Wayne with ex-stuntman Rudy Robbins, now a Bandera resident and OST regular. Grub (that's "cuisine" in Texanese) is good country cooking and a variety of Tex-Mex, from real chicken-fried steak with cream gravy to chile rellenos and fajitas. The breakfast menu offers a diverse selection from cinnamon rolls or waffles to migas and egg enchiladas. Service is friendly and prices are reasonable.

305 Main St., 830-796-3836

You'll have to look for **Brick's** because it's behind River Oaks Inn at the west end of town. Overlooking the Medina River, the family-run, full service restaurant offers a varied menu from burgers and sandwiches to steaks and seafood. The food is fresh and well prepared and the service efficient.

www.bricksrivercafe.com

1205 Main St., 830-460-3200

Busbee's BBQ serves up some of the best barbeque in Texas. Period. The aroma lures folks into the corner restaurant with red-checkered tablecloths and ranch décor. The lean beef, sausage, ribs and chicken are well prepared and portions are large. Other offerings include burgers, sandwiches, and salads. Save room for the homemade pecan pie or peach cobbler. Service is Texas friendly and prices are reasonable.

319 Main St., 830-796-3153

The China Bowl, directly across from the Bandera County Courthouse, serves good Chinese food from a menu, not a buffet.

1203 Pecan St., 830-796-8494

In the midst of Bandera's cowboy grub, Chef Jason Boyd at **The Grotto Grille & Coffee Bar** has created an oasis of creative cuisine using fresh seasonal organic ingredients. Almost everything served is made on site. His hand-made pizzas are out of this world. The coffee bar serves only organic fair-trade coffee. Dinners on Friday and Saturday nights feature gourmet specials that would cost a fortune in a big city. The ambiance is a bit funky with local artwork and Jason-built tables, casual enough to encourage a nice lunch of dinner conversation. Shaded outdoor picnic tables are crowded in nice weather.

907 13th St., 830-796-9555

Sleep

Of course, there are motels, Bed and Breakfasts, guesthouses and cabins in and around Bandera, but most folks come for the **Dude Ranches.**

Since Roy Rogers and Dale Evans rode across the silver screen, folks have dreamed of living the cowboy life. Pretend to be dudes and dudettes while enjoying a similar lifestyle at one of the dude ranches and guest ranches around Bandera. Some are rustic, others could aptly be called resorts. Most offer an all-inclusive package consisting of overnight lodging, meals, horseback riding and/or instruction, swimming, fishing, nature trails, chuck-wagon cookouts and campfires. Nightly entertainment may include rodeos, hayrides, singing or storytelling around the campfire. But no two are alike; choose one based on your expectations and budget.

Five of the best are listed here, in alphabetical order. Most rates include lodging, three meals a day, horseback riding and activities. All have lower children's rates; most have group or weekly rates and/or special packages. Call for details. Without exception, the friendly owners and staff want their guests to enjoy themselves and experience the "cowboy lifestyle."

Hill Country Equestrian Lodge: the purpose here is not to keep you busy with a whirlwind of activities, but to offer a tranquil, idyllic place in an unspoiled, natural area of the Texas Hill Country. Diane and Peter are friendly hosts and will make you feel at home on this 275-acre ranch. Lodge guests also have access to the magnificent scenery and more than 40 miles of hiking and riding trails in the adjacent 5,500-acre primitive **Hill Country State Natural Area.** You may bring your own horse or ride one of the ranch's fine quarter horses. Western or English private lessons are available.

Guest accommodations are in luxury suites or secluded cabins nestled among live oaks. The décor is Early Texas Ranch and each has a kitchen, central heat/air, sunroom and wide porches; in addition, cabins have cathedral ceilings with limestone fireplaces. Dianne and Peter can arrange personal requests from spa services to romantic candlelight dinners.

The equestrian facilities feature first class accommodations for horses also, with a new horse barn with 8 stalls, tack room, and wash rack. Hookups for horse trailers with living quarters are also available. The ranch's Whole Horsemanship Program offers five and seven-day riding clinics for riders of any skill level.

www.hillcountryequestlodge.com

1580 Hay Hollar Rd., 830-796-7950

Mayan Dude Ranch: guests say it's the "part-of-the-family" feeling that sets this dude ranch apart—maybe because it really is a true family affair. Owners Don & Judy Hicks bought the Mayan in 1951 and reared 12 children here; all now help run the ranch and there are at least 30 grandchildren "in training." Just as remarkable . . . some of the guests are fourth generation! This ranch gets consistently high ratings for their hospitality, meals and activities.

Scenic trails wind through the 350 acres from the scenic Medina River to high atop the hills for a spectacular view of the valleys. Days and evenings are full of activities, food, fun, and entertainment.

Accommodations are in native rock cottages or more modern lodge rooms, comfortably furnished and equipped with microwaves and televisions (no phones or data ports), some with fireplaces.

You might be tempted to skip a trail ride to lounge by the pool or go swimming in the crystal clear Medina River, but don't skip any meals here—the Mayan is well known for its tasty grub, from outdoor barbecues to world-class dinners in the dining room.

www.mayanranch.com

830-796-3312, 830-460-3036

Rancho Cortez: here guests may enjoy traditional dude ranch fun or an invigorating fitness program or both. Larry & Mary Cortez's family-run guest ranch caters to personal service, horseback riding and fitness training. Riding is a great way to enjoy the rugged beauty of the landscape and since Rancho Cortez is adjacent to **Hill Country State Natural Area**, guests have access to over 40 miles of unspoiled trails. Ranch hands match horses to guests' riding levels, whether experienced equestrians or real city slickers and private riding lessons are available.

Modern accommodations, a large dining room and lodge, spacious porches, two pools (indoors and outdoors), and an outdoor covered deck and hot tub offer relaxation and relief from the Texas sun. A variety of accommodations include multi-bedroom Family Suites, hotel-style one-room units, individual cottages, and two bunkhouses for groups. Rates include three healthy, home-cooked Texas-sized meals a day, mostly prepared from scratch with fresh ingredients.

With abundant wildlife, meandering walkways, benches and swings, the ranch is an ideal escape from urban life. Another option is unwinding in the air-conditioned lodge with books, TV or games. The ranch offers activities for everyone from hayrides to birding to tubing. The Fitness Center includes classes with trained instructors, an air-conditioned gym, and water aerobics. The ranch chef even prepares "fitness cuisine."

www.ranchocortez.com

872 Hay Hollar Rd., 830-796-9339

Running R Guest Ranch: the focus at this small ranch is on their individualized horseback riding program. Guests of all skill levels are welcome and the friendly folks there are experts at matching horse to riders. A herd of 35 horses includes Paints, Appaloosas, Mustangs, Quarter Horses and children's ponies. Guests have direct access to the adjacent **Hill Country State Natural Area**, a 5500-acre primitive area with 40 miles of riding trails.

Accommodations are in western-style cabins, tastefully furnished with handmade cedar post furniture and with air-conditioning, refrigerator, sitting area, private front porch and lovely view.

The lodge is open 24 hours a day with its spacious gathering room furnished with cedar furniture and a comfortable seating area around the fireplace, satellite TV, pool table and board games. Freshly prepared, delicious breakfasts and lunches are usually served in the lodge (except when there's an outdoor BBQ or Cowboy Breakfast). They do not serve evening meals at the ranch so guests can explore on their own or try some of the many restaurants in Bandera.

Facilities include a lovely pool, badminton court, ping-pong table and walking trails lead through fields of wildlife, birds and wildflowers. Go for a late night swim, watch the sunset, or gaze at a bazillion stars after dark. Congenial owners, Ralph & Iris, also speak German.

www.texas-dude-ranches.com
9059 Bandera Creek Rd., 830-796-3984

Silver Spur Guest Ranch: here themed guest rooms and cabins are named after famous or notorious western characters like Wyatt Earp, Buffalo Bill and Calamity Jane. Each has a private bathroom and TV. Several are connecting to accommodate families and groups.

The 14,000 sq. ft. western lodge encourages relaxation with comfy couches in front of a rock fireplace, billiards table, player piano and a cabinet full of puzzles and games. A "hospitality room" at one end provides vending machines, a refrigerator, ice machine and pool towels. Perfect for family reunions, weddings or special events, the dining room seats up to one hundred.

Speaking of eating, you'll never go hungry at the Silver Spur. Breakfast, lunch, and dinner are served family style, often outdoors with campfire cooking or barbecues. Meals are home cooked and hearty comfort foods, finished off with homemade desserts like buttermilk pie or peach cobbler.

There's a 250,000-gallon Junior Olympic-sized swimming pool and a playground with swings, badminton, volleyball and horseshoe pitching area. Go horseback riding or hiking to explore the beauty of the 300-acre ranch. Or be lazy and relax in one of the rocking chairs lining the massive front porch which, incidentally affords a great place for watching the sunset or stars.

www.ssranch.com
9266 Bandera Creek Rd., 830-796-3037

Hill Country view. (courtesy Al Buckner)

Special Attraction

On Hwy. 173, about midway between Bandera and Kerrville, **Camp Verde General Store** is all that remains of Camp Verde, a one-time Army post on the banks of Verde Creek. The post was most famous for the "camel experiment" that was the brainchild of U.S. Secretary of War, Jefferson Davis. The idea was to use camels to carry supplies as the soldiers traveled west to El Paso and on through the desert to California because they could travel fast and needed little water. Camp Verde was established as operations headquarters and the first shipment of thirty-three camels and their Arabian and Turkish drivers arrived in 1856, followed the next year by a second shipment of forty-one more beasts.

The experiment was successful, but the project was abandoned. The general store, open only on payroll days, was built a mile from Fort Camp Verde because Army regulations prohibited the sale of intoxicants on the post. After the fort was deactivated in 1869, the store and post office continued to serve ranchers and settlers. The present two-story stone building was constructed after a turn-of-the-century flood swept away the original building.

Today, the store stands alone, a remarkable one-of-a-kind treasure. Inside you'll find an amazing array of products and upscale gift items from around the world: jewelry, artwork, collectibles, pottery, kitchenware and accessories, toiletries, purses, luggage, garden shoes, old-fashioned candy, jams & jellies & salsas, dips and chutneys. And camels, camels, camels. It's an adventure just to wander around and absorb the history. But the best time to go is lunch time – the café serves divine Deli sandwiches. Arthur's Delight is a yummy combination of turkey, grilled onions, Swiss cheese, and cranberry-jalapeno compote on sourdough bread.

A picturesque park just across the street on Verde Creek makes a great spot for a picnic or just to eat your ice cream and relax a while.

www.campverdegeneralstore.com

285 Camp Verde Rd. East, 830-634-7722

About 15 miles west of Bandera, Medina sports the title **"Apple Capital of Texas."** Love Creek Orchards' **Apple Store** is chock a block with innumerable apple- themed gift items, souvenirs, and other goodies. Choose fresh-baked apple strudel or pastries or a gargantuan apple pie from the bakery. Sample apple butter or dozens of jam varieties (apple pie jam is scrumptious), or enjoy a cone of apple ice cream or some fresh apple cider. And, of course, fresh apples are always for sale. The **Patio Cafe** also offers a nice lunch menu of specialty sandwiches, salads, and burgers.

www.lovecreekorchards.com

14024 Hwy. 16, 830-589-2588, 800-449-0882

Boerne

Convention & Visitors Bureau

1407 South Main St. in the Historic Kingsbury House

830-249-7277; 888-842-8080

visitboerne.org

Boerne (pronounced BURN-ee) is a fast-growing town just twenty miles northwest of San Antonio. Nestled among gently rolling hills, live oaks, and lakes, it boasts a less hurried pace and total escape from the big city treadmill.

It's a charming city with a character of its own, full of history and a rich German cultural heritage, still strong today. Dozens of antique shops, boutiques and specialty shops, restaurants, and galleries, mostly in restored historic buildings, line the main street of the rejuvenated downtown. Lovely pastoral parks with benches and fountains and tree-shaded neighborhoods invite you to sit a spell.

Every Second Saturday, Boerne comes alive with art. Galleries and restaurants around town showcase art from 5 pm to 8 pm. Enjoy a glass of wine and the latest offerings on the Boerne Art Scene.

Straight out of the Old West. (courtesy Enchanted Springs Ranch)

Attractions

The **Cave Without a Name** is one of Texas' best-kept secrets, probably because of the off-the-beaten-path location, about 11 miles from Boerne. But it's well worth finding because it's one of the prettiest caves anywhere. A big part of its attraction is the natural setting—no glitz or neon here. The living cave is privately owned and the owner is dedicated to education and preservation. Tours descend steps near the original opening, then follow well-lighted walkways to view the cave's spectacular crystalline formations—awesome stalactites and stalagmites, delicate soda straws, and polished flowstone. See the 40-scoop ice cream cone, the "Leaning

Tower of Boerne," and zillions of fossils from 100 million years ago when this area was part of the Gulf of Mexico.

So how did it get its funny name? In a contest held to name the cave when it opened to the public in 1939. The winning entry, from a local student, said it was "too pretty to have a name." So be it.

www.cavewithoutaname.com
325 Kreutzberg Rd. 830-537-4212

Enchanted Springs Ranch is an 86-acre working ranch that contains an "Old West Town" originally designed as a western movie set. Visitors enjoy seeing the buildings and facades as well as taking a tractor-wagon ride around the ranch to see some of the exotic animals. During the year, events include chuckwagon dinner shows, Wild West Days celebration, and a spectacular Cowboy Christmas. Check before you go because they may be filming a movie or having a private party.

www.enchantedspringsranch.com
242 Hwy. 46 West, 830-249-8222, 800-640-5917

The Guadalupe River near Hunt. (courtesy Al Buckner)

Outdoors

About 13 miles east of Boerne, **Guadalupe River State Park** sprawls over 1,900 acres of the most scenic, rugged landscape of the Texas Hill Country. The crystal clear Guadalupe River, lined with magnificent ancient cypress trees, bisects Guadalupe River State Park, always among the favorite spots for campers. With four miles of river frontage, it's perfect for swimming, tubing, canoeing, and fishing. Other activities include hiking, picnicking and bird watching. Visitors often encounter some of the park's abundant wildlife like white-tailed deer, coyotes, foxes, and armadillos.

Those who find some of the river towns too commercialized for their tastes will enjoy the more wilderness atmosphere at Guadalupe River State Park. The adjacent Honey Creek preserve offers nature programs and guided tours. A Texas State Park Store has quality gifts, nature-related items and books.

www.tpwd.state.tx.us/park/guadalup/guadalup.htm
3350 Park Rd. 31, 830-438-2656

Wine

Sister Creek Vineyards has been making award-winning Texas wines since 1988. The winery is located in a restored 1885 cotton gin between East and West Sister Creeks in an incredibly scenic area of the Hill Country. The Sisterdale Valley Historic District is listed in the National Register of Historic Places.

www.sistercreekvineyards.com
1142 Sisterdale Rd., Sisterdale, 830-324-6704

Shop

Girls, the historic downtown area offers almost unlimited shopping and browsing opportunities. A few good places to begin; **A Little Nature Store** is heaven for bird and nature lovers.

106 E. Theissen, 830-249-2281

The Tall Pony offers an eclectic assortment of gift items and collectibles and has a wonderful Ice Cream Parlor inside.

www.thetallpony.com

259 S. Main, 830-249-2009

Jac's has an incredible selection of splendid home décor and gift items.

170 S. Main, 830-249-3443

If you like to browse antique malls, check out **Boerne Emporium**.

179 S. Main, 830-249-3390

You'll find that **Simple Treasures** offers lots of vintage items for you to peruse.

195 S. Main, 830-249-5454

Mary Brogan's Irish Cottage displays all things Irish and features the Texas Tartan Tearoom which would make a lovely place for an afternoon tea break.

www.marybrogansirishcottage.com

455 S. Main, 830-249-6818

Rosewood Yarns has a fabulous selection of fine yarns, patterns, books, and notions.

www.rosewoodyarns.com

455 B S. Main; 830-248-1195

The Pewter Store has an excellent selection of, you guessed it, pewter items.

463 S. Main, 830-249-2765

It's Christmas every day at **The Christmas Shoppe**, where you will find everything you need for a festive yuletide.
132 S. Main, 830-816-2176

Calamity Jane's Trading Company offers a selection of home furnishings from around the globe.
www.calamityjanestradingco.com
322 S. Main, 830-249-0081

Ewe and Eye is an interesting needlework shop and toy store.
www.ewe-and-eye.com
512 River Rd., 830-249-2083

Eat

El Rio Mexican Restaurant offers a nice selection of tasty Mexican dishes. The folks at this family owned and operated restaurant hand make as much as possible on site and fresh, including the thin, crunchy chips and freshly made salsa. The spinach enchiladas are the best on the planet! Service is efficient and friendly. It's located in a strip shopping center so there's plenty of parking.
1361 S. Main, #601, 830-249-9846

Aromas entice folks to **Bear Moon Bakery** and its fresh-from-the-oven pastries and bread. Glass display cases near the front exhibit gorgeous cakes, pies, cookies, scones, muffins, and teacakes. The breakfast buffet is a winner with scrambled eggs, bacon, pancakes, fruit, yogurt, organic oatmeal and more. A favorite place for locals, Bear Moon serves organic, healthy, wholesome sandwiches and fresh soups for lunch. It's a great place for a shopping break to enjoy delectable pie and coffee, consistently voted the best coffee in Boerne.
401 S. Main, 830-816-2327

The **Cypress Grille** in the heart of historic downtown, features an upscale menu of innovative and well-prepared steaks, seafood, and chicken entrées. Chef Tom has quite a culinary pedigree, beginning as a graduate of the Culinary Institute of America. His creative lunch menu offers a nice array of salads, sandwiches, soups and a daily special; his signature dessert is Warm Bittersweet Chocolate Cake. The restaurant also presents an exceptional wine list. Since it was voted "Best New Restaurant in Boerne in 2006", the Cypress Grille has quickly become a popular dining destination.

www.cypressgrilleboerne.com
170 S. Main, Suite 200, 830-248-1353

The **Dodging Duck Brewhaus** serves up bratwurst, fish & chips, wraps and burgers. The menu features lots of snack foods to accompany beer like pretzels and nachos. Choose from a variety of award-winning brews made fresh on premises and enjoy them on the inviting deck with a nice view of the ducks hanging out in the creek.

www.dodgingduck.com
402 River Rd.; 830-248-DUCK

The hugely popular **Hungry Horse Restaurant** has a unique dining concept – small, medium and large entrée portions, a whopping variety of side veggies, home-style food and reasonable prices. All in all, a winning combination. Entrées include comfort food like chicken fried steak, liver & onions, fried catfish, meatloaf and pork chops. Choose from 18 sides from baked potatoes to fried broccoli. There are salads and sandwiches and burgers, too. And cobblers and pies and . . .

www.hungryhorseboerne.com
109 S. Saunders, 830-816-8989

Seven miles north of Boerne, **Po-Po Family Restaurant** serves home-style comfort foods, steaks, and seafood, but is best known for its fried chicken. An enormous collection of over 1700 commemorative plates covers the walls.

www.popofamilyrestaurant.com
829 FM 289, 830-537-4194

Between Boerne and Comfort lies a blue-ribbon destination for discriminating diners from around the Hill Country: The **Welfare Café & Biergarten**. In this rustic former general store and post office, German-born Gabrielle (Gaby) creates the most mouth-watering, divine culinary works of art from the freshest ingredients available. Gaby and the café have received rave reviews from every Texas magazine and newspaper, as well as *Travel & Leisure*, *Food & Wine*, and more. Choice steaks, seafood, and authentic German fare paired with fine wines, excellent service and intimate setting, it equals an unparalleled dining experience.

www.welfaretexas.com
223 Waring-Welfare Rd., 830-537-3700

Sleep

Ye Kendall Inn has been welcoming guests since 1859. Today the inn has 36 historic guest rooms, suites and cabins, all individually and tastefully appointed with modern comforts and luxurious amenities. Porches overlook Boerne's Town Square and Cibolo Creek. In addition to the guest accommodations, the property includes the noted **Limestone Grille** restaurant, **Tavern 128** with its historic bar and large double-sided fireplace, **The Aveda Spa**, **Studio YKI**, a wellness and fitness center, and **Kendall Provisions Co**, with a nice selection of wine, art, jewelry and books.

www.yekendallinn.com
128 W. Blanco, 800-364-2138

Paniolo Ranch – see Distinctive Destinations

Comfort

Chamber of Commerce
630 Hwy. 27
830-995-3131
www.comfort-texas.com

A small group of "freethinking" German immigrants traveling from New Braunfels in 1854 found this scenic site with its lush green hills and clear waters of Cypress Creek and the Guadalupe River so attractive, they named it Camp Comfort. Or they told their relatives to "komm fort" to join them in this area. Both tales sound believable, so take your pick.

Today this tiny town with its German heritage and historic High Street is a popular tourist area. Girls, you can shop until you drop in the antique shops and art galleries. Families can enjoy outdoor activities such as fishing, swimming, and camping. Comfort's downtown has one of the best-preserved business districts in Texas with over a hundred structures dating to the 1800s. Most of these buildings are listed in the National Register of Historic Places – pick up a self-guided walking tour map. Until it burned in 2006, the **Ingenhuett General Store** was the oldest continuously operating general store in Texas.

Old Tunnel Wildlife Management Area features... bats! Up to 3 million bats emerge from the abandoned railroad tunnel each summer evening. It's a spectacular sight! Predators also wait for them to emerge. You may see owls or red-tailed hawks catch the bats in flight.

As the smallest Wildlife Management Area in Texas, containing only 16.1 acres of land, it was acquired for the specific purpose of protecting and managing the seasonal colony of Brazilian free-tail bats. Educational exhibits give information on the life and history of the bats and the Wildlife Management Area.

The public may watch nightly, May through October, from an observation deck adjacent to the parking area. Two viewing areas are accessible to the handicapped. From Comfort, take Ranch Road 473 east. When it makes a right turn to Sisterdale, continue straight on Old Highway 9 (Old San Antonio Rd.) approximately eight miles. Old Tunnel Wildlife Management Area will be on the right.

tpwd.state.tx.us/huntwild/hunt/wma/find_a_wma/list/?id=17
10619 Old San Antonio Rd., 830-990-2659

Wine

The tasting room at **Comfort Cellars** is in a lovingly restored circa 1904 home. Winemaker Cathie enjoys creating unusual wines – orange chardonnay, raisin wine, and jalapeno wine, great for cooking or marinating – along with classic ones.

www.comfortcellars.com
723 Front St., 830-995-3274

Shop

Comfort has a Texas-wide reputation as a great place to go antiquing. Antique and specialty shops line both sides of High Street; more on 7th Street and side streets.

Eat

The inn is long gone, but the homey **Cypress Creek Inn Restaurant** remains. The small, friendly family owned restaurant has been in business more than 55 years. It serves up home cooked meals at reasonable prices – great chicken fried steak and real mashed potatoes. Homemade pies to die for.

www.cypresscreekinn.com
408 Hwy. 27, 830-995-3977

814, A Texas Bistro, in a converted post office, serves up a homemade soup, salad, burger and a few entrées for lunch, all good but nothing exceptional. Dinners, on the other hand, are definitely the creations of an innovative chef, using available fresh ingredients. Menu choices change weekly and diners may select from three entrées and three appetizers. A small, but nice, wine list offers few Texas wines.

www.814atexasbistro.com
713 High St., 830-995-4990

On historic Comfort's main street, **High's** offers great coffee and coffee creations as well as irresistible pastries. Lunchtime brings local folks for delicious homemade soups, salads, and sandwiches on artisan breads. They sell their coffee in bulk, along with mugs, kitchen accessories, and books.

726 High St., 830-995-4995

Sleep

It's romantic! It's peaceful! It's a great getaway! **Meyer Bed and Breakfast on Cypress Creek** is a grouping of a dozen historic houses, cottages and suites amid spacious grounds and ancient oaks and pecans on scenic Cypress Creek. The creekside setting is perfect for relaxing, fishing, canoeing, and enjoying nature. A hand built cedar fence surrounds the classic swimming pool and the lush landscaping recently earned the Meyer "Yard of the Month" from the Comfort Garden Club. Shane and Teresa Schleyer have created a delightful oasis, working over 13 years to extensively remodel, refurbish and update the accommodations. Each has a private bath, cable TV, WiFi, coffee maker, ironing boards, hair dryers, individual A/C and heat and antique furnishings; many have gas fireplaces, pillow top mattresses, Jacuzzi tubs for two and porches. Guests enjoy a full breakfast buffet each morning. The Schleyers are carrying on the tradition of hospitality begun in 1857 when one of the original buildings was a stagecoach stop on the Old Spanish Trail.

www.meyerbedandbreakfast.com

845 High St., 830-995-2304, 888-995-6100

Ingram – Hunt – Mountain Home

West Kerr County Chamber of Commerce
In the Bank of the Hills – Hwy. 27 in Ingram
830-367-4322
www.wkcc.com

Among the tree-covered hills and lush green valleys, along the Cypress-lined Guadalupe River, hide several youth or religious camps and guest ranches. They vary from rustic to luxurious and assure visitors an escape from the fast lane of the big cities. Kids learn to ride horses and to respect nature and its critters. The area is home to over 300 species of birds, 300 species of butterflies, 30 species of mammals, 36 species of snakes, 17 species of lizards, 10 species of turtles, 18 species of amphibians, 35 species of fish, 70 species of trees, 300 species of wildflowers, and 70 species of grasses.

It's also home to some delightful, small communities. At the confluence of the Guadalupe River and Johnson Creek, Ingram is a picturesque little community of about 2,000 people, surrounded by youth camps, vacation and retirement homes. Located on the Old Spanish Trail, it has a long history as a commercial center for the nearby area. Ingram moved away from the river after a major flood in 1932, and today the buildings of "Old Ingram Loop" now house art galleries, studios, and antique and gift shops. In the center of the "new" town at the Y at the junction of Highways 39 and 27, be sure to check out the beautiful western history murals that artist Jack Feagan of Ingram painted on the walls of the local lumber yard.

Dinosaurs once called the area home, judging by the tracks in the riverbed of the South Fork of the Guadalupe west of Hunt. Folks have been building summer vacation homes and camps in this scenic area since the 1920s. The country store is the social center and local hangout for tubers and canoers.

To early settlers driving teams pulling wagons loaded with supplies, the hills in this area must have seemed pretty high – like mountains. Mountain Home was on the stagecoach line from Kerrville to Junction and served the surrounding ranching community with its post office, churches, and facilities.

Arts

Hill Country Arts Foundation founded in 1958, has two main focuses: **The Duncan-McAshan Visual Arts Center** and the **Smith-Ritch Point Theatre**.

The Visual Arts Center consists of an art gallery, gift shop, and several studios offering year-round classes in every medium, for all levels of students. The Gallery, an 1100 sq.-ft. exhibit space, features displays of such various arts as watercolors, pottery, and quilts.

The Theatre has two venues: a modern, 722-seat outdoor amphitheater on the banks of the Guadalupe River and the indoor Pavilion Theatre, with seating for 140. During the summer, visitors enjoy lavish musicals and comedy productions at the outdoor theatre. The seats are comfortable and the scenery is superb. A variety of shows are staged inside in the smaller Pavilion during the winter months.

www.hcaf.com
120 Point Theatre Rd. South, Ingram
830-367-5120, 830-367-5121, 800-459-HCAF

In nearby Kerrville, the **Museum of Western Art** provides a splendid showcase for contemporary cowboy artists. Permanent and rotating collections as well as special exhibits give everyone access to the legend of the American West. Workshops by artists in residence are presented at the fine facility, which also contains an auditorium, museum store, and a major western art library. Educational programs for youth and adults promote a better understanding and appreciation of America's western heritage and art. The museum itself is a work of art, its bold architecture set amid ten acres of scenic Texas Hill Country. Built of exquisite wood and native stone, it presents a stately exterior and inside, polished mesquite floors are a rich complement to the western art.

www.museumofwesternart.org
1550 Bandera Hwy., 830-896-2553

This isn't what you'd expect to find in the middle of nowhere.
(courtesy Al Buckner)

Attractions

You'll find **Stonehenge II** two miles from Hunt on FM 1340. Travelers who suddenly come upon this unusual creation, without knowing it's there, gawk in amazement and joke about making a wrong turn. This replica, about half the size of the original Stonehenge in Salisbury, England is quite a surprise. It started with one big limestone rock left over after Hunt resident Doug Hill built a patio. He gave it to his friend, the late Al Shepperd who stood it on end in his yard and the rest just kind of happened. Making the other "stones" of rebar, mesh, and plaster turned into a sizable retirement project for Shepperd. The Shepperd family allows visitors, but please respect the fact that it's on private land.

In nearby Kerrville, visit the headquarters of nationally acclaimed jewelry artist **James Avery Craftsman**. Although his fine jewelry is sold in quality stores throughout the state, it's somehow more special if you buy it here. The headquarters is a complex of buildings of different architectural styles set on lovely landscaped grounds. At the Visitor Center and Showroom, you can view a short video about James Avery's rise to "stardom" from his original garage studio and see some of the specialty items created throughout the years.

secure.jamesavery.com
Harper Rd. at Avery Rd., Kerrville, 830-895-6800

The Y.O. Ranch has been a working ranch since 1880 when it was established by the pioneer Schreiner family, headed by Captain Charles Schreiner. Truly one of the great Texas ranches, it was once on a par with the King Ranch and the XIT. Still a working ranch and managed by the Schreiner family, it's committed to preserving the heritage of the ranch and the pioneer spirit for generations to come. Using careful wildlife management and conservation practices, the Y.O. is home to North America's largest collection of exotic animals, over 60 different species. On a tour, you'll learn the history of the ranch and visit ranch headquarters to see daily operations. You'll see the famous longhorn cattle as well as the exotics.

It's a place for appreciating the bounty of nature, of quiet and solitude. The Texas Friendly folks offer a variety of tour packages from day tours to horseback rides to authentic

Longhorn cattle drives – reservations required. It's a great place for group gatherings of all kinds. The ranch entrance is fifteen miles west of Mountain Home on Texas 41; ranch headquarters are eight miles north of the entrance.

www.yoranch.com

Mountain Home, 800-967-2624

Scenic Drive

West of Kerrville, Hwy. 39 wanders along the Guadalupe River and its many homes and summer camps nestled in the scenic hills. When it runs into RR187, turn south to Lost Maples State Park, Vanderpool and Utopia through the Sabinal Canyon.

Eat

Opened in 1949, the **Hunt Store** was the only meat market/grocery store in west Kerr County. The café came later, after customers begged the owners to cook something so they wouldn't have to drive to Kerrville to eat. It's still there in the back of the store. Bob's Cheeseburger is a popular favorite, but sandwiches and tacos are good, too. It's the local hangout for tubers and canoers and most everybody around.

Hwy. 39, Hunt, 830-238-4410

Overlooking the Guadalupe River, **Elaine's Table** is a gem. Elaine uses the best quality locally grown produce in creating her daily specials and offers some great sandwiches, soups, salads, and entrées at lunch. The dinner menu offers a varied selection of upscale fine dining options, from tenderloin to trout. Wednesday evenings are "Family Nights" – platters of great food are placed in the center of tables, family style. All the desserts are homemade and totally irresistible (crème brulee to die for).

www.elainestable.com

1621 Hwy. 39, Hunt, 830-238-4484

Queen B's English Tea Room and Antiques is a delightful "secret" tucked away in Ingram. Owners Bridget and John pay so much attention to detail and personal service, you'll feel like old friends by the time you leave. Specializing in fine English Tea, Queen B's serves tasty soups, sandwiches, salads and pastries. The tables are set with fine china and lace tablecloths making every meal a special occasion.

3375 Junction Hwy., Ingram, 830-367-4184

Sleep

Sunset Inn is conveniently located between Ingram, Hunt and Mountain Home and makes a great base from which to explore west Kerr County. Jane's home includes two lovely guest rooms along with her glorious art studio atop a hill overlooking the lush landscape. She shares her home with her husband, a pet Longhorn, and some miniature donkeys. The two guest rooms each feature a queen bed, satellite TV and private bath with corner soaker tub and separate shower. Guests have access to the Great Room with books and a big screen TV, the dining room and a screened back porch with magnificent views. A delicious breakfast is included, and other meals may be arranged with prior notice. The hosts serve excellent, healthy, well-presented food.

www.sunsetinn-studio.com

124 Oehler Rd., Ingram, 830-866-3336, 877-739-1214

At **Roddy Tree Ranch**, Gretchen and Keith invite folks to enjoy their "rustic oasis" with bed & breakfast ambiance in a campground resort/dude ranch-like setting between Hunt and Ingram. Thirteen cedar and rock guest cottages, on 40 acres along the tranquil Guadalupe River, are tastefully decorated and equipped with air conditioning/heating, a full kitchen with microwave and coffee maker, a VCR with video tape selection, and an outside bar-b-que grill and picnic table.

It's a place to enjoy a more peaceful way of life. If your kids are restless, teach them to pitch washers or horseshoes. They can go fishing, canoeing, swimming in the pool or the river, or play basketball, volleyball, or visit the barnyard animals at Pecan Springs Farm. Horseback riding is available for an extra charge.

www.roddytree.com
Hunt, 830-367-2871, 800-309-9868

Fredericksburg

Convention & Visitors Bureau
302 E. Austin
830-997-6523
www.fredericksburg-texas.com

Resourceful German pioneers settled Prince Frederick's town and the surrounding countryside. They constructed sturdy homes of native stone and timber that were built to last for generations. They designed exceptionally wide streets to allow a team of oxen and a wagon to turn around.

Fredericksburg still retains its German character in its architecture and cultural traditions. Many old timers still speak the language and local churches offer German services and songs. You'll probably hear as many "Willkommens" as "Howdys." The octagonal **Vereins Kirche Museum**, in Market Square, is a famous landmark (see below) and the historic downtown, with its restored Sunday houses and stone mercantile buildings, is listed in the National Register of Historic Places.

Today, visitors enjoy Fredericksburg's culture, history, food and wine. This little town is so packed with things to do that it's easy to make it a destination for several weekend getaways. There is something for Texas history buffs, military history buffs, food aficionados, outdoor enthusiasts, and especially, shopaholics.

Pick up walking tour maps and other brochures that give detailed information about things to see and do in the area or watch a 9-minute video for an overview at the Visitor Information Center, one block off Main Street at 302 E. Austin. The staff is knowledgeable and friendly – a stop there first is wise.

The surrounding hills are brilliant with spectacular wildflowers each spring and summer, drawing visitors from around the world. Summertime brings succulent, juicy, to-die-for peaches in the orchards around Fredericksburg, Stonewall, and Johnson City. Stop at any one of a number of fruit stands along U.S. Highway 290 that sell fresh peaches—some make homemade peach ice cream on site.

While you're in town, notice the street names. The first ten streets east of the courthouse—Adams, Llano, Linclon, Washington, Elk, Lee, Columbus, Olive, Mesquite, and Eagle—spell ALL WELCOME. And the streets west of the courthouse—Crockett, Orange, Milano, Edison, Bowie, Acorn, Cherry, and Kay invite you to COME BACK.

Germans enjoy life, and there's a celebration of some sort almost every weekend, but even if you can't join the festivities, you'll always find plenty of good food, music, and hospitality.

History & Museums

A "must see" for everyone is the exceptional **National Museum of the Pacific War**, dedicated exclusively to telling the story of Fleet Admiral Chester W. Nimitz and World War II in the Pacific. Nimitz was born in Fredericksburg in 1885 and spent part of his childhood in his grandfather's Nimitz Steamboat Hotel (c. 1852), now housing the original part of the museum. At his request, this historical center is dedicated to all those who served with him during WW II.

Located on a seven-acre site, the Center includes many separate parts. The **Admiral Nimitz Museum** highlights Chester and his early childhood, his appointment to the US Naval Academy, and his role during World War II. The new 23,000-sq.-ft. **George Bush Gallery** features unique, exhibits and walk-through dioramas and the Plaza of Presidents pays tribute to great men with memorial plaques mounted on monoliths.

A great place to relax, the **Japanese Garden of Peace** was a gift from the military leaders of Japan to the people of the United States, in honor of Fleet Admiral Chester W. Nimitz. A traditional Japanese garden, it was actually built in Japan, disassembled and shipped to Fredericksburg, then reassembled by the same craftsmen who built it in Japan. Outside the Japanese Garden of Peace you'll find the **Veterans' Memorial Walk**, a limestone memorial wall honoring those who served in the Pacific during WW II.

In addition to the indoor exhibits, a 3-acre outdoor museum about a block away displays an impressive collection of Allied and Japanese aircraft, tanks, guns and other large artifacts in the Pacific War Combat Zone. A recreated Pacific War battlefield, complete with foxholes, trenches, and bunkers provides a site for the Museum's living history and educational programs.

Adjacent to the museum, an outstanding bookstore offers a wide variety of books about World War II and Admiral Nimitz, limited edition signed posters and autographed prints of the Pacific War Series, as well as other WW II memorabilia.

www.nimitz-museum.org
340 E. Main St., 830-997-4379

The **Pioneer Museum Complex** was begun in 1956 when the Gillespie County Historical Society bought a pioneer home, smokehouse and barn and turned it into a small museum. Today this outstanding complex consists of a fabulous collection of authentic late-1800s and early-1900s limestone buildings set amid a natural setting on 3½ acres of land. Displays and exhibits feature impressive collections of artifacts and photographs depicting the life of early pioneers.

www.pioneermuseum.com
325 W. Main St., 830-990-8441
Hist. Soc.: 312 W. San Antonio St., 830-997-2835

Also operated by the Gillespie County Historical Society, the **Vereins Kirche** was the first public building in Fredericksburg, built by settlers in 1847. Vereins Kirche means Society Church, but it was nicknamed the Kaffeemühle (coffee mill) for its octagonal shape and is now a museum housing permanent and rotating exhibits and a gift shop offering books and souvenirs.

Marketplatz, W. Main St., 830-997-2835

Attractions

Wildseed Farms is the nation's largest working wildflower seed farm, with more than 200 cultivated acres producing 88 varieties of wildflower seeds only seven miles east of Fredericksburg. Another 800 acres are in production at the distribution center in **Eagle Lake**. Imagine vividly colored wildflowers as far as you can see! A treat any time of year, a visit in springtime is breathtaking – bluebonnets, red poppies and other springtime blooms. Stroll along the walking trails amid the flowers on a self-guided tour and take as many photographs as you wish. Create a bouquet in the pick-your-own fields. Relax on outside benches or enjoy food, beverages, and ice cream in the **BrewBonnet Biergarten's** covered patio area.

The focal point of Wildseed Farms is **Market Center,** designed after a horse barn in the Texas Panhandle. The 7,000-square-foot building has a 33-foot ceiling covering an exceptional gift shop with a gigantic selection of Texas-made products from Texas wine to hot-as-fire salsas, nature crafts and gifts, colorful pottery, birdhouses, T-shirts, gardening books, and of course, packages of flower seeds to take home. The nursery is well stocked with plants including herbs, roses, ornamentals, natives, trees and cacti.

Wildseed is the nation's largest working wildflower seed farm.
(courtesy Al Buckner)

A 3,000 sq. ft. **Butterfly Haus** was designed to create a habitat to attract, protect and nourish beautiful butterflies. Now visitors may enjoy hundreds of fluttering beauties inhabiting the Haus and learn about their amazing life cycle. Of course, butterfly-attracting plants are for sale in the nursery so you can plant them in your own garden.

Wildseed Farms has won a mile-long list of awards for its owner John R. Thomas, the company, the facility, the seeds, the flowers, the seed catalog and reference guide, Market

Center, an educational video and on and on. It's well worth a visit or two.

www.wildseedfarms.com

100 Legacy Dr., U.S. Hwy. 290 E, 800-848-0078

A trip to Fredericksburg isn't complete without a visit to the **Fredericksbug Herb Farm**. Bill Varney and his family raise organic herbs and flowers and use them to make natural products here on this environmentally conscious farm. The Texas Star garden is awesome! An antique windmill stands in the center of the five herb beds (medicinal, cosmetic, culinary, crafting and ornamental) that form a giant star. The retail shop, located in the historic limestone cottage that was the beginning of the operation, contains a vast array of gardening supplies, books, decorative accessories, statues, dried arrangements, and live plants seasonally. In addition, you'll find dozens of herbal lotions and potions, vinegars and seasoning mixes for your kitchen. The restaurant/tearoom menu reflects the fresh garden produce and herbs. A Day Spa in the garden, the **Quiet Haus** offers various services by appointment.

www.fredericksburgherbfarm.com

405 Whitney, 800-259-4372

Entertainment

Return to the golden era of Rock & Roll at **Rockbox Theater**. This awesome high-energy, talent-packed live musical comedy show is rated the number one tourist attraction in Texas on *Trip Advisor*. And it's G-rated – you may safely take your grandkids or grandma. Incredibly talented cast members sing, dance, play instruments and do amazing impersonations of Elvis, Sonny & Cher, appearing to have as much fun as the toe-tapping audience. A moving patriotic tribute closes every show. A real Blast from the Past!

www.rockboxtheater.com

109 N. Llano, 866-349-6688

Carey Dyer and Wendy Hearn perform at Rockbox Theater.
(courtesy Rockbox Theater)

Outdoors

Enchanted Rock State Natural Area – what a sight to see! It's truly a magical place. Listen carefully—can you hear the faint creaking and groaning the early Tonkawa Indians heard? The voices of spirits? Today, scientists explain that the moaning is made as the rock heats by day and cools by night—you may believe whatever you choose. Early Indian legends said this massive dome was the site of human sacrifices. Some tribes feared to set foot on it, some worshipped there, others used it as a meeting place because its height was visible for miles. Some believed ghost fires flickered along its crest on moonlit nights. All held it in awe and reverence.

The Rock is a huge, solid, pink granite dome that rises 425 feet above ground and covers 640 acres. It's the second-largest granite rock in the U. S. – the biggest being Stone Mountain in

223

Georgia. Its formation, as well as that of the surrounding Llano Uplift, began more than a billion years ago. A very short, very non-technical explanation is that tremendous pressure built up inside the earth but instead of erupting like a volcano, the molten magma stayed below the surface (some of it oozed through cracks) and gradually cooled, the minerals in it crystallizing to form granite. This also resulted in the formation of a unique area of rare minerals found only in a 30-mile radius around Llano. Llanite, a rare type of brown granite with sky blue crystals and rusty-pink feldspar, is found nowhere else in the world except in Llano County.

Designated a National Natural Landmark in 1970, Enchanted Rock was placed in the National Register of Historic Places in 1984. Owned by the Texas Parks and Wildlife Department since 1978, Enchanted Rock State Natural Area consists of more than 1,600 acres on the border between Gillespie and Llano Counties.

Today, it's a very popular site for picnicking, bird watching, hiking, rock climbing and rappelling. The diversity of "the rock" offers leisurely walks as well as challenging climbs. The climb is fun and the views are extraordinary! Weekends are extremely crowded. The parking lot has 270 spaces and when it's full, the park is closed.

But Enchanted Rock State Natural Area encompasses much more than just one rock. Huge granite boulders, hidden caves, and other fascinating formations are everywhere. Interpretive pamphlets available at park headquarters will help you identify some of them. An amazing variety of plants and flowers appear to grow out of solid rock. This nature lover's paradise is home to more than 500 species of vegetation and at least 150 species of birds.

Trail guides and maps are available at park headquarters. If you're planning a serious trip to the rock, you might want to pick up a copy of any of these: *Enchanted Rock State Natural Area: A Guide to the Landforms* by James F. Peterson, *On*

Your Way Up: A Trail Guide to the Top of Enchanted Rock by John Williams, or *Roadside Geology of Texas* by Darwin Spearing.

www.tpwd.state.tx.us/spdest/findadest/parks/enchanted_rock
16710 RR 965, 830-685-3636

Willow City Loop – see also Johnson City

About thirteen miles north of Fredericksburg on Hwy. 16, you'll come to FM 1323 and a small sign that says "Willow City." If it's springtime, turn right and begin a scenic drive through one of the most spectacular displays of bluebonnets and other wildflowers in the state. Turn left in **Willow City** and follow the signs. The narrow road crosses creeks and meanders through pastures and granite hills for about a dozen miles before it joins up with Hwy. 16 again. This entire route wanders through private land, so don't even think about climbing fences for better views or to see wildlife up close. You'll see plenty from your car. Keep a close eye out for whitetail deer, armadillos, jackrabbits, and other critters.

A short scenic drive leads to perhaps the most famous tiny Texas town, thanks to a song recorded by Waylon Jennings and Willie Nelson in 1977. **Luckenbach, Texas** was established as a trading post in 1849. Today, it consists of a general store and the historic 1887 Dance Hall. Storytellers, singers, and musicians may be found congregating around the store and strumming on Sundays.

www.luckenbachtexas.com
RR 1376, 8 miles SE of Fredericksburg, 830-997-3224

Shop

Fredericksburg is a true shopper's paradise! Blocks and blocks of Main Street, and connecting side streets are lined with more than 150 boutiques, art galleries and one-of-a-kind shops. Most do not carry "tourist kitsch," but fine quality goods of all kinds and descriptions. Several artists live and work here, crafting their marvelous jewelry, dulcimers, quilts, candles, etc. After you shop until you drop, stop in at one of the coffee shops or eateries where you can renew and keep going.

Don't be limited by this small list of favorites. Explore on your own – that's half the fun!

Dooley's 5-10-25 Store is an honest-to-goodness old-fashioned variety store established in 1923. You'll find yourself exclaiming, "I didn't know they still made those!" over and over as you walk the aisles through kitchen gadgets, ribbons and hats, ladies' hankies, toys and dolls, washtubs and cloth diapers. It's a nostalgic experience for adults, but you may have to explain some items to kids. They don't accept credit cards.

131 E. Main, 830-997-3458

Der Kuchen Laden is located in the historic Keidel Memorial Hospital building on Main Street. The upscale kitchen shop has several rooms stuffed with fine cookware & bakeware, kitchen tools, cutlery, gadgets, cookbooks, tableware and linens, cookie cutters and molds, gourmet foods and teas.

www.littlechef.com
258 E. Main, 830-997-4937

Rustlin' Rob's Texas Gourmet Foods has an enormous variety of gourmet foods, homemade fudge, salsa, BBQ sauces, syrups, desert toppings, jams, jellies, preserves, marmalades, meat rubs and sauces, jalapeno products, dips, soup mixes, pickles, honey, peanut butters, sugar free items, and a special room chock a block with nothing but a zillion kinds of hot sauces. The best part – you can taste most of them!

www.rustlinrob.com
121 E. Main, 830-997-7969

226

Don't miss a visit to **Chocolat.** In 1984, Lecia Duke began making truffles based on a centuries old European process known as Liquid Praline (liquid center chocolates) after apprenticing under a Swiss master Chocolatier. Each batch is handcrafted using her own variation of the Swiss technique of spinning a fine sugar shell around the liquid center, then covering it in top-quality chocolate. The centers are usually good alcohol, fruit nectar or coffee. What all this means to you is a first bite of rich chocolate, followed by a burst of sugar and warm liquid. Heavenly! Try something exotic like Crema d'Almendrado Tequila, a zingy combination of tequila, almond and chocolate.

www.chocolat-tx.us
330 W Main St., 830-990-9382, 800-842-3382

The Grasshopper & Wild Honey offers an extensive selection of quality German nutcrackers and beer steins, collectibles, crystal, gifts, and fine art, pottery, bronze sculpture and wood art.

www.grasshopperfbg.com
113 E. Main, 830-997-5012

Stonehill Spinning has a wonderful selection of materials and books for weaving, knitting, or rug hooking. The owner and staff are knowledgeable and helpful. They offer some great classes, too.

www.stonehillspin.com
109 E. Ufer, 830-990-8952

Salt Branch Outpost displays antler art as well as other fine home décor, mesquite furniture and gift items.

www.saltbranchoutpost.com
257 W. Main, 830-990-4449

One of the most unique shops has to be **Phil Jackson's Granite and Iron Store.** It's amazing what Phil can do with granite and iron, creating incredible furniture of all kinds and home décor accent pieces.

www.granite-iron.com
206 E. Main, 830-997-4716

Fredericksburg Coffee & Tea offers a great selection of coffees and loose teas, including certified organic Fair Trade coffees. They serve breakfast and lunches featuring vegetarian wraps, Gyros, German sausage wraps, Panini grilled sandwiches, not to mention freshly baked scones and apple strudel.

www.fredericksburg-coffee.com
338 W. Main, 830-997-8327, 800-558-3193

Wine

Several vineyards and wineries surround Fredericksburg (see also Stonewall and Johnson City) including:

- **Bell Mountain Vineyards**, 463 Bell Mountain Rd., 830-685-3297, www.bellmountainwine.com
- **Chisholm Trail Winery**, 2367 Usener Rd., 830-990-2675, www.chisholmtrailwinery.com
- **Fredericksburg Winery**, 247 W. Main St., 830-990-8747, www.fbgwinery.com
- **Grape Creek Vineyards**, 10587 Hwy. 290 East, 830-644-2710, www.grapecreek.com
- **Torre di Pietra Vineyards/Winery**, 10915 Hwy. 290 E, 830-644-2829, www.texashillcountrywine.com

Eat

One of the best reasons to visit this charming Old World town is to dine at restaurants offering German, Italian, Mexican, Southwestern, and Texas cuisine. Others specialize in home cooking, bar-b-que, or bratwurst and beer. Be sure to visit one of the great bakeries on Main Street for German pastries and fresh breads. Note: many restaurants are closed on Sunday and/or Monday.

For authentic German food, try **Der Lindenbaum**, featuring schnitzel, steaks, homemade breads and scrumptious strudel and Black Forest cake. The restaurant is located in a beautiful historic limestone building built by the German pioneers who founded Fredericksburg over a century ago. There is live music in the Biergarten on weekends.

www.derlindenbaum.com
312 E. Main, 830-997-9126

Auslander Biergarten & Restaurant serves German cuisine, as well as award-winning steaks, seafood, sandwiches, and homemade desserts. It also features the largest selection of beers in the Hill Country, and live music every Thursday through Saturday.

www.theauslander.com
323 E. Main, 830-997-7714

Engel's Deli serves breakfast and lunch only and is known for homemade strudel and desserts.

320 E. Main, 830-997-3176

Girls, for a lovely lunch, visit **The Peach Tree Restaurant and Gift Gallery** for a nice selection of freshly prepared soups, salads, sandwiches, quiches and decadent desserts. The gift shop sells gourmet foods, cookbooks, body care products, handbags, pottery and a variety of gift items.

www.peach-tree.com
210 S. Adams, 830-997-9527

Another good choice is **Rather Sweet Bakery & Café** featuring luscious pies and cakes, huge cookies and brownies and melt-in-your-mouth scones, all made from scratch. Pastry Queen Rebecca Rather also serves delicious soups, salads, hot and cold sandwiches and a daily special for lunch.

www.rathersweet.com
249 E. Main, 830-990-0498

Touted as the oldest brew pub in Texas, **Fredericksburg Brewing Company, Inc.** specializes in brews, but serves a wide variety of burgers, sandwiches, chicken fried steak, and German sausages and schnitzels.

www.yourbrewery.com
245 E. Main, 830-997-1646

Another casual place, **Cranky Frank's BBQ** has great Texas barbecue with all the fixin's.

www.crankyfranksbbq.com
1679 S. Hwy. 87, 830-997-2353

Hondo's on Main is part bar, part live Texas music venue, and part restaurant with great burgers, sandwiches, salads, Mexican food, and a wide variety of proper entrées as well as tasty bar food.

www.hondosonmain.com
312 W. Main, 830-997-1633

Fredericksburg also has some fine dining establishments with award-winning chefs. **August E's** offers gourmet cuisine with a European flair, quality steaks and seafood, and exceptional service.

www.august-es.com
203 E. San Antonio St., 830-997-1585

Hill Top Café is a former gas station/beer joint and just funky enough to be chic. The décor features an old jukebox and mounted deer heads. The food is outstanding, the menu an interesting combination of Texas-Cajun-Greek. You'll hear live jazz, blues, or boogie-woogie on the piano Friday and Saturday nights.

www.hilltopcafe.com

10661 U.S. 87 North, 11 miles NW of Fredericksburg

830-997-8922

The Southwestern-inspired **Navajo Grill** features a fine seasonal menu New American cuisine served on white tablecloths in the formal dining room or in a more casual ambiance of the stone patio by a courteous and efficient staff. Extensive wine list and full bar.

www.navajogrill.com,

803 E. Main, 830-990-8289

Austin's – The Restaurant at Rose Hill Manor – see Distinctive Destinations below

Troisi's Italian Ristorante – see Trois Estate, Distinctive Destinations below.

Sleep

Many visitors come to Fredericksburg to stay in one of more than 300 bed and breakfast inns and guesthouses scattered about the area.

B&Bs and guesthouses are distinctively different. Some travelers like the pampering, service, and interaction with hosts and other guests at a traditional B&B, others prefer the privacy of a guesthouse. They're both worlds away from chain motels.

With traditional B&Bs, expect a full, sometimes family-style breakfast. The owner or innkeeper usually lives on premises, and other guests will usually be present. If you decide to stay in a guesthouse, you'll find that if breakfast is included, it will be a continental breakfast left in the refrigerator. On the other hand, guests have use of the whole house to themselves.

"Sunday Houses" are unique to the German farming communities of Texas. Early settlers in the Fredericksburg area were given ten acres in the country and a half-acre town lot for each man 21 years of age or older. They built tiny one-room homes on the town lots so their families could come into town to shop and socialize on Saturday, spend the night and go to church Sunday morning before returning to their farms. Today, people are renovating many of the remaining Sunday Houses to create charming guesthouses.

No two are alike – you might choose a restored country barn, a rustic log cabin, a turn-of-the-century rock cottage or Sunday House. Aside from basic comforts, amenities and décor may differ greatly. Some are frilly and romantic with wine, cheese and whirlpools for two; others may be more rustic and family oriented with TVs and horses. Do your homework to match one with your needs, or use one of the several reservation services in town.

Gastehaus Schmidt is one of the oldest and the largest.
www.fbglodging.com
231 W. Main, 830-997-5612, 866-427-8374

The Fredericksburg Convention and Visitors Bureau operates an all-inclusive lodging website for Fredericksburg and Gillespie County.
www.fredtexlodging.com

Some exceptional B&Bs are: **Palo Alto Creek Farm** offers total luxury in a peaceful country setting under ancient Live Oaks; historic landmark property on Palo Alto Creek. Fabulous Barn Suite and Log Cabin, each with a private spa room (packages available), fireplace, Jacuzzi.
www.paloaltocreekfarm.com
90 Palo Alto Ln., 800-997-0089

Historic Palo Alto Creek Farm now offers luxurious accommodations.
(courtesy Al Buckner)

The **Schandua Suite** is an elegant 1340-sq. ft. suite on the second floor of the historic 1897 Schandua Building in the heart of downtown. Every amenity imaginable, fine antique furnishings, private balcony overlooking a secluded courtyard.
www.schandua.com
205 E. Main, 888-990-1415

Das Garten Haus, a traditional B&B only a few blocks from Main Street, has three guest suites with private entrances and lovely landscaped New Orleans-style courtyard (owner is a horticulturist). Gracious hosts serve a full breakfast in the dining room each morning.
www.dasgartenhaus.com
604 S. Washington, 800-416-4287

Camp David Bed & Breakfast would be perfect for girlfriend getaways! Five amenity-laden private cottages, appointed with English Country décor, surround a secluded garden patio area. Cottages have fully-equipped kitchens, lots of space to gather and lovely porches.

www.campdavidbb.com
708 W. Main, 830-997-7797, 866-427-8374

The Cottages at Limestone on Main offer three private cottages, each with luxurious linens, cable TV, full kitchen and rocking chairs on the front porch. A covered pavilion is an ideal place for groups to gather. Congenial hosts deliver a gourmet breakfast each morning on a silver tray.
www.cottagesatlimestone.com
706 W. Main, 830-997-8396, 866-330-1736

Rose Hill Manor – see Distinctive Destinations

Trois Estate at Enchanted Rock – see Distinctive Destinations

Johnson City - Stonewall
Visitor & Tourism Bureau
406 W. Main
830-868-7684
www.lbjcountry.com

About 30 miles east of Fredericksburg, Johnson City became famous in 1963 when native son Lyndon Baines Johnson was sworn in as the 36th president of the United States. He boasted constantly that he hailed from the most beautiful land in the Texas Hill Country. While he was in office, he brought important guests from around the world to his "Texas White House." The ensuing publicity and increased tourism brought new life to Johnson City. LBJ's boyhood home is open to the public, as well as the LJB State and National Historical Parks.

In the spring and summer, a colorful kaleidoscope of wildflowers, so beloved by Lady Bird Johnson, carpet the countryside. A popular Wildflower Loop from Johnson City goes north on US 281 to FM 1323 to FM 1320 to US 290 and back to Johnson City. Most of the attractions of this area are related to the natural beauty of the land.

Attractions

Lyndon B. Johnson National Historic Park and LBJ State Park – to appreciate the childhood of former President Lyndon B. Johnson, visit both districts of this National Park, the Johnson City district and the Johnson Ranch district near Stonewall. Although born on the ranch in Stonewall, he spent many years in Johnson City, named after his pioneer ancestors. The frame house where he lived while attending public school is furnished with family items and period furniture. The Visitor Center features information and exhibits telling the story of our 36th President, his roots in his beloved Texas Hill Country, and its influence on him. About 15 miles west of Johnson City, near Stonewall, is the Johnson Ranch where LBJ was born. Along the banks of the Pedernales River, you'll see the "Texas White House," several original and reconstructed buildings, and the family cemetery.

www.nps.gov/lyjo
830-868-7128
www.tpwd.state.tx.us/spdest/findadest/parks/lyndon_b_johnson
830-644-2252

At **Pedernales Falls State Park** you can swim, tube, fish, hike, ride your horse or mountain bike, picnic, camp, bird-watch, or just relax and enjoy nature at its best in this 5200-acre State Park along the banks of the **Pedernales River**. Pedernales means "flint" in Spanish, and although it doesn't look like it, most locals pronounce it "pur-den-alice." The park harbors abundant wildlife (white-tailed deer, armadillos, rabbits, coyotes, raccoons) and more than 150 species of birds.

A covered bird viewing station with feeders offers a chance for an excellent up-close and personal experience.

www.tpwd.state.tx.us/spdest/findadest/parks/pedernales_falls
2585 Park Rd. 6026. 830-868-7304

Willow City Loop – see also Fredericksburg

If you're going to drive the **Willow City Loop** from Johnson City rather than Fredericksburg, take Hwy. 281 north from Johnson City a few miles to FM 1323, then turn left. This takes you through nearly 25 miles of scenic countryside to Willow City. Follow the signs for the loop.

Wine

Between Fredericksburg and Stonewall, **Becker Vineyards** boasts 46 acres of vineyards, a 3-acre lavender field reminiscent of Provence, a 10,400 sq.-ft. winery in a reproduction of a 19th-century stone barn, tasting room and gift shop, and a reception hall/ event center – all surrounded by peach orchards and fields of lavender and native wildflowers. Their award-winning wines are popular in Texas and have been served at events and competitions around the globe, including the White House.

www.beckervineyards.com/index2.htm
464 Becker Farms Rd., Stonewall, 830-644-2681

Texas Hills Vineyard, located in the gentle hills of the Pedernales River Valley, produces wines with an Italian influence. When Kathy and Gary saw that the soil and land were much like the Tuscan countryside, they planted grapes associated with Italian wines. They have a wine club and several culinary events throughout the year and an annual grape stomp in August – remember that *I Love Lucy* episode?

www.texashillsvineyard.com
878 RR 2766, Johnson City, 830- 868-2321

Shop

Eclectic doesn't begin to describe the offerings of The **Black Spur Emporium**. A seemingly endless variety of items includes cowboy hats, metal art, lamps and shades, hand-carved tables, kitchen items, jewelry, paintings, candles, pottery, Western home décor, cowhides and horns, Mexican glass, furniture, chandeliers, mirrors, crosses, greeting cards and live plants. And more!

www.blackspuremporium.com
100 W. Main, 830-868-7675

Several antique malls and gift shops are scattered about town. **The Historic Pearl Antique Mall & Tearoom**, located in a former 1890s hotel, is bursting with lovely antiques and collectables.

www.historicpearl.com
201 N. Nugent, 830-868-2711

Eat

Don't let the rustic appearance inside the old lumber yard complex fool you. Inside **The Silver K Café**, you'll find white tablecloths and the motto: "Rustic Elegance with Texas Pride." This is a nice restaurant with excellent food and great Texas wines. The Sunday buffet is extremely popular, as are the many special events held at the Silver K.

www.silverkcafe.com
209 E. Main, 830-868-2911

Recently featured in a *Texas Monthly* magazine article about the Top 40 Small Town Cafés, **Hill Country Cupboard** has menus glued on paper bags. Friendly waitresses serve up comfort food like chicken-fried steak and hand-breaded pork chops with a large selection of sides including fried okra and black-eyed peas, cornbread muffins and German potato salad.

An in-house bakery fills two dessert cases with freshly baked strudels, pies and cookies.

www.hillcountrycupboard.com

101 Hwy. 281, 830-868-4625

Blanco

Chamber of Commerce

312 Pecan Street

830-833-5101

www.blancochamber.com

Touted as the **Lavender Capital of Texas**, Blanco is a year-round destination for those wanting a peaceful getaway, yet still be in the midst of the many attractions of the Texas Hill Country. Twelve miles south of Johnson City, Blanco hosts a Lavender Festival each June drawing visitors from all over the state. The rest of the year, it's a quiet little town of about 1,500 folks with a few B&Bs, shops and eateries and a delightful state park.

Lavender farms in the area include:

- **Texas Lavender Hills Farm & Market**, 5110 Kendalia Rd., Blanco; 830-833-9183; www.texaslavenderhills.com
- **Lavender Hill**, 1378 River Run, Blanco; 830-833-9097; www.lavenderhilltx.com
- **Blanco River Lavender Company**, 4136 RR 1623, Blanco; 830-833-4494; www.blancoriverlavenderco.com
- **Hill Country Lavender**, 4524 Hwy. 281, Blanco; 830-833-2294; www.hillcountrylavender.com
- **Miller Creek Lavender**, 8453 Miller Creek Loop, Johnson City; 512-934-1616; www.millercreeklavender.com

- **The Meadows at Flat Creek**, 852 Flat Creek Rd., Johnson City; 830-385-5336; www.lavendermeadow.com
- **Hummingbird Farms**, 9340 Hwy. 290, Johnson City; 830-868-7862; www.hummingbirdlavender.com

Attractions

An excellent example of Second Empire style architecture, the **Old Blanco County Courthouse** (1885-6), a Recorded Texas Historic Landmark, sits proudly in the heart of downtown Blanco. Used only four years as a courthouse – the county seat was moved to Johnson City in 1890 – it's been used as a bank, school, office building, opera house, and even a hospital. Today it serves as a Visitor Center and gift shop.

Blanco State Park sits nearly in downtown Blanco, the only state park inside a city limit and the second smallest state park in Texas. It's a beautiful park with crystal spring waters and centuries old Live Oaks. Original developments were made along the banks of the Blanco River by the CCC in the mid-1930s.

www.tpwd.state.tx.us/spdest/findadest/parks/blanco
830/833-4333

Shop

Jan and John Brieger showcase their stunning handcrafted stoneware pottery as well as works of more than 20 other artists in their huge store on the north side of the town square at **Brieger Pottery**.

www.briegerpottery.com
town square, 830-833-2860

Two Friends offers gifts, jewelry, clothing and accessories.

405 Main St., 830-833-1300

239

On the Square sells clothing, shoes and gifts.
405A 3rd St., 830-833-0405

Find antiques and home décor at **The Vintage Cottage**.
508 4th St., 830-833-5709

Heron's Nest Herb Farm specializes in high quality herbs for culinary and medicinal uses, classes and events.
www.heronsnestherbfarm.com
1673 River Bend Dr., 830-833-2627

Eat

Located on the town square, **Riley's Bar-B-Q** serves up really great Texas barbeque.
www.rileysbarbq.com
318 4th St.; 830-833-4166

The **Rockin' R Steakhouse** offers fine steaks, seafood, chicken and pork, grilled on an open flame grill. As much as possible is made fresh on site, including the delicious homemade bread. The lunch menu features sandwiches, burgers, soups and salads as well as daily specials. Recently opened for breakfast, the Rockin' R's chef makes gooey sticky buns and other fresh pastries in addition to traditional breakfast offerings.
www.rileysbarbq.com
318 4th St., 830-833-5783

Oso's Mexican Grill & Cantina features good fresh, handmade Mexican dishes. The lunch menu also includes burgers, sandwiches, soups and salads.
306 Pecan, 830-833-1304

Uptown Blanco is a unique facility with big plans. In one of the oldest buildings on the square, the restaurant is open Thursday-Sunday, offering a wide variety of well-prepared food and a nice wine list. Billing itself as an Entertainment Center, plans include an art center, theater, ballroom and tavern in addition to the restaurant. Currently, the lovely park-like courtyard is available for weddings, concerts and community events and the Uptown Blanco Art Center and Frame Shop offers painting and pottery classes and custom framing at reasonable prices.

www.uptownblanco.com

317 Main St., 830-833-1579

Sleep

If you'd like to stay, motels, guesthouses, B&Bs, and cabins offer overnight accommodations in Blanco and nearby Johnson City.

Red Corral Ranch – see Distinctive Destinations.

Wimberley

Chamber of Commerce

512-847-2201

www.wimberley.org

Nestled among picturesque hills, fields of spring wildflowers, magnificent live oaks, and giant cypress trees along Cypress Creek and the Blanco River, Wimberley is a charming little village. Its business area (not a town square, more like a triangle with branches) is a treasure trove of artists' studios and galleries, specialty shops, and eateries. Special events take place throughout the year and **Wimberley Market Days**, held on the first Saturday of each month, is the second largest outdoor flea market in the state.

241

Arts

The Emily Ann Theatre, named for a local high school student killed in a car wreck, was built entirely by community volunteers, friends, and family. Now one of the largest permanent outdoor stages in the country, it's the perfect venue for concerts, plays, reunions, and parties. Each summer, Wimberley High School's "Shakespeare Under the Stars" productions are held here. The facility also includes beautifully landscaped grounds and picnic areas with spectacular views.

www.emilyann.org
512-847-6969

Located on Rocky River Ranch, the **Corral Theatre** is a unique outdoor walk-in theater that shows first-run movies Friday and Saturday from Memorial Day to Labor Day, and Sundays, too, on holiday weekends. The shows start at dark-thirty; take your own lawn chair. Refreshments are available at the concession stand. Check the website to see what's playing. All films are family rated.

www.corraltheatre.com
100 Flite Acres Rd., 512-847-5994

Attractions

Bella Vista Ranch, designed to emulate a traditional Tuscan farm, is home to the family-run First Texas Olive Oil Company. With more than 1000 olive trees and an Italian olive press, they have been producing fresh olive oil since 2001. True to the Italian image, the farm also has grape vines and a winery – **Bella Vista Cellars**, a boutique winery handcrafts a few wines, including a popular Blackberry Wine.

www.texasoliveoil.com
3101 Mt. Sharp Rd., 512-847-6514

Wimberley Glass Works was established by glass artist Tim deJong in 1992 after he fell in love with the Hill Country while on vacation the year before. What began as a small shop with a few lawn chairs has grown to an air-conditioned facility with seating for ninety. Tim has built his little business into the Southwest's award-winning premier Art Glass studio. Watch free glassblowing demonstrations to explain the tools and techniques of crafting molten glass into fabulous art.

www.wgw.com
6469 RR 12, 800-929-6686

Scenic Drive

RR 32 runs along a ridge called the **"Devil's Backbone"** from RR12 about 4 miles south of Wimberley to U.S. 281 south of Blanco. Overlooks provide spectacular views.

Shop

Girls, here's another shopping paradise! Spend the day on the town square – which isn't really a square, more like a triangle – and Ranch Road 12 going through town.

Kiss the Cook displays an amazing array of the latest, top-quality kitchenware and accessories, great gadgets and gift ideas. They also present fabulous cooking classes with guest chefs and culinary experts.

www.kissthecooktx.com/5039042_13735.htm
201 Wimberley Square, 512-847-1553

The River House is chock a block with great home décor and gift items – colorful pottery, linens, tableware, glassware, furniture, folk art, soaps and lotions, designer jewelry and handbags, and special candies and goodies.

www.riverhousewimberley.com
104 Wimberley Square, 512-847-7009

Interior Elements offers excellent interior design services, fine furniture, lighting and accessories.

www.interiorelements.net

13600 Ranch Rd. 12, 512-847-8440

Wall Street Western is an upscale western boutique featuring the latest in apparel and accessories for the urban cowgirl.

www.wallstreetwestern.com

13904 Ranch Rd. 12 #2, 512-847-1818

Dovetails of Wimberley features high quality ladies wear, fine lingerie, custom accessories, jewelry and fragrances.

www.dovetailsofwimberley.com

13701 Ranch Rd. 12, 512-847-1263

On the square, the **Old Mill Store** encompasses more than 7,000 sq. ft. of merchandise – furniture, lamps, accessories, jewelry and handbags, candles, gifts, artwork, gourmet foods.

www.oldmillstore.com

14100 Ranch Rd. 12, 512-847-3068

Star Antiques displays vintage lamps, chandeliers, and light fixtures. They also offer repair and restoration services.

www.starantique.com

301 River Rd., 512-847-9970

Just north of Wimberley, **The Old Oaks Ranch Fiber Arts Center** is a working alpaca ranch that offers classes by talented instructors in spinning & weaving, dyeing, knitting, felting, and more. The shop carries a magnificent collection of fibers and fabrics as well as instruction and pattern books, looms and wheels, and accessories.

www.theoldoaksranch.com

601 Old Oaks Ranch Rd., 512-847-8784

Eat

There's a lot to choose from – Bar-B-Q, pizza, fast food, a deli, tearooms, and a couple of fancier places. Several pizza and fast food chains have names you'll recognize. **Juan Henry's** features great gourmet burgers, sandwiches, salads, beef, chicken and seafood entrées and Tex-Mex inside or on the outside deck.

www.juanhenrys.com
500 River Rd., 512-847-1320

The **Leaning Pear Café** specializes in fresh soups, salads and sandwiches.

www.leaningpear.com
111 River Road; 512-847-7327

Ino'z is a sports bar offering great burgers and casual dining overlooking Cypress Creek.

14004 Ranch Rd. 12, 512-847-6060

Miss Mae's Bar-B-Q serves up mouth-watering Texas barbeque for indoor or outdoor dining or carryout.

www.missmaesbbq.com
419 FM 2325, 512-847-9808

Marco's Italian Restaurant is the place for authentic Italian food and great pizzas. The Tiramisu is awesome!

303 Wimberley Square, 512-847-0742

Wimberley Pie Company is a hard place to resist. Pastry Heaven – an amazing array of pies, cookies and cheesecake.

www.wimberleypie.com
13619 RR 12, 512-847-9462

Sleep

Wimberley is one of those little towns with dozens of cabins and cottages and cute B&Bs scattered about. Some are in town, others on the river or secluded in the countryside. To find one that meets your needs, call one of the Reservation Services: **All Wimberley Lodging** or **Hill Country Accommodations**.

www.texashillcountrylodging.com
800-460-3909, 512-847-3909
www.texasvacation.com
800-926-5028, 512-847-5388

Named one of the "Top Twelve Romantic Inns of Texas" by the *Dallas Morning News*, **Blair House Inn** provides gracious hospitality at the Bed and Breakfast, an acclaimed cooking school and fine art gallery. Each individually designed guest room and suite has a private bath with luxurious linens, TV/VCR/DVD and special touches like fresh flowers, fine chocolates and plush robes. The inn offers a variety of spa treatments – a private massage room is available, or services may be arranged in some of the cottages. Exceptional dining is a large part of a visit to Blair House Inn. Every evening, overnight guests enjoy a homemade dessert delivered to the room and each morning, a full gourmet three-course breakfast served in the dining room. Special five course dinners are offered every Saturday evening, open to the public with reservations. Owners, Mike and Vickie emphasize quality of service and have designed some fabulous romance packages with roses, bubbly and relaxing massages.

www.blairhouseinn.com
100 W. Spoke Hill Dr., Wimberley, 877-549-5450

Red Corral Ranch – see Distinctive Destinations

San Marcos

San Marcos Convention and Visitors Bureau
202 N. C.M.Allen Parkway
512-393-5900
www.sanmarcostexas.com

Tourist Information Center
617 I-35 North
512-393-5930

San Marcos is renowned for water recreation activities on the crystal clear **San Marcos River**. Halfway between San Antonio and Austin, it remains a world away from the fast lane of big city life. Ladies however, know it only as the best shopping on the planet.

As with any college town (Texas State University), there's always something going on – festivals, rodeos, trade shows, garden shows, arts & crafts shows, walks, marathons, sporting events, tours, holiday celebrations, musical performances, performing arts and cultural activities.

At the heart of the city is the San Marcos River, a longtime favorite for tubing, kayaking, or snorkeling – the water is 72° year round. Aquarena Springs is the headwater of the river, bubbling up from an underground lake along the Balcones Escarpment.

Attractions

At **Aquarena Springs Center** the glass bottom boats let you view an underwater archaeological site and the bubbling springs at the headwaters of the **San Marcos River**. Owned by **Texas State University**, the focus is preservation and education with classrooms, lab and research facilities. Aquarium displays include a special Endangered Species Exhibit which gives visitors an up-close look at unique species of aquatic life, some that live nowhere on earth except in the San Marcos River. Educational programs include tours for school children, teachers, Boy & Girl Scouts, and the Diving for Science has courses such as Underwater Photography and Underwater Archaeology. With the park's focus on nature, Aquarena Springs is a new destination for nature tourism.

www.aquarena.txstate.edu
921 Aquarena Springs Dr., 512-245-7570

Wonder World is yet another one-of-a-kind place. Fun and educational for the whole family, this is the only earthquake-formed cave in the U.S. that is open to the public. Instead of stalactites and stalagmites, you'll see the Balcones Fault from the inside. Unlike water-formed caves, it's not harmed by touch or light and visitors may take photos and experience the cave close-up. In a dark room, minerals imbedded in the cave walls glow in various colors. The 110-foot Tejas Observation Tower gives an awesome view of the Balcones fault line, formed when a mighty earthquake rocked this area 30 million years ago, and created the Hill Country beyond. Younger children will enjoy other activities like the miniature train ride through Mystery Mountain into the large petting park. They'll love playing in the topsy-turvy anti-gravity house. There's also a souvenir/gift shop, snack bar, and game room.

www.wonderworldpark.com
1000 Prospect St., 512-392-3760

Shop

San Marcos' two outlet malls DEFINE "shop until you drop," combining more than 240 name-brand shops in one enormous area. **Prime Outlet Mall** and **Tanger Outlet Mall** are across the street from each other, so walking from one to the other is easy. With amazing discounts, claiming up to 70% off retail, the prices are hard to resist.

www.tangeroutlet.com/sanmarcos
4015 IH-35 South; 512-396-7446
www.primeoutlets.com/locations/san-marcos.aspx
3939 IH-35 South, 800-628-9465, 512-396-2200

Downtown, just off the town square, **The Paper Bear** is a monstrous Texas-sized store crammed with an awesome array of toys, T-shirts, games, beads, old-fashioned candy, party goods, candles, and gifts.

www.paperbear.com
214 N. LBJ; 512-396-2283

New Braunfels

Chamber of Commerce Visitor Center
390 S. Seguin
800-572-2626; 830-625-2385

Highway Visitor Center
I-35 at Exit 190C
830-625-7973; 830-625-7975
www.nbcham.org
www.downtownnewbraunfels.com

Established in 1845 by German settlers led by Prince Carl of Solms-Braunfels, New Braunfels still exhibits the area's rich German heritage – tasty German food, pride in workmanship, old-world hospitality, and celebrations of fun and festivity.

At the Chamber of Commerce, pick up a book of discount coupons for Schlitterbahn, Natural Bridge Caverns and Wildlife Ranch, and other attractions. Also get a complimentary copy of the Visitor Guide, *Prosit*, and a historic walking tour map to guide you around the downtown area with more than 30 historic buildings. The heart of the community is the plaza with its roundabout, or traffic circle. Note that in downtown, "Streets" run east-west and "Avenues" run north-south. Germans like things organized.

New Braunfels, along with its well-known Gruene historic district (see Gruene), offers unlimited water-oriented recreational activities along the **Guadalupe and Comal Rivers**. Dozens of outfitters rent tubes, canoes, and rafts. Trivia: The Comal River is the shortest river in the world (less than two miles), starting and ending within the city limits of New Braunfels.

History

The recently restored, historic **Brauntex Theater** offers a variety of performing arts programs and concerts throughout the year. Call to see what's playing—it could be anything from a tribute to Elvis or a banjo concert to a performance of Dickens' A Christmas Carol.

www.brauntex.org
290 W. San Antonio St., 830-627-0808

A well-kept secret, **The Museum of Texas Handmade Furniture** doesn't get nearly the attention it should. Paying tribute to the German cabinetmakers of the mid-19th century who crafted fine furniture on the Texas frontier, it displays over 70 examples of Texas Biedermeier furniture (circa 1845-1880). There's also an outstanding collection of over a hundred pieces of white English ironstone. Knowledgeable and enthusiastic guides make a visit here an interesting and valuable experience. The museum is the nucleus of **Heritage Village**, a living history museum.

www.nbheritagevillage.com
1370 Church Hill Dr., 830-629-6504

The New Braunfels Conservation Society saved several historic buildings slated for demolition in the name of progress and moved them to a site known as "**Conservation Plaza**," adjacent to Heritage Village (above). Conservation Plaza has the largest collection of German fachwerk, or half-timber, buildings anywhere in Texas. Now completely restored and furnished with period pieces, the buildings, dating from 1849 – 1870 depict a typical German village. A gift shop offers a fine selection of handmade items.

www.nbconservation.org
1300 Church Hill Dr., 830-629-2943

Outdoors

Schlitterbahn means "slippery road" in German. Consistently rated the top waterpark in the country by amusement businesses and publications, Schlitterbahn provides 65 acres of great family entertainment with its collection of world-class rides and activities in six themed areas, tube chutes, river rapids, water slides, water coasters, five swimming pools, hot tubs, five children's water playgrounds, water and sand volleyball courts, five gift shops, two restaurants, 20 snack bars, and cool, shady picnic grounds. The natural riverfront setting with trees, beautiful landscaping, and picnic tables set it apart from other waterparks. The family-owned, family-friendly park offers free parking, free tubes, free lifejackets, and allows you to bring your own picnic (no glass or alcohol).

www.schlitterbahn.com/nb
305 W. Austin, 830-625-2351

The 200-acre **Landa Park** is as popular today as it was over 100 years ago when visitors came on trains from San Antonio. In addition to the spring-fed wading pool and Olympic-sized swimming pool, it now includes a miniature golf course, paddle boats, rowboats, volleyball and tennis courts, playgrounds, a snack shop, picnic areas shaded by ancient oaks, and scenic nature trails. Chug around the park on the miniature train or watch critters from below during a ride in the glass bottom boat on Landa Lake.

830-608-2160

The Kings' Throne room in Natural Bridge Caverns
(courtesy Natural Bridge Caverns)

At **Natural Bridge Caverns**, wind through a vast subterranean maze–gigantic rooms and corridors stretch more than a mile–leading to fantastic cave formations and an underground creek. Named for its 60-foot natural limestone bridge, this remarkable cave is 140 million years old and still growing. One of the state's largest caverns, it's also one of the seven Texas show caves and is both a Texas State Historical Site, and a Registered U.S. National Natural Landmark.

Knowledgeable guides will point out a few of the 10,000 different formations. Visitors may choose from the original Discovery Tour, the new Illuminations Tour, or the Adventure Tour.

There's also a **Mining Company and Rock Shop** with a sluice where you can pan for gems, minerals, or even fossils. Test your climbing skills on the 50-ft. Watchtower Challenge, one of the largest public outdoor climbing towers in Texas. The view from the top is spectacular. So is the return trip on a zip cord! The Visitor Center provides a gift shop, interpretive exhibits, a snack bar and picnic grounds.

www.naturalbridgecaverns.com
FM 3009, 210-651-6101

Adjacent to Natural Bridge Caverns, **Natural Bridge Wildlife Ranch**, this family-owned ranch is currently home to more than fifty species from every continent except Antarctica and is constantly adding new animals. Visitors drive through as exotic, native, and endangered species roam freely around 400 acres of native limestone, massive live oaks, and clear streams. Look for the highly endangered white rhinoceros or South American jaguar. Since the facility has a highly successful breeding program, you'll probably get to see baby animals year round, but especially in the spring. There's also a visitor center, petting zoo, snack bar and picnic area.

www.wildliferanchtexas.com
830-438-7400

253

Scenic Drive

An eighteen-mile stretch of River Road meanders between New Braunfels and Canyon Lake Dam. It provides an incredibly scenic drive with several low water crossings, rapids, dams and waterfalls, campsites, and wildlife. Loved by floaters and canoe enthusiasts, this part of the river is a controlled recreation area. The upper stretch of the Guadalupe that lies just below Canyon Lake Dam, where the water temperature is a chilly 54 degrees, offers a grand opportunity to fly-fishing enthusiasts. The river is stocked with speckled, brown, and rainbow trout by the Guadalupe Chapter of Trout Unlimited. For rules and regulations and a good map, pick up the pamphlet "Guadalupe River Scenic Area" at any tourist information site.

Fifteen miles northwest of New Braunfels on Hwy. 306, **Canyon Lake** is a large Corps of Engineers lake, one of most scenic in Texas, surrounded by steep, evergreen hills. Recreational activities year round include fishing, boating, sailing, water skiing and scuba diving, depending on lake levels. Public parks along the shore provide camping and picnic areas and boat ramps. Two yacht clubs, two marinas, a ski club, and fishing groups schedule a host of activities.

www.canyonlakechamber.com

3934 FM 2673, 830-964-2223, 800-528-2104

Special Event

This is a German community, meaning the residents love festivals and celebrations, and you'll find one almost every weekend. The major one is **Wurstfest**, an annual, fun-filled 10-day salute to the sausage. It's the third biggest festival in the state, behind Fiesta San Antonio and the State Fair in Dallas. Gemuetlichkeit means fun and fellowship in the German tradition. Families come to sample tasty sausage and strudel, pretzels and potato pancakes served up by friendly folks.

Others come to polka to oompah music performed by German bands. There are dozens of entertainment groups plus art shows, historical exhibits, and special events.

www.wurstfest.com

830-625-9167, 800-221-4369

Wine

Dry Comal Creek Vineyards uses Black Spanish (Lenoir) grapes to produce award-winning wines unmatched in character and quality. In addition to a tasting room, gift shop, special events and activities, they offer "Winery U," a series of non-pretentious classes designed to take the snobbishness out of wine. What a great idea!

www.drycomalcreek.com

1741 Herbelin Rd., 830-885-4076

Eat

You'll find nearly all the major chains and fast-food places here, but you really should try some German food.

Huisache Grill and Wine Bar serves creative contemporary cuisine in an intimate setting. The innovative menu offers a nice selection of salads, sandwiches and well-prepared main courses from grilled steaks to Seattle-style salmon in parchment paper, all made with as many fresh regional ingredients as possible. The shrimp and crawfish bisque is to die for. So are the made-from-scratch desserts, especially the Italian Cream Cake. Boasting an impressive wine list, this delightful eatery has received deserving accolades in major publications from coast to coast.

www.huisache.com

303 W. San Antonio, 830-620-9001

Liberty Bistro serves contemporary American cuisine in the basement of the 1929 City Hall building in historic

255

downtown. The chef uses fresh, seasonal ingredients and everything is made in the bistro kitchen. Themed dining areas have names like the Senate and House, the Supreme Court, the Executive Branch (a private room for meetings or parties), and the Treasury (a 1929 vault holding the wine cellar). Live jazz with Sunday brunch.

www.mylibertybistro.com
200 N Seguin Ave., 830-624-7876

Naegelin's Bakery celebrated 140 years in 2008, making it the oldest continuously operating bakery in Texas. Recipes have been perfected for over a hundred years – German breads, cakes, sausage and fruit-filled kolaches as well as legendary apple strudel, cream puffs, chocolate éclairs, and bear claws. A vast array of cookies includes traditional iced molasses squares, pfefferneuse, springerle, and the popular Lebkuche. A "must" stop for everyone.

www.naegelins.com
129 South Seguin, 830-625-5722

New Braunfels Smokehouse has been a local institution for more than 50 years. A new building retains much of the rustic look of the original restaurant and features a deli that continues to serve all the favorite smoked meats, sausages, hams and turkeys.

www.nbsmokehouse.com/about/restaurant.asp
1090 N. Business 35, 830-625-2416

Oma's Haus serves traditional German dishes like Wiener schnitzel, grilled sausages and German potato salad, plus a full American menu. The bakery specializes in strudels, Black Forest cakes and homemade fudge. The gift shop stocks imported beer steins and gourmet foods and gift items.

www.omashaus.com
541 S. Hwy. 46, 830-625-3280

The Vineyards Restaurant at Garden Ridge is tucked away in a lovely setting between New Braunfels and San Antonio. This multi-award winning restaurant and its patio offer incredible views of vineyards and rose gardens. Or choose an intimate dinner in the candle-lit wine cellar. As glorious as the views are, it's the incomparable food that makes The Vineyards so special. The chefs perform magic with everything from prime rib to rack of lamb to salmon. The sinful homemade German Chocolate cake is awesome. If you propose to that special someone at this romantic restaurant, there's a pavilion that's perfect for the wedding. Choose the "Vineyards Romance Package" or let the accommodating owners prepare a special treat for a birthday or anniversary.

www.thevineyards.org
27315 FM 3009, San Antonio, 830-980-8033

Shop – see also **Gruene**

Grassmarket – the folks from Huisache Grill renovated several buildings on what was the Tietz family homestead behind the restaurant. They relocated buildings and created a "village" of unique retail shops and named it Grassmarket.

A New Braunfels tradition since 1857, **Henne Hardware** is the oldest hardware store in Texas, Henne's has original tin ceilings and wood floors, as well as rolling ladders and other old fixtures. Whether you're looking for hard-to-find items, windmills, cast iron cookware, tools, new hardware stuff, or just browsing, it's a fascinating place.

246 W. San Antonio, 830-606-6707

Browse the **Downtown Antique Mall** with 12,000 sq. ft. chock-a-block with antiques, jewelry, furniture and artwork.

www.downtownantiquemall.com
209 W. San Antonio, 830-620-7223

Gruene

Information Center
1601 Hunter Rd.
830-629-5077
www.gruenetexas.com

Only three miles from New Braunfels' downtown Plaza, the historic district of Gruene (pronounced green) has been developed into a charming little tourist area with artisan studios, boutique shops, antique shops, and fine restaurants. **Gruene Hall**, the oldest continuously operating dance hall in Texas, circa 1880, regularly offers weekend performances by well-known country-western celebrities.

Listed in the National Register of Historic Places, Gruene is usually a quiet little place during the week, but fills up on weekends with tourists, antique shoppers, and in the summer, zillions of "toobers." It's an easy place to walk, with only two main streets and a compact clustering of shops and restaurants. Located high on a bluff overlooking the **Guadalupe River**, it's an immensely popular recreational site for tubing, canoeing and other water activities. **Old Gruene Market Days** (a shopper's paradise) lures visitors from miles around the third weekend of each month from February through November and the first weekend in December.

Night Life

Legendary **Gruene Hall** boasts distinction as Texas' oldest, continually operating dance hall – since 1878. There's no glitz or décor of note, but the steady stream of local and nationally recognized performers paired with a down-home setting makes this well-worn dance hall one of the hottest spots along the Guadalupe River.

www.gruenehall.com
1281 Gruene Rd., 830-606-1281

Shop

Oh, my . . . girls, this is another "shopping paradise." With only two main streets, it's so easy to spend the day browsing, lunching and even wine tasting. Galleries and antique, specialty, and gift shops furnish plenty to buy. Definitely too many to list, but here are a few to whet your shopping buds.

The **Gruene Antique Company** housed in what was once H.D. Gruene's mercantile building, displays more than 8,000 sq. ft. of antiques, collectibles, memorabilia and gift items.
1607 Hunter Rd., 830-629-7781

Black Swan Antiques features Old World European antiques and collectibles.
1720 Hunter Rd., 830-625-7122

Hampe House has a nice collection of antique furnishings and accessories.
www.hampehouse.com
1640 Hunter Rd., 830-620-1325

The old **Gruene General Store**, built in 1878, sells sodas from the old fashioned fountain and stocks tons of "stuff" from antiques and vintage signs to cookbooks, jalapeno candy and jelly, gourmet coffees, and all sorts of wonderful edibles.
www.gruenegeneralstore.com
1610 Hunter Rd., 830-629-6021, 800-974-8353

Don't miss **Buck Pottery**, located in a turn-of-the-century barn where Dee and Terry Buck have a showroom of exquisite hand thrown clay dishes, oil lamps, vases, and other items. Both are highly acclaimed potters, committed to preserving their craft and educating the public about its rich heritage.
www.buckpottery.com
1296 Gruene Rd., 830-629-7975

Gruene Outfitters is a sportsman's haven with an enormous array of fly fishing rods, reels and accessories, wading boots and quality name-brand clothing and footwear for men and women.

www.grueneoutfitters.com
1629 Hunter Rd., 830-625-4440, 888-477-3474

Grandmother Moon's Magical Emporium is one of the most unusual shops you'll find anywhere. Filled with fairies and flowers and "new age" metaphysical art and gifts. A fun place to browse.

www.grandmother-moons.com
1714 Hunter Rd., 830-608-8072

The Grapevine specializes in Texas wines and has an excellent collection. The wine tasting room offers complimentary samples daily.

www.grapevineingruene.com
1612 Hunter Rd., 830-606-0093

Texas Homegrown has cute women's clothing, jewelry and accessories. Owner Paula wrote a delightful coloring book showing the history of Gruene, the early Indian tribes, haunted houses, and folk medicine.

1641 Hunter Rd., 830-629-3176

The Dancing Bear showcases a nice variety of jewelry, candles, coffees & teas, gifts, wind chimes and home décor.

www.dancingbeartexas.com
1632 Hunter Rd., 830-629-2059

Eat

Adobe Verde, located in what was once an old winery, this is a first-class Mexican restaurant serving seafood, chicken fried steak as well. Enjoy Margaritas on the outside deck or inside in the Cantina.

www.adobeverde.com

1724 Hunter Rd. 830-629-0777

The Gristmill wasn't a gristmill at all – it was a brick 1878 cotton gin. Today the three-story restaurant has multi-level outdoor decks overlooking the Guadalupe River, tin-roofed patios nestled among the trees, and dining areas inside near a cozy fireplace. It's located beneath the water tower, next to Gruene Hall. There is often a wait to be seated, but there is a wonderful grassy waiting area. The innovative menu offers delectable steaks, chicken and fish, great burgers and round cut fries. A refreshing selection of veggies is available as side orders. For an appetizer, try the Texas Torpedoes, deep fried jalapenos stuffed with cream cheese and served with ranch dressing. Dessert would be a tossup between the Jack Daniel's pecan pie and awesome strawberry shortcake.

www.gristmillrestaurant.com

1287 Gruene Rd., 830-625-0684

River House Tea Room offers casual dining inside or outside under big umbrellas. The menu features a great selection of salads, sandwiches and entrées.

www.riverhousetearoom.net

1617 New Braunfels, 830-608-0690

Sleep

For a really fun getaway, book one of the fantasy rooms at the **Gruene Apple Bed and Breakfast**. The 14 themed guest rooms are absolutely fantastic! The "Hill Country Lodge" has faux log walls, a warm fireplace, and rustic furnishings resembling a North Country hunting lodge. The "Angler Room" features whimsical hand-painted fish furniture and a cloud-and-sky ceiling. And the "Shady Lady" looks remarkably like a turn-of-the-century bordello, decorated in rich velvets and brocades and a lipstick red claw-footed bathtub. This wonderful B&B offers so many luxurious amenities and facilities: a natural stone swimming pool and hot tub, spectacular views of the Guadalupe River from private balconies, a media room with a 12-ft. viewing screen for nightly movies, a game room with billiard table, well-stocked library, and a scrumptious gourmet breakfast.

www.grueneapple.com
1235 Gruene Rd., 830-643-1234

Lamb's Rest Inn is another premier Bed and Breakfast establishment. On the Guadalupe River, less than a mile from historic Gruene, the owners of this distinctive Bed and Breakfast offer the warmest Texas hospitality. Tastefully furnished with antiques and heirlooms, the six guest rooms feature luxurious linens and down comforters, TV, WiFi, and private baths, some with spa tubs or fireplaces. Breakfast will be a true treat and Judy's award-winning chocolate chip cookies are available daily. For romance, choose the splendid Lilycott Garden Cottage, a separate cottage featuring a king-size bed, double Jacuzzi, fireplace, recessed lighting and a private balcony overlooking the Guadalupe River. You'll have to bring the wine. The landscaped back yard slopes to the river, with its fragrant English-style gardens and fountains. Rocking chairs line the back porch, and several decks encourage quiet respites or sunset watching. The lovely pool and therapeutic hot tub offer more areas to relax. Delightful owners Judy and George have created special packages like the "Lovebird Special" or "Just the Girls," but they will gladly customize a special just for you. They also have a fabulous new spa room and can arrange wonderful spa services.

www.lambsrestinn.com

1385 Edwards Blvd., 830-609-3932, 888-609-3932

In the heart of historic Gruene, the upscale **Gruene Mansion Inn** provides guests a chance to sleep surrounded by Texas history. Listed in the National Register of Historic Places and a Recorded Texas Historic Landmark, Henry D. Gruene's Victorian 1872 mansion has been renovated to its original splendor and serves as the centerpiece of a premier Bed and Breakfast. Located on the banks of the Guadalupe River, adjacent to Gruene Hall, the rest of the accommodations are in a restored carriage house, corncrib, and two barns. All rooms are spacious, magnificently decorated, and contain every luxurious amenity you can think of. Some overlook the river, others the courtyard, two are in the main mansion. Owner Cecil and his staff offer some great packages – from romance to fly fishing specials. One for girlfriends called "The Estrogen Package" includes lodging without an alarm clock, meals, spa treatments and time to "giggle and wiggle" – don't cha love it?

www.gruenemansioninn.com

1275 Gruene Rd., 830-629-2641

Sleep – Canyon Lake

Biscuit Hill Bed and Breakfast, a luxurious retreat, offers scenic views and abundant wildlife in the center of many Hill Country attractions. The owners have paid careful attention to detail and thought of every amenity to pamper their guests. Each room provides a private bath, king-size bed, fireplace, mini fridge, TV/VCR/Cable, and porch seating with a view of the garden or lake. Some rooms have private hot tubs. The owners no longer live in the home, but do live close by and gracious innkeepers Cara and Matt will attend to your comfort.

They know the area and will be glad to recommend restaurants, shops, nearby wineries and outdoors activities

Biscuit Hill offers some of the most creative romance and special event packages, self-indulgent spa packages (including a create-your-own pamper package), gourmet food & wine packages, and fabulous wedding services. They present culinary classes, wine & cheese events and craft classes.

www.biscuithill.com

717 Colleen Dr., Canyon Lake, 830-899-4800, 888-998-9909

Distinctive Destinations

Kyle: On a hilltop amid a hundred acres of quiet countryside, **The Inn Above Onion Creek** is a gracious country inn and spa in an idyllic setting. You'll never need to leave this paradise because the rates include a full hot breakfast and scrumptious three-course gourmet dinner (bring your own wine) prepared on site by the Executive Chef. Complimentary beverages and homemade cookies are available during the day. Each guest room features a fireplace, entertainment center, oversized bath, feather mattress, fresh flowers, complimentary wireless internet, relaxing porch and panoramic views of the scenic Hill Country. Enjoy spectacular sunsets and brilliant stars from your porch. Wander the numerous trails to see some of the abundant wildlife like deer, fox, wild turkeys and lots of birds. In warm weather, relax by the lovely pool and admire the gorgeous flower gardens. Already a perfect place for a romantic getaway or honeymoon, the recent addition of a relaxing Day Spa completes the enchanting ambiance at this Shangri-La. The Inn offers romance packages and specials as well as weekday discounts. Friendly innkeeper Amy will help arrange activities if you really want to explore the surrounding areas. You'll find wineries, golf courses, water sports, fishing, horseback riding, hiking and biking and fabulous shopping and market days in surrounding towns of Wimberley, San Marcos and Gruene.

www.innaboveonioncreek.com

4444 W. FM 150, Kyle, 512-268-1617, 800-579-7686

The pool at Inn Above Onion Creek overlooks magnificent scenery.
(courtesy Al Buckner)

Sisterdale/Boerne: Paniolo Ranch, A Bed & Breakfast Spa provides a tranquil escape from reality. Overlooking a picturesque lake and rolling hills, this splendid resort in the heart of the Hill Country affords a beautiful natural setting with a pool, lake, walking trails, fishing/swimming dock, art studio and full service spa. Perfect for romantic getaways, private guesthouses have satellite TV/VCR/DVD, refrigerator, microwave, coffee pot, plush robes & slippers and all the luxurious amenities you can imagine; some can sleep from 4 to 6, others have covered porches, hot tubs and magnificent views. The Spa House has a patio outside the room and a stone walkway to a private lakeside patio. The O'Hana House features a large covered porch, wood-burning fireplace, and private hot tub under the stars. Enthusiastic hostess Judy can provide planning for any intimate group gathering from anniversaries to girlfriend reunions. Her "Girls Only" package offers total pampering and self-indulgence, including a sleep shirt and pizza party, massages and chocolates – what more could any girl want! She also offers fabulous romance packages, surprise birthday parties and more creative ideas for special weekends.

www.panioloranch.com

1510 FM 473, Sisterdale, 866-726-4656

Fredericksburg: The Trois Estate at Enchanted Rock, LLC, about 16 miles north of Fredericksburg, is a European style village – a luxurious Bed and Breakfast, a lovely wedding and event venue, a European Day Spa, retail space and a fine Italian restaurant. Designed and created by Rebecca and Charles Trois, it's a magic oasis in the middle of the scenic Hill Country. Ask Charles to show you his incredible cap gun collection, the largest in the world. Overnight guests have a choice of nine opulent suites, elegantly appointed and bearing names like Da Vinci Villa, Cielo Bovedo and Troisi Pieza. Each morning, they enjoy a multi-course gourmet breakfast delivered to the suite or served in the restaurant or on the scenic rooftop. After a day of exploring or enjoying the services of the European Day Spa, relax and enjoy a glass of wine and the view from the rooftop bar before dinner at **Troisi's Italian Ristorante**. Offering fine Italian cuisine as well as filet mignon and shrimp scampi, Troisi's uses market fresh and seasonal ingredients. Save room for the seven layer triple chocolate mousse cake! Then stroll under the stars for a perfect ending to a perfect day.

www.troisestate.net

300 Trois Lane, Fredericksburg, 830-685-3090, 830-685-3415

Fredericksburg/Stonewall: Rose Hill Manor is a small luxury inn and restaurant about 15 miles east of

Fredericksburg. It's ideal for a true romantic or relaxing getaway, offering the pampering of a fine B&B and spa as well as fantastic gourmet dining. If you must get out and about, Rose Hill is in the midst of wine country and near all the shops and attractions in Fredericksburg. Guest rooms are in the main building or private cottages on the grounds – all are tastefully decorated and appointed with deluxe amenities. A delicious three-course breakfast is served in the main dining room each morning, included in the rate. **Austin's**, the upscale restaurant at Rose Hill, offers gourmet New American cuisine to guests and the public Wednesdays through Sundays. The chef creates menu choices using fresh local ingredients and serves European style . . . leisurely, with several courses, candlelight and tablecloths. There's also an extensive selection of wines from around the world.

www.rose-hill.com

2614 Upper Albert Rd., Stonewall

830-644-2247; 877-FOSEHIL

Winberley/Blanco: About halfway between Wimberley and Blanco off FM 2325, **Red Corral Ranch** sprawls across 1,100 acres of the prettiest scenery in the Hill Country. With nature trails and abundant wildlife, an organic farm, an aquifer-fed swimming pool, butterfly garden, hike & bike trails, horseback rides, yoga and culinary classes, massages, and an extraordinary outdoor walking labyrinth, this is not your average B&B. Attention to detail and personal touches make the rooms and cabins delightful places for a romantic weekend, spiritual retreat, family or girlfriend gathering. The Limestone Lodge is ideal for a gathering with 6 bedrooms and 5 baths, living room with rock fireplace, dining room and full kitchen. Each cabin has a full kitchen and guests are welcome to bring food, or visit the restaurants of nearby Wimberley and Blanco. The Big Red Party Barn is a large special events facility, perfect for any casual celebration, barbecue or party while

James' Pavilion Meeting Hall is designed for weddings, parties, dances and more formal gatherings of up to 100 guests.
www.redcorralranch.com
505 Red Corral Ranch Rd., Wimberley, 866-833-4801

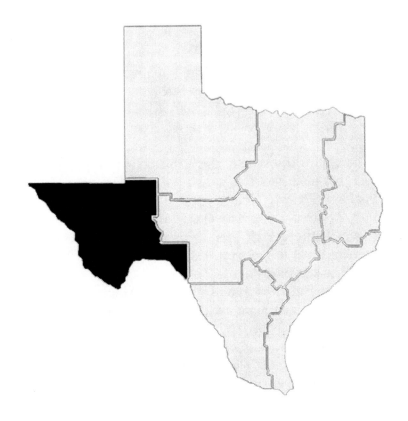

West Texas

An escape to West Texas is not exactly a "little trip" unless you're already starting from somewhere in West Texas. But it's a magnificent part of the great state of Texas! You'll return to reality refreshed and relaxed after a true getaway to a most unspoiled area of natural beauty.

Alpine

Alpine Tourism Initiative
106 N. 3rd Street
432-837-2326; 800-561-3712
www.alpinetexas.com

The seat of Brewster County, this delightful small town is cradled between the Davis and Glass Mountains and the Chihuahuan Desert. Known as the gateway to Big Bend Country because Texas 118 leads to the western entrance of Big Bend National Park near Terlingua and Study Butte. The other main route to the park, U.S. 385, goes south from U.S. 90, 31 miles east of town.

Home to **Sul Ross State University**, Alpine has a thriving arts community and more cultural resources than many towns of its size. It capitalizes on its wealth of recreational opportunities, as the mild climate allows for golfing, mountain climbing, camping, and playing outdoors year-round.

As you walk around this Texas Main Street City and its historic downtown, notice the colorful murals depicting various images of West Texas – scenes from the movie *Giant*, Dan Blocker (one of Sul Ross' most famous alumni), John Wayne, and others.

The **Texas Cowboy Poetry Gathering** in late February draws thousands of visitors from around the country. The **Hot Air Balloon Festival** over Labor Day is also worth putting on your schedule.

History & Museums

The comparatively small, but outstanding **Museum of the Big Bend** is located in a remarkable building on the campus of Sul Ross State University (use entrance #2 or #4). Showcasing the four cultures that shaped the history and heritage of the Big

Bend area with well-done exhibits, dioramas and paintings, it offers an excellent introduction to the vast area reaching from the Davis Mountains to the borderlands of Mexico. There's also a great gift shop.

www.sulross.edu/~museum
432-837-8730

Attractions

Whether or not you're a rock hound, you'll enjoy a visit to **Woodward Ranch**. More than 60 different kinds of gemstones are found on this 3,000-acre ranch, including the rare red plume agate, found nowhere else in the world. You may buy what you find, and experts will help grade it. There's also a lapidary shop with rocks, gems and one-of-a-kind jewelry from around the world. But the real treasures here are Trey and Jan Woodward, owners of the land heritage ranch that has been in the family for 109 years. They welcome visitors and happily tell stories, show off their "heritage room" and explain what to look for when you go rock hunting. Sometimes, guided tours to remote areas and jeep tours are available. In addition to rock hunting, the ranch offers great birding, hiking and photo opportunities. There's a small RV park, tent sites and two rustic cabins if you'd like to stay a bit.

www.woodwardranch.com
Hwy. 118 S., 432-364-2271

Entertainment

The **Big Bend Players**, a local drama group and Sul Ross' outdoor Theatre of the Big Bend present a variety of stage performances throughout the year. Most weekends, you'll find live music at the funky **Railroad Blues**, a local gathering place.

www.railroadblues.com
504 W. Holland, 432-837-3103

The historic **Granada Theater** has been extensively remodeled and is now a state of the art performance and event center. Check to see what's going on while you're there.

www.alpinegranada.com
207 E. Holland St., 432-837-0101

Shop

As home to quite a mélange of artists and craftsmen, Alpine has more than two dozen galleries and specialty shops that offer a diverse selection of treasures from paintings and sculptures to hand-crafted jewelry and pottery to rare books and Western Wear.

When you see the billboards advertising the **Apache Trading Post**, don't think it's just another tacky tourist shop . . . Stop! In a bright blue log cabin about four miles west of town, this is a fascinating shop with rocks, fossils, minerals, pottery, books of the west, gifts, jewelry, art work, paintings, photos, CDs and greeting cards. The gigantic collection of topographic maps and 3-D relief maps of the West Texas area is second to none. And if that's not enough, there's a special little room where you may watch a video of the famous Marfa lights.

www.apachetradingpost.com
2701 West Hwy. 90, 432-837-5506

Front Street Books has locations in both Alpine and Marathon. This independent bookseller stocks a comprehensive collection of travel and natural history of the Big Bend region, as well as West Texas and ranching heritage and Texana. It offers a nice inventory of best sellers and general interest titles, out-of-print and collectible books, calendars, note cards, and a few gift items. Across the street is a spacious reading room and the used books.

www.fsbooks.com
121 and 201 E. Holland Ave., 432-837-3360, 800-597-3360

Open the door to the fragrant smell of leather at **Big Bend Saddlery**. Two leather workers in this first-class saddlery make top quality custom saddles, chaps, belts and purses. The enormous retail store is brimming with leather goods of all kind, tack, saddle blankets, men and women's top-name Western wear, hats, T-shirts, cast-iron cookware, western music CDs and a humongous selection of books – from cookbooks to *Hank the Cowdog* series to regional history and geology to novels by Elmer Kelton and J. Frank Dobie. An in-house silversmith creates magnificent custom jewelry. A friendly staff will offer to help and they mean it.

www.bigbendsaddlery.com
2701 E. Hwy. 90, 800-634-4502

Stroll along Holland (the main street) and discover the **Kiowa Gallery** featuring "Art of the Big Bend" as well as a custom frame shop.

www.kiowagallery.com
105 E. Holland, 432-837-3067

Mi Tesoro offers antique and contemporary original sterling silver and gold jewelry and other fine arts.

109 W. Holland, 432-837-1882

Visit the **Catchlight Gallery** where you'll see works of local artists in a wide variety of media displayed.

www.catchlightartgallery.com
117 W. Holland, 432-837-9422

Quetzal International Folk Art Gallery showcases colorful handcrafts from Mexico and around the world.

302 W. Holland, 432-837-1051

The Spirit of the West Gallery is located in the Apache Trading Post (described above) and features fine art

273

photography, original gemstone jewelry, stained glass and clay pottery by artists of the area.

In addition to the excellent galleries, several eateries, including La Trattoria and the Bread and Breakfast Bakery (described below) have changing art displays of local and regional artists.

Eat

La Trattoria espresso bar & ristorante is an authentic Italian espresso bar and café serving home-cooked Italian dishes and fabulous pizza, great deli sandwiches and Panini, fresh salads, and several vegetarian and organic selections. A favorite of locals for more than 8 years, La Trattoria has created a friendly, inviting atmosphere, with newspapers and WiFi available. The comfortable café serves the finest gourmet coffee, cappuccino, espresso, fresh fruit smoothies, and an extensive selection of beer and wine, not to mention fresh bakery items. . . all at reasonable prices.

www.latrattoriacafe.com

901 E. Holland, 432-837-2200

The original **Reata Restaurant**, named for the ranch in the 1955 epic *Giant* was opened in 1995 in Alpine. Allegedly the birthplace of Western Cuisine created by cowboy chefs of culinary fame, Reata remains a destination for those seeking a special dining experience. Menu selections include Pan-seared Pepper Crusted Tenderloin with Port Wine Sauce and Carne Asada Topped with Reata's Cheese Enchiladas. One of the raved-about signature appetizers is Tenderloin Tamales with Pecan Mash.

www.reata.net/reata_alpine.html

203 N. Fifth, 432-837-9232

Located in a small remodeled house, **La Casita** serves great Tex-Mex food. Nothing fancy – just good food, homemade salsa, fast and efficient service.
1102 E. Ave. H, 432-837-2842

Pick up some divine pastries or sausage rolls at **Bread & Breakfast Bakery** or stay and enjoy a breakfast of eggs Florentine or a veggie omelet. Locals crowd in at lunchtime for tasty sandwiches, friendly service and good-value prices.
113 W Holland Ave., 432-837-9424

The **Alpine City Limits** is a local favorite with a friendly staff and great food. The menu offers a wide selection of steaks, chops, chicken, seafood, barbecue and burgers. Eat outdoors on the new patio for a lovely view of the mountains.
www.alpinecitylimits.com
2700 W. Hwy. 90, 432-837-9088

Big Bend National Park
432-477-2251
www.nps.gov/bibe

Big Bend is about as far away from anywhere as you can get. Dozens of books have been written about this area of magnificent contrasts! Truly an outstanding collection of ecosystems, it's a geological showplace sprawling over 800,000 acres. It is a vast land that invites exploring, not a park that can be seen in just a few hours.

Big Bend is one of America's great National Parks, still largely unknown to non-Texans, but gaining popularity among nature lovers who come to gaze upon the stark landscape and enjoy the wild beauty of the **Chihuahuan Desert**. The variation in elevation and temperature makes Big Bend an ideal year-round park.

A hundred million years ago, this area was ocean. Sixty-five million years ago, dinosaurs roamed the area. You'll see an incredible diversity of plants (more than 1200 types), over 450 species of birds, and animal life just as varied.

Rafting the Rio Grande. (courtesy Al Buckner)

Explore more than 150 miles of trails, 100 miles of paved roads, and 170 miles of dirt roads. Permits are required for all backcountry and primitive camping, also for all river users, but they're free and may be obtained at park visitor centers. Pets are not permitted on any trail or outside developed areas and must be kept on a leash at all times in developed areas.

The main Visitor Center is in the middle of the park at Panther Junction at the intersection of U.S. 385 and Texas118. Basic facilities in the park include National Park Service campgrounds, a trailer park, store/gas station, post office, and lodge/gift shop/restaurant in the Chisos Mountain Basin.

Visitor Centers throughout the park offer information, maps, and exhibits. **Panther Junction** is open year round while the ones in Chisos Basin, Persimmon Gap, and Rio Grande Village are open seasonally.

Several licensed outfitters provide river rafting or float trips and wilderness excursions. One of the most popular, **Far Flung Outdoor Center** offers canoe, raft, Jeep or ATV adventures.

www.ffoc.net
800-839-7238

Fort Davis

Chamber of Commerce
Town Square in the Library building
432-426-3015; 800-524-3015
www.fortdavis.com

Voted the Best Small Texas Town 2009 by the "Official Best Of" folks, this little town radiates character! Much of its early frontier atmosphere has been preserved with a number of original buildings and the longest remaining stretch of the famous **Overland Trail**. Buildings dating from the early 1900s surround the stately **Jeff Davis County Courthouse**. The Davis Mountains provide plenty of recreational activities for outdoor lovers – biking, hiking, glider rides, horseback rides and jeep tours.

www.officialbestof.com

History & Museums

Fort Davis National Historic Site, at the foot of Sleeping Lion Mountain, is considered one of the best-preserved surviving examples of a frontier military post in the Southwest. Established in 1854, it was the first military post to guard the route between San Antonio and El Paso. After the Civil War, it was home to the Buffalo Soldiers, many of them former slaves from Southern plantations. During the summer, park rangers and volunteers, dressed as soldiers, officers' wives, and servants, provide information and answer questions in some of the buildings. The Visitor Center, in a restored barracks, contains an excellent bookstore, museum and theater.

www.nps.gov/foda
432-426-3224

Fort Davis National Historic Site (courtesy Al Buckner)

The **Overland Trail Museum** (Fort Street) contains exhibits depicting early life in West Texas and vintage photographs of pioneer settlers. Owned and operated by The Fort Davis Historical Society, it has limited hours but special tours may be arranged.

Special Attraction

Romantics, go stargazing with your sweetie! A visit to **McDonald Observatory** is totally overwhelming, or as kids say "awesome!" The magnificent site, atop the 6791-foot peak

Mount Locke, was selected because of the clear air, high number of cloudless nights, and distance from a large concentration of artificial lights. Astronomy exhibits and a short orientation video are featured at the outstanding new Visitor Center. Its gift shop sells astronomy-related items, T-shirts, and lots of books. Participate in guided or self-guided tours, solar viewing, star parties, and special events. Once a month visitors may look through the giant 107-inch telescope by making reservations with the Visitor Center. This event is very popular and sometimes booked months in advance.

www.mcdonaldobservatory.org

877-984-7827

Outdoors

The **Chihuahuan Desert Research Institute**, located in the rolling foothills of the Davis Mountains, is a living desert museum, with outdoor exhibits, gardens, and walking trails. The Nature Center and Botanical Gardens exist to educate and promote public appreciation for the natural diversity of the desert and to encourage conservation. The Research Institute offers a wide variety of nature-related seminars, educational programs and special events throughout the year. The Visitor Center houses interpretive exhibits and the "Leapin' Lizards Nature Shop."

www.cdri.org

432-364-2499

The 2,700-acre **Davis Mountains State Park** is one of the most scenic state parks in Texas with an elevation change of 1000 feet. Don't miss Skyline Drive, a paved road that climbs steeply on the eastern side of the park to two overlook areas where you can see the roads to Alpine and Marfa, parts of Fort Davis, and Limpia Creek far below. Bird life is abundant, especially during spring and fall migrations. Several miles of hiking trails pass through oak, pinon pines, and juniper, and lead to a canyon formed by Keesey Creek. Lodging is available at **Indian Lodge** (see "sleep" below) or the campground.

www.tpwd.state.tx.us/spdest/findadest/parks/davis_mountains
432-426-3337

Other activities include Jeep Tours (432-426-2500) and horseback riding at Fort Davis Stables (800-770-1911).

Scenic Drive

Fort Davis is the starting point for one of the most scenic and uncrowded drives in Texas. Seventy-five miles long, the Scenic Loop Drive leaves Fort Davis on Texas 118, proceeds up Limpia Canyon past Mts. Locke and Fowlkes and the McDonald Observatory and then into Madera Canyon and a quiet, pine shaded picnic area. After a left turn on Texas 166, the road passes Mt. Livermore and Sawtooth Mountain, then gradually descends past a prominent ridge lined with wind generators toward the southeast side of the mountains, with broad views to the Sierra Viejo Mountains along the Rio Grande to the south. As you approach Fort Davis again on Texas 166, the Puertacita Mountains and Miter Peak are straight ahead. Highest elevation on the Loop is about 6700 feet, making it the highest public highway in Texas. For a detailed narrative on the Loop, which takes about 1.5 hours to drive, ask at the Fort Davis Visitor Center.

Shop

Adjacent to the hotel (see Sleep below), the **Hotel Limpia Gift Shop** is overflowing with high-quality gifts, garden items, soaps and lotions, western home furnishings, gourmet foods and colorful kitchen pottery, candles, baby gifts, greeting cards and an extensive selection of books – regional, history, nature, cookbooks and more.

Across the street from the Hotel Limpia, **Javelinas and Hollyhocks**, a nature store, features educational and fun children's toys and books, T-shirts and hats, candles, bath products, and home accessories.

107 State St., 432-426-2236

Visit the **Davis Mountains Broom Shop** to see live demonstrations and learn the fascinating history of broom making. The shop sells handcrafted yucca and cholla walking sticks and beautiful brooms made as they were in the 1800s.

401 State St., 432-426-3297

Davis Mountains Nut Company has been making fabulous flavored pecans for 12 years. Candy coated or marinated and roasted, the delicious pecans are handmade, one batch at a time. Flavors include Sassy Sinnamen, Hot-N-Spicy, Mocha Madness and the most popular Vanilla Almond. Yum.

www.allpecans.com
610 State St., 432-426-2101, 800-895-2101

The eclectic **Old Fort Country** features antiques, western art, local crafts, a wonderful collection of antique and new maps, a "West Texas Wine Corner" and a popular homemade fudge shop.

www.oldfortcountry.biz
1250 N. State St., 432-426-2742

Eat

The menu at Hotel Limpia (see Sleep below) **Dining Room** offers excellent beef, chicken, fish and pork selections as well as salads and fresh vegetables . . . and melt-in-your-mouth honey buttermilk biscuits. Save room for the homemade pies. The Hotel Limpia Cookbook is available at the gift shop.

Sutler's Club, upstairs over the dining room, has a nice wine list and cocktails for private club members.

Murphy's Pizzeria and Café serves great thin-crust pizza, sandwiches, burgers, salads and pasta entrées. In nice weather, enjoy eating on the lovely partially enclosed patio.
Hwy. 17 at Hwy. 118; 432-426-2020

The Caboose serves Blue Bell ice cream in homemade waffle cones, banana splits, malts and shakes, shaved ice and other cool treats from an old green Burlington Northern caboose.
www.thecaboose.biz
1250 N. State St., 432-426-2742

Sleep

The **Hotel Limpia** is much as it was when judges, doctors, and politicians came to Fort Davis to escape the sultry summers a century ago. Built in 1912 of pink limestone, it retains its original pioneer character. In the main hotel building, ten rooms and three suites exhibit 12-ft. pressed-tin ceilings and are furnished with Victorian reproductions. A parlor with a fireplace and comfy couches welcome guests in the lobby area and rocking chairs and wicker furniture fill expansive porches and a glassed-in veranda. Owners Joe and Lanna Duncan also offer a "Suites Annex," a remodeled tourist court, and several guesthouses and cottages around town.
www.hotellimpia.com
Town Square, 432-426-3237, 800-662-5517

The **Old Schoolhouse Bed and Breakfast** offers three delightful guest rooms in this historic 1904 adobe schoolhouse. The building has undergone several renovations and now has modern plumbing and electrical systems, while still exhibiting

22-inch adobe walls, bead board paneling and ceiling-high windows. Situated in a peaceful pecan grove, the B&B features a large, shady deck, off-street parking and broadband internet access. The guest rooms, named Reading, 'Riting and 'Rithmetic, offer modern conveniences with old-fashioned comfort and lovely furnishings. Helpful owners Carla and Steve serve up a massive dose of West Texas hospitality and Carla serves a delicious full breakfast each morning. Their new property, Hope's Ranch Guesthouse, offers a 3-bedroom, 2-bath ranch house for small groups.

www.schoolhousebnb.com
401 N. Front St., 432-426-2050

Indian Lodge located within Davis Mountains State Park (see "outdoors" above), is a striking multi-level pueblo-style adobe hotel. The historic section was built by the CCC in the 1930s and features the original hand-carved cedar bed frames, dressers, and chairs, fireplaces and ornate stonework. Since it opened in 1935, it has been expanded and extensively remodeled and upgraded. There's a pool, landscaped patio courtyard, and rocking chairs for watching the spectacular West Texas sunsets. With its unmatched mountain scenery and abundant wildlife, Indian Lodge is one of the most unusual inns in the Southwest.

www.tpwd.state.tx.us/spdest/findadest/parks/indian_lodge
432-426-3254

Marfa

Chamber of Commerce
207 N. Highland Ave. in Hotel Paisano
432-729-4942
www.marfacc.com

Enjoy the beauty of nature, the vastness of the sky and the brilliance of the stars in Marfa, situated on a high plateau of the Chihuahuan Desert between three mountain ranges.

The legendary **Marfa Mystery Lights** were first reported by early settlers in 1883. The playful lights, sometimes called "ghost lights," still defy explanation. The historical marker at the prime viewing area, nine miles east of the city on U.S. 90, gives details. Every visitor to Marfa must look for the lights!

Marfa's other claim to fame is that the 1955 Warner Brothers motion picture, *Giant*, starring Rock Hudson, James Dean and Elizabeth Taylor, was filmed here. The cast and crew stayed in the El Paisano Hotel that still operates today.

Marfa's cowboy heritage can still be seen, but today an influx of artists from around the country has added cultural diversity. Galleries, coffee houses and bookstores exhibit a cosmopolitan flair. Marfa's 9-hole municipal golf course is the highest golf course in Texas.

Activities

Soar through the high country! Marfa is celebrated for its excellent soaring conditions and has attracted pilots and soaring enthusiasts since 1960. The little town has hosted numerous national contests, including the World Soaring Championship in 1970. Sunny weather and scenic mountain ranges create glorious soaring conditions with strong thermal updrafts. At **Marfa Gliders**, Master Flight Instructor and FAA Designated Pilot Examiner, Burt Compton, will give rides or lessons.

www.flygliders.com
Marfa Municipal Airport Hwy. 17, 800-667-9464

Art & History

The late artist Donald Judd acquired several acres of land near Marfa in the early 1970s with a vision to create a showplace to exhibit his large sculptures and those of other kindred spirits. After his death in 1994, the **Chinati Foundation** was formed and the exhibits are accessible by guided tour only. Call for information.

www.chinati.org
1 Cavalry Rd., 432-729-4362

Located in an old home, The **Marfa and Presidio County Museum** contains a nice collection of artifacts and photographs detailing the history of the Marfa region.

110 W. San Antonio St., 432-729-4140

The *Giant* **Museum** at the **Hotel Paisano** (see Sleep below) pays tribute to the 1955 epic movie. A small viewing room off the lobby plays the movie all day and there are wall hangings and displays showcasing memorabilia from the set. The gift shop offers many *Giant*-related souvenirs.

Shop

You can feed your artsy soul in more than a dozen Art Galleries and Studios scattered about Marfa, offering an eclectic variety of contemporary and funky artwork in various media. Those along Highland Ave. include the **Greasewood Gallery** at the Hotel Paisano showcasing regional artists in varied media.

207 N. Highland, 432-729-4134

The **Highland Gallery** features fine art photography.

115 N. Highland, 432-729-3000

Along San Antonio Street, browse **Galleri Urbane** showing diverse art by artists across the country.

www.galleriurbane.com
212 E. San Antonio, 432-729-4200

Inde/jacobs gallery features fine photography.
www.indejacobs.com
200 E. San Antonio, 432-729-3939

Marfa Book Company is part bookstore, part art gallery
with changing exhibits of Texas artists – a place to browse and
relax, to gather with friends for book signings, readings and
special events.
www.marfabookco.com
105 S. Highland, 432-729-3906

Luz de Estrella Winery is located 3 miles east of Marfa.
Picturesque desert mountain ranges surround this vineyard,
winery and tasting room. The wine collection includes wines
with names like Big Bend Red, Paisano Rojo and Big Bend
Blush as well as classics like Chenin Blanc and Cabernet
Sauvignon.
www.luzdeestrella.com
E. Hwy 90 at Starlight Way, 432-729-3434

Eat

The Food Shark serves up fantastic "Mediterranean-by-
way-of-West-Texas" food out of a funky converted 1974 Ford
delivery truck. Usually open Tues. through Fri. from 11:30 -
3:00 under the pavilion between the railroad tracks and Marfa
Book Company, Krista dishes out amazing gourmet foods like
a roasted chicken sandwich with brie and pesto on Ciabatta
bread, shredded pork tacos or tasty homemade falafel. Eat at
large communal tables and visit with fellow diners.
www.foodsharkmarfa.com
no address, no phone

The Food Shark serves great food from this funky converted 1974 Ford delivery truck. (courtesy Al Buckner)

In an adobe cottage in the heart of Marfa, the **Brown Recluse Cafe** specializes in organic ingredients and healthy offerings like freshly baked apple cinnamon empanadas and yummy muffins served with Marfa-roasted organic coffee and fresh fruit juices. Cowboy breakfasts and daily specials are served amid local art, used books and classic records.

www.brownreclusemarfa.com

111 W. San Antonio St., 432-729-1811

Another health conscious choice is **Squeeze Marfa**. Across from the Presidio County Courthouse, this European-style deli and café offers smoothies, soup, Panini sandwiches, freshly squeezed juices and other healthy cuisine in the friendly café or on the lovely patio. The chocolate corner offers melt-in-your-mouth Swiss Vollenweider chocolates. Yum.

www.squeezemarfa.com

N. Highland at W. Lincoln St., 432-729-4500

For a special dinner, try the upscale **Jett's Grill** in the **Hotel Paisano** with menu selections of well-prepared steaks, chicken, pork tenderloin, trout and shrimp entrées. Finish with a rich dessert or after dinner specialty drink. Dine on the patio in nice weather and enjoy occasional live music in the courtyard.

Sleep

Around Marfa, several guesthouses and B&Bs offer distinctive accommodations for visitors.

The El Paisano Hotel, now **Hotel Paisano** was built in 1930. Ornate ceramic tile and wrought ironwork adorn the Spanish Colonial style hotel. The hotel became famous when the cast and crew of the 1955 film *Giant*, including Elizabeth Taylor, Rock Hudson, and James Dean came to town. The hotel was used in several of the scenes and the cast and crew hung out at the hotel's restaurant, bar and swimming pool. After many years of neglect, the owners of the Limpia Hotel in Fort Davis purchased the old hotel in 2001 and restored it to its former splendor. Guest accommodations are in the original historic rooms and suites, deluxe historic rooms and mezzanine patio rooms. All are handsomely furnished and feature luxurious amenities.

www.hotelpaisano.com
207 N. Highland Ave., 432-729-3669, 866-729-3669

Distinctive Destinations

Marfa (near): Escape the world of today and journey back to the days of the Old West at **Cibolo Creek Ranch** in far West Texas, 25 miles from the Texas-Mexico border. Originally built by early cattle baron Milton Faver in the mid-1800s as an adobe fort, it was meticulously restored to its late 19th century appearance by John Poindexter. The restoration has earned unending accolades, historic national and state designations and markers.

The striking Cibolo Creek Ranch. (courtesy Al Buckner)

No money was spared to create an intimate, idyllic world-class getaway for an affluent clientele – from the traditional Mexican architecture with spacious verandahs and Saltillo tile floors to the fully equipped exercise facility and spa with its rich Mesquite flooring, regional artwork and lovely pool overlooking the scenic vistas of the vast Texas wilderness.

In the midst of the natural beauty of the **Chinati Mountains**, surrounded by dramatic canyons and an endless sky, the remote 30,000-acre working ranch offers privacy and seclusion with warm Texas hospitality and first-class cuisine. The low humidity, altitude and clean air contribute to the enjoyment of outdoor activities like swimming, fishing, hiking and horseback riding in the mountains and canyons.

Each individually designed and tastefully furnished guest room features a comfortable bed with down pillows and comforter, fireplace, Western art and luxurious bath toiletries. An accommodating resort staff and outstanding executive chef pamper the most discriminating traveler. Each day, three scrumptious gourmet meals are prepared with the freshest regional ingredients from Texas and Mexico.

www.cibolocreekranch.com

432-229-3737

Texas Travel Resources

Travel Tex – the official site of Texas Tourism:
www.traveltex.com

Texas Association of Convention & Visitor Bureaus:
www.tacvb.org

Texas Parks & Wildlife:
www.tpwd.state.tx.us

Texas Parks & Wildlife magazine:
www.tpwmagazine.com

Texas Highways magazine:
www.texashighways.com

The Handbook of Texas Online:
www.tshaonline.org

Texas Beyond History (a virtual museum):
www.texasbeyondhistory.net/index.html

Texas Almanac:
www.texasalmanac.com

Texas Escapes Online:
www.texasescapes.com

Festivals of Texas:
www.festivalsoftexas.com

Texas Less Traveled:
www.texaslesstraveled.com

Guide to Texas Outside:
www.texasoutside.com

AAA Texas:
www.aaa-texas.com

Mileage Guide:
ecpa.cpa.state.tx.us/mileage/Mileage.jsp

Texas Travel Industry Association:
www.ttia.org

Texas Scenic Drives:
www.trails.com/stateactivity.aspx?area=12302

Texas Top to Bottom – U.S. Hwy. 281:
www.ushwy281.org

No Place But Texas:
www.noplacebuttexas.com/window.htm

Texas Pronunciation Guide:
www.texastripper.com/pronounce

Texas Hill Country Wine Trail:
www.texaswinetrail.com

LaVergne, TN USA
22 June 2010
186982LV00010B/63/P

9 781933 177199